Your Head In The Tiger's Mouth

Talks in Bombay with
Ramesh S. Balsekar

Books by Ramesh S. Balsekar:

- *Consciousness Speaks*
- *Consciousness Writes*
- *A Duet of One*
- *From Consciousness To Consciousness*
- *The Final Truth*
- *Experiencing The Teaching*
- *Explorations Into The Eternal*
- *Pointers From Nisargadatta Maharaj*
- *Experience Of Immortality*
- *Ripples*
- *The Bhagavad Gita - A Selection*

Your Head In The Tiger's Mouth

Talks in Bombay with
Ramesh S. Balsekar

Edited by
Blayne Bardo

First Published in March 1998
Chinese Year of the Tiger

Advaita Press

First Published in India by
ZEN PUBLICATIONS
9 Raja Bahadur Building, 156 J. Dadajee Road, Tardeo,
Mumbai 400 034. India. Tel.: (91 22) 492 3446. Tel/Fax: (91 22) 492 2429

Published in U.S.A. by
ADVAITA PRESS
PO Box 3479
Redondo Beach, CA   90277

Photo Credits:
Front Cover: **E. Hanumant Rao/PORPOISE PhotoStock**
Back Cover: **Dr. Joahnn Dham**
All photographs accompanying text pages by **Justin Pumfrey**

ISBN: 0-929448-17-0
Library of Congress Catalog Card Number: 98-071393

Dedicated to Ramana Maharshi

CONTENTS

    Effort—intellectual understanding—concepts—I Am, the only Truth—the Source—deep sleep—flip-flops—suffering—no individual entities, no choice—life is a reflection—will of God—no doer—programming—destiny—acceptance and surrender—seeking just happens—Potential Energy

    Involvement—expectation—tiger's mouth—life is nothing but seeking—what Ramesh says is not the Truth—does the Guru love the disciple?—love and impersonal Love—"who" is seeking?

reaction—Consciousness is all there is, so "who" is to ask "what" question?—no "one" is reborn—concept—I Am is the Present Moment—Consciousness aware and unaware of Itself—life is a movie—the Heart—parenting—meditation

Enlightenment—experiencing I Am—vertical arises, horizontal is involvement—seeking is a process—working mind, thinking mind

Ego and enlightenment—individual can do nothing—living life as it happens—body-mind organism programmed—Nisargadatta meets his Guru—no doer—arising of thoughts, involvement—identification and witnessing—effort—no goal to life— karma—the only Truth—do what you like—tiger's mouth

Upanishads—surrender—understanding is everything—not this, not that—I Am That I Am—all knowledge is subject-object— *jnana, bhakti*

Way to look at the Guru—predictions and destiny—why the sense of doership—no choice—ego— *sadhana*—meditation—I-I, I Am, I am so-and-so

Love, love—Knowledge (*Jnana*), Love *(Bhakti)*—relationships—"you" are the obstacle—concepts of enlightenment—doership—intellectual understanding

ACKNOWLEDGEMENTS

I am grateful to everyone who has helped with the preparation of this book—from Ramesh's affectionate pats on the back and smiling encouragement following our numerous editorial meetings to the wonderful enthusiasm and eager impatience of those who would ask how the book was progressing.

The polish of the book is due to the many devoted hours of seven people. Numerous errors were caught and editorial suggestions made by Jennifer Claire Moyer and Sajjana during their caring and critical proofreading. And I deeply appreciate the final reading of the completed manuscript by Wayne Liquorman, Chaitan Balsekar (Ramesh's brother), Jaya Nagarkatti (Ramesh's daughter), Heiner Siegelmann, and Tukaram Nantel.

Consciousness kept Its editing manifestation in rent and food by the generosity and kindness flowing through the following body-mind organisms: Dilip Desai, Dr. Verena Jegher-Bucher, Nico Stavropoulos, Yogesh Sharma, Luzius Jegher, Andre and Eveline della Casa, Ramcharan, Gert Seglitz, and Philippe de Henning.

A heartfelt thanks to Mahrouk Vevaina for her friendship, calmness, sense of humor, and generosity—letting me pass in and out of her home all hours of the day and night for weeks while I used her computer and enjoyed many delicious meals—always with dessert.

The huge amount of time and effort required for transcribing *satsang* tapes was accomplished by Mandie

Armitage (over half), Mahrouk Vevaina, Jock Millenson, Beatriz Anabitarte, Giovanna Dalle Rive Carli, Philippe de Henning, Manjushree, Luzius Jegher, and Gion Jegher. The transcript used for the scene devoted to the Upanishads was specially edited by Ananda Wood, author and lecturer on the Upanishads, who had the original *satsang* conversation with Ramesh.

Wolfgang and Ines Schröder have devotedly taped the *satsang*s during their visits. Wolfgang immediately responded to my urgently faxed plea for tapes. Taping was also done by Manjushree, Kanwarjit Singh, and Udo Schindler.

The *bhajan*s at the close of each scene were provided in Marathi by Rajiv M. Naik and in English interpretation by Shirish S. Murthy.

Thanks to Justin Pumfrey, master artist with the camera, for the inspiring and beautiful photographs of Ramesh contained within the book and to Dr. Joahnn Dham for his photograph of Ramesh on the back cover. The purchase of the rights to use the photograph of the tiger on the front cover was made possible by a generous gift from Salila.

And my appreciation to: Yogesh Sharma and Vijay Surve for all of their assistance—almost always at a moment's notice during busy office hours; Mr. Gurudyal for so generously loaning me a computer to use in my room; and Peter Paull for his professional adjustments to this out-of-shape body's reactions to being hunched on the side of a bed over the computer on a coffee table.

Editor's Notes

Present Moment is all there is—
Consciousness manifesting a sage
and listeners in a little room.
Yet, all there is is Consciousness—
no separate sage,
separate listeners,
separate little room.

Dreamed sage, real to dreamers—
Dreaming they are seekers
seeking something sought.
Yet, It is Consciousness dreaming—
separate sage,
separate seekers,
separate little room.

Your Head in the Tiger's Mouth is fifteen scenes within the Great Play. These scenes took place in a little room in Bombay where seekers sat listening and speaking with Ramesh Balsekar: awakened sage, tooth in the tiger's mouth, life-long devotee of Ramana Maharshi, disciple of Nisargadatta Maharaj, householder, father and grandfather, graduate of the London School of Economics, retired successful banker, body builder, one-time golfer with a twelve handicap, cricket enthusiast—and an infinitely generous heart and warm, sparkling sense of humor.

You, the reader, may never have had, as part of your role in the Great Play, the blessing of being in Ramesh's presence. But in the scenes which follow you can experience the wisdom of his concepts—a spiritual feast. And speaking of nourishment, since you are reading this play at your leisure, the thought may arise to take an intermission and feed the body-mind organism. By all means do so and enjoy! But keep in mind that in the little theatre where these scenes originally took place there were no concessions.

◻ ◻ ◻

The thought came to Ramesh that there was nothing published which captured, in the form of transcribed dialogue, the concepts he had been sharing for the past few years in the little room in his home. I was completely caught off guard when he asked me to assemble and edit such a book and insisted I include a brief account of my own journey. I am deeply grateful.

Early in the process of the book's development it evolved into being presented in the format of a play. While I worked assembling and editing the scenes, a number of thoughts continuously arose. It was Consciousness speaking and Consciousness listening in that little room in Bombay, and Ramesh and the seekers were playing both roles. But *only* he—totally immersed in the Love which has no expectations and no knowing of separateness—is awake in the dreamed play, sharing concepts for which each of us thought we had made the individual decisions to come and hear. However, while listening to him it became startlingly clear that we were there *only* because it was the impersonal functioning of Consciousness, or God's will. All there is is Consciousness—no separate doers, no separate anything.

Ramesh's express editorial policy was to keep, as much as possible, exactly what had been spoken during the original *satsang* dialogues. Also, his intent was to convey the flavor and texture of the happening in the little room. "As much as possible" was the key, because the dialogues, transcribed verbatim, were sometimes unclear or confusing. This is perfectly natural since the simple, everyday rush of asking a question or delivering a response can create a word pattern that is excessively awkward or which does not read as originally intended. As a result some editing was necessary and Ramesh agreed to occasionally add words for clarification or completion of a thought. Most importantly of all, I always kept in mind that there was the noumenal Presence creating a rare setting and subtle atmosphere through the lead player who, as you either know, suspect, or hope, is an awakened sage. So I've approached the editing as I would the dusting of an ancient Chinese bronze—handle it, if at all, as little and as gently as possible, taking care not to damage or intrude upon the beauty and value of its rare patina. I know that these dialogues have lost none of their patina, because Ramesh did a final reading of the manuscript.

Organization of the Play

The play opens with two quotes—one from Ramana Maharshi and one from Ramesh. These establish the feeling for the entire play. A setting follows. If you never visited Ramesh, this will hopefully give you a feeling for the venue. The fifteen scenes come next, each with a simple structure. A scene opens with a number of thoughts which recently flowed through the pen Ramesh was holding. These set the tone. They are followed by the transcribed *satsang* dialogues which are the core. Each scene closes with one or two of the *bhajans* which were daily sung by

Kalindi. They appear in original Marathi and in English interpretation using Ramesh's concepts and vocabulary.

Selection of the Dialogue for Each Scene

The first scene is an entire *satsang*. However, most of the scenes are a single block of dialogue taken from a *satsang*. The remainder of the scenes are comprised of sections of dialogue which were assembled from different *satsangs*. Except for the scene devoted to the Upanishads, the scenes are not thematic, although some are partially subject-oriented by having juxtaposed blocks of dialogue dealing with the same concept. In this way Ramesh's thoughts on a specific concept are presented as completely as possible. A good example of this would be the Guru-disciple relationship. By having brought together blocks of dialogue on this concept from different *satsangs*, the reader gets a more thorough single presentation of Ramesh's thoughts. This does not mean that a subject so treated does not appear in other scenes. For example, Mother Teresa and the psychopath make numerous entrances and exits. In fact, there is lots of repetition. Why not if you haven't "gotten" it yet? But of course there is no "you" to get" "anything." Indeed, this was one of the dominant flavors of the little room.

回 回 回

If it is your programming to do so, sit back and relax. Relax not just the body, but also the mind. Let it become receptive. It can always resume its old concepts. The sage always enjoys when a member of the audience wakes up.

The curtain is rising on the pre-play entertainment. If you are one of those who do not enjoy such things, then turn the pages to the first scene.

Enjoy the play!

Bittersweet Journey
A Seeker's Tale

A giant cumulus cloud preciously hued by the last rays of the day's sun hovers in a clear sky above Mumbai. As these few sentences are typed on a borrowed computer in a rented bedroom of a private flat fifteen minutes' walk from Ramesh's home, the inspiring colors fade, accompanied by the last, seemingly desperate conversations of crows. The hour of cow dust, seldom remembered in the teeming cities, passes like all things...

The simple rudimentary fact that seeking is inherent and primary in the programming of all body-mind organisms escaped me until I heard it from Ramesh. This was humbling and continues to be very humorous when I think how wise I thought I was becoming over the years. Even funnier is that for fifty-four years, one month, and one day, I thought I had at least a little free will!

The seeking for the ultimate answers through this body-mind organism began with a few questions to my parents just before I started my school years. Purposeful seeking started in the early teens and by my early twenties it was in full swing. At twenty-six appeared the first spiritual teacher with whom I studied. There followed many years of determined "soul growth," meditation, and doing. Then came a great surge of devotion to the Mother in many of her aspects. But I always remained unfulfilled even with the visions and ecstasies, hugs and *kriyas*, disappointments and despair. Expectations grew. I *must* do and then I would get. Doership—a ship that can only flounder.

So much effort and frustration, yet where was the answer? I definitely knew there was no choice but to keep seeking because I had tried quitting. There always seemed more things to do, and most importantly, don't do!— prescriptions, practices and spiritual poultices to be applied. Eventually, I understood intellectually that there would be no peace if there remained even the slightest shadow of conceptual thinking or volitional action. But this understanding remained a product of the intellect. Here was the apparent puzzle. So I continued shopping among Gurus and teachers and reading. Finally my mind grasped with certainty that there is no one to find anything—yet paradoxically, the Guru finds the seeker!

回 回 回

And so, the telling of my bittersweet seeker's journey begins with a taste of the end of it. After almost twenty-eight years of searching, on the morning of June 29, 1997, I opened the door into Ramesh's home. Remarkably, my first step into his home was accompanied by the sudden vivid memory of the first vision I had after meeting my initial spiritual teacher.

Ellen Resch held public meetings on 57th Street in New York City. They began with a short, practical, spontaneous talk that her Tibetan spirit teacher brought her, his words being filtered through her concepts of what was appropriate and inappropriate. This inspired lesson was followed by a brief meditation, after which she would ask if anyone had had a vision. Those who wished to do so could share it and she would interpret. Following the interpretations she would come to each person with a channeled message.

My first of few visions was of an elegant European dining room with a long table perfectly set with china, crystal, silver, lighted candelabras, and magnificent flowers. There was a feeling of expectancy for unknown guests to arrive and a meal to be served. When the potent vision ended I wondered if there would be dessert, my favorite part of any meal. Ellen interpreted my vision as the spiritual feast that lay before me. Little did I know then, nor could I have handled the knowledge, that almost three decades would pass before dessert was served!

But I mustn't get too hasty with the recollections of my spiritual journey if I'm going to share with you the major highlights. When I was fifteen there were two important events. I had been in the habit of saying the Lord's Prayer every night before I went to sleep. For many years it had been comforting, but eventually it also became disturbing. The "debts" or "transgressions" were not at all clear. My readings and studies had begun to make it abundantly evident that transgressions depended upon who, where, and when they were defined. I poignantly remember that part-way through the prayer one night I was visually confronted with an immense, roughly-hewn, dark, impenetrable rock wall. I can still recall it clearly although it no longer exists. It was too high and sheer to climb. It extended infinitely in either direction, and there was the sense that it was embedded so deeply in the earth that I could not dig beneath. In utter frustration and despair I knew that the God I was seeking and yearning for was on the other side. Bitterly discouraged, I stopped saying the prayer.

The second event was soon after this. Two characters, not beings, suddenly presented themselves to my mind, Ironicus and Saint If. These two new friends, whom I regarded as a lesser Roman deity and a Christian saint, filled the void left by the prayer. They emerged from my frustration with history, personal and otherwise. There were so many ironies, and I often indulged in the entertaining consideration of "if this or that had or had not happened." I was initially eager to use them as interlocutors in a story of history, but they repeatedly let me know that I wouldn't be writing anything until my mid-fifties. And how ironic that the prayer I'd left behind held the key—Thy will be done.

Well, Thy will was being done and the destiny was to study under Ellen, a well-intentioned and sometimes wise matriarch in New York City. I was living in the first of many apartments when suddenly I was plagued by doubts about leaving the Judeo-Christian West for the Tibetan Buddhist East. I, a confirmed existentialist during my recent military and hippie years, was worrying about leaving Christ for Buddha! I consulted the *I Ching* and the answer was clear, but I was not entirely convinced. The resolution was provided by two visitations.

One afternoon with my head just touching the pillow, I sensed something, opened my eyes and looked across my small studio apartment. There was a tall figure forming which immediately became as real as any friend walking into the room. It was Christ in blue robes. He was smiling, looking directly at me, and said very clearly, "You are trying to make a difficult decision. You will make the right one." There was a brief pause as I continued to look at him, and then he was no longer there. His presence, both manifested and lingering, was so friendly and accessible that I didn't feel any fear or awe, but rather a sense of gratitude and a lessening of worry. Although I'd never experienced anything like this before, I only thought about it briefly and then went to sleep. When I awoke I remembered all of the details about him and what he had said. For the next few days I lived with this experience and the quandary which had induced it. Suddenly I just knew with certainty that I would embrace Tibetan Buddhism and the woman who was leading the way. As soon as this knowing occurred he came again, in the same way, only this time he was dressed in white and felt more authoritative and unapproachable. He looked at me kindly but without smiling and said, "You've made a good decision. Work hard. Good luck!" He didn't visit me again for twenty-three years, and then he would be standing next to the Buddha!

During my first few months in New York City, I would occasionally share a joint with friends. Then came a fateful party where I overdosed on an experimental synthetic substance. Vaguely I remember the room disappearing, then crawling on my hands and knees through an inky, black space. Suddenly there was a commanding voice, "Do you want to go back?" I thought desperately over my entire life, my gratitude for being on a spiritual path, the visits from Christ, and the fear of what this "bad karma" would earn me in my next incarnation. I said, "Yes. I want to go back." The voice replied, "You have to earn it." The speed and direction I had been crawling slowed and torturously reversed itself, and there in the far distance was the earth. An exhausting effort was required for the return. I suffered the after-effects for over a week and never took drugs again. I didn't even take an aspirin for years.

It was January, 1970 and the decisions were made. For the next eighteen years my life was formatted around Ellen, her twice-weekly public meetings, my private weekly meeting, group activities, and meditating for fifteen minutes twice daily. For devotional focus most of us who studied with Ellen had an altar with the image of the Buddha, and many had Tibetan thangkas.

In our private meetings *everything* could be discussed, and there was almost always an answer or suggestion for any question asked. She taught us astrology (for self-study and "to avoid the pitfalls of karma") and tarot. Some of us became readers and taught as well. The basis of her teaching was soul growth predicated on karma, emphasis on good and bad, with all of the implications. If we asked, she gave us the names of our spirit teacher and spirit guide. Some could see them with varying degrees of clarity and frequency, and a few of the students had a clairaudial relationship. I had neither. For those of us who could not perceive them, she assured us they were our constant companions helping and guiding us in every aspect of our lives. *De facto*, Ellen directed most of our lives, and we willingly and devotedly let her do so. Of course, there were degrees and fluctuations of willingness and devotion.

She absolutely did not encourage visiting other teachers; however, she did approve of the Dalai Lama. In 1981 many of us, along with Ellen, attended his Kalachakra initiation. One of the things he spoke about at the Kalachakra was in complete contradiction to Ellen's approach. She encouraged the development of psychic gifts and their positive use. Her teachings and guidance mostly proceeded from her clairaudiance, clairvoyance, and past-life readings. His Holiness instructed quite otherwise. He said that most of the many wrathful deities depicted on the road to Shambhala represented *siddhi*s or psychic gifts. His advice was not to get involved with them. If they happen, let them happen, but it is unwise to pursue them as they are potentially traps on the road to liberation. Since then, I have come to know exactly of what he spoke. Years later I was stripped of "mine" when I entered the presence of a sage in south India. I felt suddenly deprived, and my ego longed for the gratifying and well-intentioned involvement.

The first two of my journeys to India were with Ellen and a few members of the group in 1979 and 1982. We were seriously involved in raising money for the Tibetan refugees in India. In addition to the Tibetan communities in the north and south, we also visited Buddhist and Hindu pilgrimage sites and the usual tourist spots.

Our fund-raising activities eventually included feeding the homeless and HIV/AIDS victims. The AIDS situation was tragic and frightening, especially for those of us who were gay. One-night stands became fewer. Until this time I had never lost anyone close to me except for a few beloved pets. Even when my father died in the early seventies I was not sad nor did I grieve, because there was a permanent end to the cause of early physical abuse, ongoing non-understanding, and one-way communication. Now, with friends dying all around me, there was always brief sorrow, tears, and prayers, but to my surprise, no grief.

I didn't get HIV; I got hepatitis B instead. It was a shock to get a major disease, especially when the body did not immediately defeat it. The illness became chronic and lasted for eight years. Initially there was an ever-increasing debilitation, and by September 1985 I was down and out in bed. It took me a while to realize I was experiencing a remarkable blessing in disguise. It was an absolute, abrupt change—no work and no play.

I seldom remember dreams and have had few visions. However, these have usually been major signposts or teachings along my seeking way. For this reason my story seems to naturally divide itself into the phases which they presaged. Also, I seem to remember these experiences more vividly than the months or years of events in-between. Case in point: about two months after being forced into bed by the hepatitis, I awoke early one morning sensing something. My dog, who always slept with me, was rigid with an unwavering stare across the room. As I looked, the room filled with a mist. A friendly and instructive voice said from within it, "Read mythology. Don't memorize!" That was it. The mist slowly disappeared and I recall thinking, "How, in my exhausted, hardly-able-to-let-the-dog-out condition, was I going to get to the book store?" However, I did and discovered Joseph Campbell. I read all of his works and leapt through the windows of symbols—never again to stop at the symbols themselves. One in particular contained them all for me—Shiva Nataraj, King of Dancers dancing endlessly the manifestation and dissolution of space-time. And this dance is a dreaming!

Shortly before I became sick I realized that I was going to leave Ellen. This came as a blow. I don't think it had ever seriously occurred to me before, and it was more than leaving just Ellen. The group members had intimately shared their lives with each other for years. Her many devoted students, to one degree or another, had come to need her, and I realized she needed them. This changed my perspective and my feelings.

I didn't speak to her of my growing intention for three years. In the meantime the hepatitis would periodically lessen its grip and I could become cautiously active. At other times it threw me back into bed or forced long periods of minimal exertion. I studied, thought, prayed and meditated (or sat there), went broke, sold everything, was relentlessly pursued by creditors who would not negotiate, was forced into bankruptcy, and received welfare. Through all of this was unwavering encouragement and support from Ellen, family, and group friends. But inside, the unrelenting patterns of change were in motion.

Within a year of becoming ill I had a dream which instructed me to "soak in hot waters in New Mexico." That morning I called a friend in Santa Fe who told me about Ojo Caliente. Within a week I was submerged in its healing waters, experiencing the separation from the New York City patterns, and opening to the energies and expansiveness of the high desert. My interest in the dynamic symbols of mythology continued, and like the healing waters of Ojo Caliente, there were both subtle and obvious effects. I was not healed from the hepatitis virus or the twin viruses of dualism and doership, but now when I look back I can see that the cures were progressing.

A few months after returning from New Mexico and a brief trip to Kathmandu, I left Ellen after eighteen years. It hurt and it was a relief. The conclusion was a series of events which resulted in my no longer being able to trust her completely. What a shock! Also, the relationship between us had grown tired and there was little or nothing I had to discuss at my meetings. She was locked into goals, approaches and concepts which I could no longer share.

Now, for the first time in many years, I had no teacher. It was a strange feeling and a little frightening after being so dependent for so long. Months went by with no sense of direction until one afternoon when I was riding on the subway. I suddenly realized I was fed up with the spiritual search. What a relief! I felt like laughing. What a sense of freedom, or more accurately, being unencumbered. Gone was an ingeniously constructed load of differing teachings, practices, methods, recipes, *do's, don'ts*, thinly veiled and sometimes outright threats, outrageous promises and contradictions. Almost all of these were from books, some from Ellen. I suspect this load seldom entirely collapses under its own weight, because within it there are also a few precious jewels of wisdom, inspiration, and glimpses of the Love which has no expectations.

With a few of these jewels embedded in my being I seemingly floated out of the subway car, skipped down the dimly lighted platform, and took the steps two and three at a time up to street level into the sunlight. Everything seemed brighter! I could do anything I wanted! I was so intoxicated in my new freedom that as I crossed the street I didn't realize the abrupt disappearance of the sun. Suddenly there was a rain shower which became a downpour. I ducked into a doorway, within a couple of minutes the cloudburst ended, and I carefully continued on my way along a muddy, sodden, broken sidewalk.

Cautiously placing each step, I looked up ahead a few yards to see how far the clean sidewalk might be. I was startled to see a rolled up tube of paper precariously balanced on top of a small mound of wet dirt. Approaching, I could see that it was neither wet nor soiled. How was it possible? Obviously it must have been dropped, but there was nobody behind or ahead of me. I was still super-charged from my minutes-old resolve to no longer be a seeker. I bent down to rescue it. Standing up, I realized it was like a large calendar and again looked around for its owner. Seeing no one I held it at arm's length and unrolled it. Shiva's eyes were staring directly into mine! I blurted out, "Okay, I'll continue!" Understanding now that all of this is destiny does not detract from having had such an experience or the memory of it. I knew then for certain, and still do with deep gratitude, that there would always be guidance and protection. I always hang this picture wherever I stay long enough to unpack.

Within two years after my first visit to New Mexico, I moved there. A close, spiritually-minded friend called to say he was deeply concerned about the sudden development of uncontrollable and often extreme *kriyas*. He asked if I could come and stay for a while. We both prayed fervently for some sort of guidance. It came within a few mornings in the form of a flier on a telephone pole. That night Asha Ma, now Anandi Ma, was holding a meditation gathering, and the following morning was going to offer *kundalini shaktipat* initiation. We attended the meditation, took the initiation, and both had deep, lasting experiences. His *kriyas* continued, but not as overwhelmingly.

During *shaktipat* I had a vision which has ever since been a comfort and reassurance—when it's remembered! In the vision I became aware of sitting in full lotus posture on the back of a huge white bull. As he walked his backbone was painfully coming in contact with my tailbone. Also, I was frightened of falling off. I desperately grabbed hold of his hump. This was both startling and soothing, because rather than the firmness I hoped for, my fingers and hands were holding onto sweetly fragrant, soft, velvety skin. At the same moment I noticed his long white ear as he turned his head to the right to look back at me. He clearly said in a deep, gentle, commanding voice, "I will never let you fall." I was riding on Nandi, Shiva's bull! I relaxed, he picked up speed, and then we harmlessly passed through numerous threatening obstacles.

Shortly after this I moved back to New York City. I was still living with hepatitis. Months would go by during which my energy and endurance were almost normal, and then unexpectedly my immune system would begin the battle all over again. As a result I would be in bed or not far from it for days or weeks. During this period my home became a center for Anandi Ma's meditations. We meditated to a forty-five minute taped mantra chanted by her Guru. He was 115 years old and living in Gujarat, India. He appeared to me, almost overwhelmingly, one night after meditation. There were three others present, one of whom, as usual, had arrived late. I got angry and furiously told him to sit down and to never be late and interrupt the session again. Shaking with adrenaline I rewound the tape and started the meditation over again. I knew for sure I wouldn't be able to meditate. At the end I opened my eyes to look at the altar. There, about three feet in front of me was Guruji smiling. I felt I would melt.

Silently he invited me to look into his eyes. I knew I was being offered a transmission, and I looked. Instantly I was lifted up and thrown about five feet across the room. I landed on my back laughing, crying, and sweating profusely at the feet of the two people sitting on the couch. I struggled to turn over and crawl back to my meditation seat. I pushed myself into an upright position and looked directly in front of me. Guruji was still there smiling with the same invitation. Again I was thrown across the room as before, and then a third time. It felt as if there was almost nothing left of me except the burden of a physical body. After struggling again to return and sit up, I looked at Guruji and silently told him if he did it again I would not survive. He smiled so warmly and tenderly. From heart to heart I said I was not his disciple but would forever be thankful and grateful to him. Looking out through his eyes was Love. His smile widened, he slowly turned his head away from me, and looked up to his right.

Where Guruji had been an instant before was now myself walking up the steep, grassy side of a mountain. I was approaching a ring of people who appeared to be completely encircling the mountain just beneath its sharp peak. The grass ended at their feet. Instantly I was aware of who these people were— *all* of the ones with whom the energies in this body-mind organism had ever studied spiritually! Right in front of me was Christ and Buddha looking at me and smiling welcomingly. Suddenly I experienced an embarrassing dilemma: which one do I offer obeisance to first? Almost simultaneously with the occurrence of this troubling thought, I stepped between them. I turned around, but they were still looking down the mountain as others approached. Briefly, I gazed at the back of all their heads with intimate recognition. Slowly turning around I realized I was standing on bare rock facing the steep ascent to the pointed peak just ahead. I looked for a moment and then gently returned to my sense of presence in the room. I was soaking wet and exhausted. The others were asking me questions about what had happened. They had only seen me jerked off the floor and sailing across the room. I briefly recounted what had taken place. The fellow who had come late looked at me with wide eyes, didn't come near me, and never came back.

Shortly after this I met Amritanandamayi, Ammachi, when she toured New York City in 1990, and I immediately became submerged in *bhakti*. Now, what had been gestating for so long became consuming devotion to the Mother in general and specifically to her manifestation as Ammachi. Anandi Ma continued as an intimately comforting and guiding presence. My long relationship with Kuan Yin and Tara intensified, and for the first time Mary softly touched my life. But there was also a slowly growing confusion as to which manifestation of the Divine to focus on. Again, as had happened a few times before, there was resolution with the appearance of a teaching vision.

One year later while en route to Ammachi's ashram in Kerala, I stopped for a couple of nights in Juhu Beach, Bombay. I was in a terrible emotional state. I felt unsure and uncertain about *everything*. I thought it remarkable how the negative, undermining moods continued to arise even after so many years of hard work. Regardless of the wisdom teachings and practices I knew, these times would just happen with always some degree of self-recrimination and guilt afterward. Now again I was that miserable seeker as the tiresome old demons of doubt and fear had a hold on me. A thought came to use an oracle. I picked up a copy of the *Bhagavad Gita* I had been given that day. I held it, prayed, and opened it at random. The sentence was a lightening bolt of clear wisdom and promise. I calmed down and much of the mood receded, but there remained the nagging, lingering confusion as to "which" part of the path and on "whom" to focus.

I went to bed and immediately saw myself standing in front of Anandi Ma seated in a chair. I looked into her eyes as I bent down to *pranam*. Just as I got to the floor, in my peripheral vision appeared Ammachi approaching. As she walked towards Anandi Ma she smiled at me, reached Anandi Ma and blended into her. They were sitting there as one. I could see both, yet only one. I *pranam*ed. They, the Mother, reached for my hands and pulled me into them, her. I momentarily lost all sense of presence and then came back to myself lying in bed smiling. All confusion had dissolved. Where's the difference unless you differentiate? There is no separateness!

Ammachi's was the first ashram I lived in. The first day I was assigned the *seva* of caring for and milking the cows. My favorite was Nandini who, after her scrubbing, always allowed me to lie over her wet back. We would both sigh contentedly. This was the best part of every day except for Mother's *darshans* and singing. Other than being physically close to Mother, I did not find it particularly inspiring to be in the ashram. My expectations were not being met. Poor me.

Within four weeks of arriving I started to get impatient and frustrated with almost everything, including myself. One morning, sweaty and dirty after finishing with the cows, I was stomping back to my room determined that if I were to come face to face with Ammachi I would not pay respects. Just as I was turning a corner, she turned it first and stood only a couple of feet away looking directly at me. It was all I could do to keep my resolve, but I just stared at her. She broke into a smile and continued on her way laughing. I immediately packed and tearfully left in a couple of hours.

During the eight months until her next U.S. tour I often worried how she would receive me. When the time came

I made a garland, and with pounding heart got close to the beginning of the *darshan* line. She penetratingly looked into me and then beamed as she leaned forward to receive it. What a hug that was, and her singing was so sweet into my ear. Devotion consumed me. After the tearful farewell in Boston ten weeks later, I returned to Santa Fe to work and attend her *satsangs*. The following year I also toured with her and then returned to her ashram in Kerala.

This time it was different for me. One of her swamis said, "Why pay attention to anything here but Mother?" How simple! Like the flip of a switch my whole attitude changed. It was almost as if I had a teflon coating. Nothing stuck except Mother. Also, I made a wonderful Swiss friend who introduced me to Wei Wu Wei's book *All Else Is Bondage*. Yeow! I almost hemorrhaged mentally. I put it in my suitcase for later study. The next four months flew by. I laughed a lot, my energy was high. I was told by a number of people that I was not supposed to be enjoying myself so much! There were intensities and confrontations, but I reacted differently. I took my leave from Mother with her blessing and invitation to return some day.

I returned briefly to Santa Fe and then went to New York City to do a research, rewrite, and editing job. Great to be back! Time flew and with it increasing thoughts of Ramana Maharshi and Tiruvannamalai. I had been reading David Godman's book. Finally, I said a prayer to Ramana that I needed a sign if I were going to again return to India. He came to me in a dream in which I was standing talking with some of Mother's *brahmacharini*s at the checkout stand in a familiar supermarket. I heard the entrance door open and looked at Ramana as he walked in. I left my friends and went to him. While I was approaching I saw only his bare right leg. I *pranam*ed, touching the arch of his right foot with my forehead. I woke up that morning and gave notice that I would be leaving for India as soon as I finished the book.

At this point in time there was a major shift in the mode of seeking—from devotion to knowledge. However, I am very much both a *bhakta* and *jnani*. Does this mean knowledgeably devotional or devotionally knowledgeable? So many involved seekers vehemently defend their approach against other ones. Why not just let the seeking happen? Now I know the answer—it's destiny and the programming. But this age-old foolish and immature argument by the insecure and unknowing can still upset me. I am programmed with an intolerance for intolerance! For many years one of my favorite jewels has been an *abhanga* from the *Kena Upanishad*:

> He who knows that It is incomprehensible,
>   comprehends;
> He who conceives of It comprehends It not.
> It is unknown to the knowing ones;
> Known to the unknowing.

I returned to India and rented a little grass-roofed house one-quarter of the way around Arunachala from Ramanasramam. From my small verandah Arunachala filled the view. Breathtaking! It became an intimate part of me while living there, always filling and promisingly fulfilling. However, I was not fulfilled.

I read numerous writings by and about Ramana. I ended up concentrating on Wei Wu Wei's book, which required supreme patience and determination. Once I even threw it across the room. I laugh as I remember this because it turned out to be great preparation for Nisargadatta Maharaj and Ramesh who were to come. Regularly I did *pradakshina* around Arunachala and visited the ashram for meditation and *pradakshina* around Ramana Maharshi's *mahasamadhi* shrine.

A friend invited me to accompany her to Tirupatti where the presiding deity is Venkateshwara, a manifestation of Vishnu. We stood in the long waiting line to see the image. With my first glance I received a powerful jolt, staggered, and was helped towards the exit. It is traditional to request something of Venkateshwara, and the boons he grants are as legendary as the offerings by supplicants. I had nothing to ask for because I had come to realize that I didn't necessarily know what I truly needed. My prayer was simply, "Thy will be done." Two days later the friend I had accompanied gifted me *I Am That*. I said a prayer of thanks to Venkateshwara and proceeded to devour Maharaj's teachings as presented in this book. My daily routine continued in Tiruvannamalai, and I could feel a dramatic change within as I absorbed Nisargadatta Maharaj's concepts.

One month later I decided to visit Ammachi for the holidays, but when I arrived in Bangalore to purchase a train ticket, every seat was sold for days. It was late afternoon, I didn't know where to stay, and suddenly Sai Baba popped into my mind. When I got to the last bus of the day there was one seat left. This was my first visit to Puttaparthi, although I had visited Sai Baba in Whitefields once before.

During this visit a relationship quickly developed with a Turkish doctor and his wife. They had been reading only *I Am That* for two and one-half years. Nothing else! Our conversations—mostly between the doctor and me in the kitchen from four to six each morning—developed into seriously wondering if Maharaj's teachings were the be-all and end-all we had come to believe. We agreed to concentrate on our question in that afternoon's *darshan*. Baba walked directly to the doctor, reached over, and patted the top of his head while clearly saying three times, "I am happy you are reading that." The significance of what had happened spread like wildfire, and before long there were no more copies of *I Am That* in Puttaparthi book stores.

I wasn't sure when I should leave Sai Baba's, so I silently asked him in one morning's *darshan*. That afternoon I was invited to attend a small group being addressed by the chancellor of Baba's university. This gentleman was not able to come, so he sent a woman who had been a secretary for Sai Baba, often traveling with him. She told wonderful stories and then asked if anyone had been to Tiruvannamalai. Someone told her I rented a house there. She looked at me with surprise and said, "What are you doing in this laboratory? Return to Tiruvannamalai and graduate school!" I laughed. He had given me my answer.

Even though I did not become a permanent, involved disciple of Anandi Ma or Ammachi or Sai Baba, we formed deep, penetrating relationships which last to this day. I feel their presence often and am ever lovingly appreciative and grateful.

I went back to Tiruvannamalai for a couple of more months and then left India as unfulfilled as ever. I didn't feel depressed, but I certainly felt disillusioned. So many years of seeking and there still remained a Blayne thinking and doing. I returned to Santa Fe with no funds and no plans except to find work and a place to live. At one job I had access to a computer so I extracted seventy-five pages of Maharaj's answers from *I Am That*. I arranged them by subject, and it made a perfect study book at the time. Almost three years went by "waiting for something to happen"—it always does.

I was happily baby-sitting an old wolf and not so happily fasting in the mountains outside Santa Fe when it began— the undeniable, sudden insistence that it was time to return to India. No, no, no, not again! And why? Yet I somehow couldn't help it, and in spite of the inner arguments and protesting I made the necessary arrangements.

Late spring 1997 and I was back in Tiruvannamalai. Again I rented a house in the countryside, equipped it with all the necessities, and with little enthusiasm slipped into a routine similar to the one of my first visit. Restless and a little bored after only a few weeks of my arrival, I went into town one day. While sitting deep in the shadows of a roadside store I was suddenly jerked out of my thinking by an excited voice shouting from the street, "Blayne!" I didn't recognize the person who exuberantly engulfed the little remaining space in the shop. He eagerly told me that he had wanted to continue the conversation we had had three years previously. He said the *only* place he knew of where he could possibly find me was in Tiruvannamalai. During the ensuing couple of weeks we continued "the conversation" and initiated many others. He finally announced that he would soon be leaving for Italy. On the way to New Delhi he was planning to stop in Bombay and see Ramesh Balsekar. When I heard Ramesh's name I *knew instantly* why I'd returned to Mother India.

I locked up my house and we caught the train to Mumbai. While riding I mused, remembering the first couple of times I had heard of Ramesh. The first was while milking the cows at Ammachi's ashram in Kerala. My friend and head cowherd mentioned one early morning between udders that he was reading *Consciousness Speaks*. He enthusiastically spoke about what he understood from Ramesh. The only thing I honestly remember from this first encounter was that Ramesh had told a seeker to just go back and play golf and not be concerned about enlightenment. I couldn't believe my ears. As I had not at that time read either Ramana Maharshi or Nisargadatta Maharaj, this bit of arcane wisdom completely went over my head. I didn't understand then that the instant the golfer intuitively understands in the heart that there is no golfer golfing, the process of seeking ends—whether driving down the fairway (or freeway), putting on the green, or relaxing in the clubhouse.

The next time I remember hearing about Ramesh was the day I happened to take a road which I was not sure led to where I was going. Little did I know! I halted at a stop sign just as the high desert sun over Santa Fe emerged from behind a cloud and brilliantly lighted a display of jars filled with honey. I had been meaning to replenish my supply so I pulled into a parking space. The guardian of this golden hoard and I became friends soon after the first handshake and eye contact. These were followed by five hours of non-stop conversation that included a discussion of Ramesh's concepts and the sharing of Gary Starbuck's hand-rolled cigarettes, kambucha tea, and bee pollen. I left with a jar of star-thistle honey, not aware that the real sweetness was still a little more than two years away—in Bombay.

For many years I had avoided, if at all possible, traveling to Bombay. With one exception, earlier visits had not proved kind. In fact, I ranked it with Newark, New Jersey as my least favorite city. But the seeking brought the apparent seeker back. With eager anticipation I arrived at Victoria Station. It was afternoon and purpose was postponed until the following morning.

Amazing! I simply walked into Ramesh's home and my first thought was: "Dessert to a long spiritual feast." There was a feeling of being home. Then I immediately felt twenty-eight long, bittersweet years collapse into the Present Moment.

回 回 回

May the reader twice mistaken
with the belief that something's read,
Vanish in the *reading*
of the Wisdom that's ahead—

At the feet of my living Guru,

Blayne Bardo
Mumbai
December 1997

Your head is already in the tiger's mouth.
There is no escape.

— Ramana Maharshi

The speaking happens as part of the impersonal functioning of Totality. The speaking and the listening—conversation—are part of life. It means really there is no one asking and no one explaining. The asking and the explaining
are one movement in Consciousness.

— Ramesh Balsekar
January 15, 1998

THE SETTING

10 Sindhula, Gamadia Road, Bombay, India—the home of a sage. He lives on the top floor overlooking the Arabian Sea. It's a white residential building five floors high, two flats wide, set into the side of a steep hill and facing the street. Tight against the front wall, the full width of the building, is a narrow lushly planted garden. The entrance, in the center, is open to the street and reached by crossing a flagstone sidewalk. A friendly, smiling doorman sits on a gray-metal folding chair. Stepping up two white marble risers accesses a short entry hall. This leads to marble steps and an old, metal-grilled, wooden elevator.

First time here? The elevator will carry only three people; just try to also bring on an extra heavy piece of luggage. Push the button for the fourth floor. Upon arriving you see how many shoes and sandals have preceded yours. Off with the footwear. Leave the baggage out here? Don't see any other bags, better take it in.

Pulse increases. Knock first or just walk in? Hand on the blue door handle, push and enter into the tiger's den. Open carefully in case someone is drinking a glass of water with their back to the door while reading the Far Side calendar.

Speaking of water, you're hot and thirsty from the adventure of getting here. Can you drink this water? After all, it's in the home of a sage. Maybe better check to see if it's boiled, filtered. Oh well, small surrender or wish you had.

Pulse increasing. Do others feel this way? There's a gray-haired Indian gentleman in whites walking this way. Is this

Ramesh? What should I say—Nameste*? Should I* pranam *or just pretend to be relaxed and say, "Hello"?*

"Hello!" he says, smiling. "Is this your first time here? You called? Oh, just go in." He gestures to a doorway and off he goes, continuing his morning walks from the back bedroom the full length of the house to the front living room, and looking out the windows momentarily.

Wow, the room is small. Sit on the floor or on a chair? There's the ocean and the horizon. It feels intimate and comfortable here. Oh, what if he talks to me, asks me questions.

Ten o'clock exactly. Following a few devotional moments in front of Ramana Maharshi's picture, Ramesh enters the little room, walking directly to his corner chair. The room is quiet except for the occasional street vendor calling out his wares, the tune from a taxi in reverse, the sporadic cries from eagles, and the intermittent chattering of small green parrots and gray hooded crows.

RAMESH   You're new? What is your name—the name on your passport? What can I do for you?

SCENE 1

All seeking is based on the insecurity of separation. The fact of the matter is that the seeker is already what he is seeking.

Do you want to escape the suffering of life? There is only one way—become the spectator of your life.

There never has been a seeker, only seeking; therefore, don't worry, be happy.

RAMESH   What brings you here? Your names are...

VISITORS   *Gitanjali, Marge, and Nina.*

RAMESH   Have you come together?

NINA   *Yes.*

RAMESH   Any particular place you have come from?

9

NINA *Churchgate. We live in Bombay.*

RAMESH And how do you happen to be here?

NINA *I met Peter and Kavita, and we talked about this. I wanted to come, and he said it would be okay for us to come and hear you.*

RAMESH I see. What is your interest? What did Kavita tell you about what happens here?

NINA *She said I can just be quiet and hear you, that if I want to talk I may, or that others may talk.*

RAMESH Yes, but did she tell you what I am talking about?

NINA *Yes, she said you were talking about* Advaita *and duality.*

RAMESH In which you are interested? How long have you been interested?

NINA *For a long time in spirituality, but not in* Advaita *specifically.*

RAMESH Oh, for a long time. In other words you are seeking? You have been a seeker for a long time? Nina, what have you been seeking?

NINA *Inner serenity. Maybe less confusion in my life.*

RAMESH I see. No problem about material things?

NINA *Not major, but yes.*

RAMESH I see. So what have you been doing so far, Nina? Since when did this search start?

NINA *Well, I don't know consciously, but I have listened to Krishnamurti since I was a young girl.*

RAMESH You were interested in Krishnamurti when you were a young girl? That's unusual isn't it?

NINA *I went to Rishi Valley.*

RAMESH Oh, you studied at Rishi Valley? Your parents sent you there? They were interested in Krishnamurti's philosophy?

NINA *Yes.*

RAMESH So it's hereditary, then? *(everyone laughs)*

NINA *Yes, and before that my grandmother took me to the Theosophists.*

RAMESH So it's *really* hereditary then! *(laughter)* Now, since you came out of Rishi Valley, do you think it prepared you for life, or is the teaching you received in that school so different from the average school that you are not prepared for life? Is that what is happening or not? I mean, it's just a question.

NINA *No, I don't think so. I think you lose some of it when you come back into the environment that doesn't foster it. So you tend to forget some of it, but I think certain things stay within you, and they do prepare you for life.*

RAMESH I see. So what was it that you learned in Krishnamurti's school?

NINA *I thought* I *was going to hear* you *talk!* (laughter)

RAMESH But what I talk about depends on what people want to hear. That's why I asked you what you wanted to know.

NINA *Anything you say. I just wanted to see you.*

RAMESH What I am trying to get at, Nina, is what is it that you need?

NINA *I need some wisdom.*

RAMESH You see, wisdom you can't buy, can you?

11

NINA *I know. I know that.*

RAMESH So what kind of wisdom did you have in Rishi Valley? What kind of wisdom did you get from reading Krishnamurti? You read Krishnamurti? It must have been quite a lot. So from what you have read and what you have been taught in Krishnamurti's Rishi Valley school, what is the wisdom?

NINA *I think that you have to look within yourself for the answers, and I suppose, to be as aware of yourself as possible and just watch yourself without judging. Just be with yourself rather than fragmented. So, to try and just keep that sort of awareness full.*

RAMESH Yes, but were you told how you get that?

NINA *No, he never tells you how.* (both laughing)

RAMESH Have you personally met Krishnamurti at all?

NINA *Many times.*

RAMESH In fact, my impression of him is that if people asked "how," he would get very angry.

NINA *Well, he would just say that there is no "how." And the first thing he would say was, of course, "No Gurus. Don't make them your Guru, no Gurus. You have to look..."*

RAMESH So if the Guru doesn't tell you how, then how are you to know?

NINA *That's what you have to find for yourself. You have to center. You have to be with yourself. You have to create it for yourself. I mean if someone tells you how, it still doesn't necessarily mean that you can do it. You have to find your own way.*

RAMESH So you try to find out the *how* all your life, and then it is possible that you won't "get it." That is possible, isn't it?

NINA *Of course it is. It depends on how devoted you are to it.*

RAMESH Oh, you are very devoted. I mean, you are trying to get your wisdom all day, all night.

NINA *But I haven't been so sincere.*

RAMESH So that means, if you don't get your wisdom in your life you have not been trying hard enough? (*everyone laughs*)

NINA *Sometimes, I'm sure, people get it without trying. So I don't know.*

RAMESH That is the whole point, Nina. So the question really is why do you suppose it happens that some people get it without trying, some people get it with a little bit of effort, and many don't get it even after having tried all their lives? It's not fair, is it? It's not fair. It's not just.

NINA *But many things are not just. Most things are not just, in the sense that we look at them.*

RAMESH Quite correct. Therefore, if you are saying that this is what happens and that's all that happens, do you mean that you have to accept the unfairness? All your life you work at it and don't get it, but some get it, and you accept this unfairness? Is that what you are supposed to do?

NINA *Yes. Well, I think one thing is you don't compare with other people.*

RAMESH Yes, all right, then in your own case if you get it, no problem. So the problem arises if you *don't* get it. (*laughing*)

NINA *But it's not your problem. If somebody else gets it, then that's where they are in their life, and you don't compare.*

13

RAMESH   So if you get it and someone else doesn't get it, there must be some reason. I'm not talking of fairness. All I am saying is that someone gets it with a little effort, someone gets it with a little more effort, and someone just doesn't get it at all. What would you say? Why do you suppose it happens? I mean, you have been trying and you haven't got it. Someone else has been trying and he or she got it very easily. So is there some explanation for it?

NINA   *I don't believe in them particularly, but there is karma, or where you are in your particular stage of your life, or whether you were meant to receive it or not.*

RAMESH   Yes. Now whether you were meant to receive it or not—meant by "whom," Nina?

NINA   *The Universe, the Energy, Cosmic Intelligence. Whatever It is. I don't know.*

RAMESH   Sure, whatever It is, I agree with you. Call It Energy, call It Consciousness, call It Cosmic Intelligence, call It God. It makes no difference. You accept that it happens because of Consciousness, or the Universal Energy, or the Source, or God. Isn't it?

NINA   *I don't agree.*

RAMESH   You don't accept it?

NINA   *No, I'm not sure. You're asking me why. I don't really know. I have heard these things, but I'm not sure why I don't get it, and I think maybe it's more within me.*

RAMESH   So it's "your" fault?

NINA   *Fault or not, I don't say fault.*

RAMESH   Then where did you "buy" that fault? How did you get that fault?

NINA   *I don't see it necessarily as a fault.*

14

RAMESH   All right, then the problem still is three people are trying. One gets it fairly quickly, one gets it with a little difficulty, and the third one just doesn't get it in spite of real effort. That is where we start from. You see? So what I'm saying is it does not really depend on the extent of the effort. Someone gets it with hardly any effort. Someone else in spite of effort doesn't get it. I mean there must be some reason for it, and the reason could only be either a fault in you or that Power, or Consciousness, which manifested everything. You say you don't think the Energy has created these differences. You said you don't accept it.

NINA   *I'm not sure because I haven't experienced it. I know it at an intellectual level, but I don't know it as a reality for me.*

Ramesh   Sure. But wherever you start, it can only be at the intellectual level, isn't it, Nina?

NINA   *Yes.*

RAMESH   Now, you read Krishnamurti's books. At what level are you reading them?

NINA   *Mostly intellectual.*

RAMESH   It has to be....

NINA   *But, some of it has sunk into who you are.*

RAMESH   So it has to begin at the intellectual level. And it seeps in you said. Seeps into *where*, Nina? Again, this is a concept.

NINA   *I think, to a deeper level.*

RAMESH   "To a deeper level" is a concept. So you say from the intellect, to a certain extent, the intellectual understanding has seeped in somewhere towards the heart—a concept. But the point is that the intellectual understanding has to go deeper, deeper into a personal

15

experience. Isn't it? And what you are saying is that it is not in your hands, it is not in your control. Someone gets it without effort, someone doesn't get it at all, and someone else with great effort.

NINA *But it is in your hands.*

RAMESH It *is* in your hands? Then why don't you get it?

NINA *Obviously you're not doing it right, or there's something within you that's blocking you.*

RAMESH But, you are not supposed to go to a Guru who tells you how to do it, right?

NINA *No, but you can hear and you can hope that when you hear something it might just happen. You have to be open. You can't say, "I haven't got it so that's it, I'm not going to do anything."*

RAMESH I see. So what do you do, Nina?

NINA *I try to come, and hear, and see, and read, and do something.*

RAMESH Yes, so you come here, and what I say you will tell me, "But that is a concept."

NINA *No, I won't say that. I'm willing to listen to your...*

RAMESH Why? It is a concept. I say it, Nina! I say it! *(everyone laughing)* You see, whatever I say, make no mistake, it is a concept.

NINA *Until it becomes reality for me?*

RAMESH That's right. So whatever any sage has said at any time, whether it is Jesus Christ or Ramana Maharshi, whoever has said anything is a concept—a concept being something which some people may accept, some people may not. You see? Now, even there we can go deeper. Why is it that some people accept it and some people don't?

The fact remains that some people accept it, some people don't. That is what I call a concept. I repeat, whatever any sage has said at any time, whatever any scripture of any religion has said at any time, is a concept. Make no mistake. That is where I begin. It's a concept.

NINA *But would you say Universal Truth is a concept?*

RAMESH Now, Universal Truth *is* a concept because where is the Universal Truth? In fact my point is if you know what that Universal Truth is, then It is no longer a concept. And there *is* a Universal Truth, Nina. There *is* a Universal Truth and you *know* it. You cannot *not* know it, Nina. Therefore, it is *not* a concept.

So what is it that you cannot not know? Very simple, Nina. You *are*, you exist—I Am. You don't doubt that you exist. You don't doubt that you are. You don't have to ask any Guru, "Do I exist?" You *know* you exist. I know—I Am, I Exist. I Am is indeed the Universal Truth, and the *only* Truth. Everything else is a concept. I Am is the only Truth. That is why in the *Bible* it says, I am told—I haven't read it—"I Am that I Am." I Am is the Universal Truth.

What is this I Am? The answer is you can't define It—I Am that I Am. Beyond this, and that you know it, you cannot go. So this is the only Universal Truth, and you *know* it. You cannot *not* know it. Therefore, what are you seeking, Nina? You *are* that Truth. The only Universal Truth you are. You *are* That. So if you are that Universal Truth, what are you seeking?

NINA *But I don't feel I am That.*

RAMESH But you know you exist.

NINA *Yes, but that I is a limited I.*

RAMESH No, not at all. On the contrary—whether it is Nina's name or something else, would Nina not know that she exists? Would that I Am not be there?

17

NINA *It is there.*

RAMESH I Am is there irrespective of anything else. I mean, I Am is there for everybody. No one can deny it. As I told you, what Krishnamurti said may be denied. You can say, "I don't accept Krishnamurti." But nobody can deny that he or she *Is*—I Am. That, nobody can deny. And that is why It is the only Universal Truth. If this is accepted, then whatever you see can only be part of the manifestation of What Is. It can only be part of the manifestation of Truth. There can't be more than one Truth, and whether you call It Consciousness, Universal Energy, Primal Energy, God, Totality, or whatever, It is this I Am. That is the only God, That is the only Consciousness, That is the only Truth. So the Truth is I Am, and that I Am is not different in different people.

"I am Nina" is an untruth. I Am is the Truth. You see? And all problems arise from Nina because you stray from the I Am into "I am Nina," or "I am Robert," or I am whoever. You understand? So if you don't stray from the I Am and you accept Nina as the creation of that same Truth, then Nina and the billions of other human beings are all a creation of the same I Am. And all the billions of human beings are merely objects in the manifestation of Totality. And the totality of manifestation—where could it arise except from the same Source?—the same Source being I Am, or Consciousness, or God. Nothing can exist unless it has come from the same Source. The Source is only one. From that Source has come all this totality of manifestation in which we are all objects.

That is the only corollary from the Universal Truth—I Am. That's the Truth. That's God. That's Consciousness. So whatever we see as manifestation, therefore, could only have come from that Source. And whatever happens in that manifestation, in the functioning of that manifestation, can only happen because that is what the Source intends. The manifestation cannot exist without the Source, because the manifestation has come from the Source. The functioning of the manifestation—life as we call it—can only happen because that is what the Source wants. Instead of saying Source, I would say God. Although I think Krishnamurti hated the word "God." Is that right?

NINA *Yes.*

RAMESH He never liked the word "God." Why? Why should he hate something?

NINA *I don't think he hated it.*

RAMESH No? But he didn't use it.

NINA *No, because it wasn't a truth for him. You see, he really didn't believe in it.*

RAMESH In other words, the concept of God he didn't accept.

NINA *Well, he may not have called it God because God has so many implications for people.*

RAMESH Quite right.

NINA *When you say God, it means religion and lots of other things that obviously were not part of...*

RAMESH And religion was not part of What Is for Krishnamurti? Krishnamurti used the concept What Is, didn't he? What Is at this moment. So "at this moment,"— and I repeat, this is my *concept*, Nina—is What Is which includes everything. What Is includes the good and the bad. What Is includes all the Mother Teresas and all the criminals. All is part of What Is. Isn't it? They are not separate from What Is. Whether it is a Mother Teresa or a psychopathic organism, both have come from the same Source.

That is why I maintain: whether you say God, or Consciousness, or Totality, it makes no difference to me. It is easier to use the word God because there are many people for whom God means something. Otherwise, you can use the word Source or Consciousness. I have no objection either way, so long as it is understood that by God I mean the Source and *not* an individual entity. This is important. When I use the word "God" I do not mean an independent entity like Allah or Christ or Shiva or Vishnu. I use the word "God" meaning the Source or Consciousness from which the totality of manifestation has arisen.

So everything that exists—whether we call it good or bad, beautiful or ugly—comes from the Source. And life as we know it, the functioning of the manifestation, is based therefore on interconnected opposites. These interconnected opposites are the functioning of manifestation which has come from the Source, and the Source is I Am. So as long as the I Am in manifestation accepts this, no problem, Nina.

Where does the problem arise? The problem arises when Nina says, "I like Mother Teresa, I don't like the criminal." That's where the problem arises. The problem arises with Nina *choosing* between two opposites and not accepting the existence of *both* opposites. That is the trouble. We expect and choose. But if we accept that both opposites are part of What Is, part of God's will, then there is no problem. If you truly accept that *nothing happens unless it is the will of God*, the Source, I Am, then That is What Is. That is not a concept. Is it a concept?

NINA *I think for me it is.*

RAMESH And then what is not a concept from this point of view?

NINA *That I Am.*

RAMESH So if I Am is the only Truth and you accept that I Am, then all of the rest of it is a concept. Manifestation is a concept.

NINA *No, it's a reality. You're flesh and blood.*

RAMESH   Oh, so what you call reality is something which only the senses can perceive? Only that is real for you? Is that it?

NINA   *Not only that, but it is also real. This is also real.*

RAMESH   So what the senses perceive is only real? When you are in deep sleep, do you see the world? You don't. That means the world is unreal? I thought you said that the world is real because you can touch it, you can smell it, you can hear it, your senses tell you that this is real. But your senses don't exist in deep sleep; however, you exist. I Am continues in deep sleep. Therefore, where I Am is concerned, whether there is manifestation or not, makes no difference.

The manifestation has come from the I Am. The functioning of the manifestation is in the I Am. It is like a reflection in the mirror. So what you accept is that whatever happens is merely a reflection in the I Am. All manifestation is a *reflection* in the Source—otherwise, there would be two.

PETER   *So it can't be a reflection of the Source, it's a reflection in the Source?*

RAMESH   It can only be *in* the Source. All this is a reflection *in* the Source because the Source is all there is. So whatever happens, you choose a concept. You can't do without concepts, otherwise you have to remain silent. And if the question "Who Am I?" arises, that is the very first thought which needs an answer. The answer is a concept, a concept being something which points to the Truth. The value or usefullness of the concept is only to the extent that it points to the Truth. You see? And this concept that the totality of manifestation and the functioning of this manifestation is a reflection in the Source is a pointer to the Truth—which is the Source.

My concept says nothing happens unless it is the will of the Source. Nothing happens unless it is the will of God. I repeat—God not being an entity but the Source. So if you truly accept that nothing happens unless it is the will of God, or the Source—if you truly accept this—how can there be any action which is your action?

GITANJALI *There is no consciousness?*

RAMESH Consciousness, Energy, God—same name.

GITANJALI *No, by consciousness I mean isn't this consciously done? You're saying it just happens.*

RAMESH *Yes!* Everything just happens, because if you say that you are consciously doing, then you are saying consciousness is an entity which does something. It is only an *entity* who thinks he or she is doing something.

GITANJALI *The consciousness that we have is us. It's the Gitanjali or Nina.*

RAMESH The names are different, but It is the same Consciousness. The same I Am.

GITANJALI *Yes, but I say that I am conscious of myself. I am conscious of myself really only as the conditioned person that I have become or developed.*

RAMESH That is why—I-I, I Am, and I am Gitanjali. And the process is reversed. Gitanjali hides the I Am.

GITANJALI *So the consciousness that we tend to think...*

RAMESH ...think is only your consciousness, is general Consciousness, impersonal Consciousness. So the Gitanjali during the waking state hides or covers the I Am and therefore suffers.

GITANJALI *I am talking from a personal experience that I had. I underwent open-heart surgery two years ago, had a cardiac arrest, and I died, or I stopped breathing, or whatever happened. When I came back into consciousness, or into my own mind or body or whatever, I was very, very aware that something had happened. I knew I'd gone somewhere or I'd been somewhere. I was not aware that any of this had happened to me, but it left me extremely disoriented for a long time. I still am unable really at times to come to terms with what it is that I went through. I find it very difficult to explain in words.*

RAMESH   What happened is very simple. Consciousness was on the point of leaving this body and came back again because it was not the time.

GITANJALI   *Yes. I don't know if Nina remembers this, she was with me through a lot of it. I went through a point like when you separate two things that are joined together. She was with me once when it happened. It was a strange kind of state that I was in. I remember telling her I felt like a non-person. I didn't know how else to express it in language.*

RAMESH   That's right.

GITANJALI   *I told her that I felt I was suffering from a nonidentity crisis.*

RAMESH   That is correct.

GITANJALI   *And this has really affected my life to this day. I mean, I now feel I am more merged than I was then.*

RAMESH   Would I be right in saying that now what happens is deep down Gitanjali says, "Whatever happens doesn't matter"? Would that be right?

GITANJALI   *Yes. Absolutely!*

RAMESH   Absolutely? That's the whole point. Earlier there was a strong Gitanjali. Now that strength of that Gitanjali is much less. The Gitanjali is weaker.

GITANJALI   *Yes, but I feel stronger.*

RAMESH   "I" feel stronger! Yes. Sure. Therefore, what is

23

happening is the Gitanjali which was covering the I Am now covers it off and on. And when Gitanjali doesn't cover the I Am, I Am shines in its full glory. The I Am, the impersonal Awareness...

GITANJALI *You can call it grace. I feel like I've experienced grace.*

RAMESH Of course.

GITANJALI *But I must admit sometimes it just flows through me. Other times it's a bit of a dichotomy, and I still find myself looking at things through a split image.*

RAMESH Sure. That's right. So what I would say—the flip-flop. The flip-flop is uncomfortable but the flip-flop happens. It is part of What Is. Accept it.

GITANJALI *Yes, I'm trying to.*

RAMESH Yes, quite. That's all you can do. The flip-flop happens, accept it. The flip-flop disappears, fine.

GITANJALI *Those are the quiet times.*

RAMESH Those are the quiet times when Gitanjali is not there to complain of the flip-flop. *(laughter)*

GITANJALI *Yes, you're quite right.*

NINA *I have a question. If It's all Energy, why are we different? Why is the Energy one way here and one way there?*

RAMESH You see, It's not different, It's the same Energy, but It is observed as "one way here and one way there" because otherwise life as we know it would not happen.

NINA *But why do we have life as we know it? Why should it happen?*

RAMESH It's God's *lila*. It's the Energy's game.

24

NINA *But how do we know that?*

RAMESH Oh, "you" don't *know* that. That's why it is a concept. The only thing you know is that you exist. Other than that, everything is a concept, Nina. Everything else is a concept.

NINA *So what do you do if you can't accept that concept?*

RAMESH If you don't accept that concept you will be unhappy. *(everyone laughs)* You will suffer. And suffering and unhappiness will be the destiny of that body-mind organism until the acceptance happens—until the *acceptance happens*.

MARGE *What happens to the body when people die? What happens to that Energy? It goes where?*

RAMESH Now let me put it this way, Marge. What happens to a kitchen gadget when it is "dead"? You throw it in the waste bin. What happens to the electricity? It continues functioning through other kitchen gadgets. So if this body-mind organism is destroyed, what happens to Consciousness? It functions through other instruments.

MARGE *Yes, but what happens to this Energy that is here?*

RAMESH It is the same Energy. It is not "your" Energy, just like the electricity does not belong to that kitchen gadget. The kitchen gadget doesn't say, "What happens to my electricity?" That is what you are asking. Electricity is electricity. The kitchen gadget is gone; electricity still functions through other gadgets.

NINA *So how do we understand the nature of this Energy?*

RAMESH Now look, if you want to understand something, Nina, you are the subject. And what you want to understand is the object. This subject wants to understand an object. And if you want to understand God,

25

Subjectivity, then you are an object which wants to understand its subject. Then what happens is you, an object, have usurped the subjectivity of the Source; and worse still, you have changed the pure Subjectivity into an object.

So the longer you want to understand, the longer you will suffer. Knowing something, seeing something, wanting something, are subject-object relationships—and what you want to understand is pure Subjectivity! So how can an object understand pure Subjectivity, Nina? *(pause)* How can the mind-intellect know or understand its Source?

NINA *If the Source is within me, I should be able to be in touch with It. I should be able to know It.*

RAMESH "Who" is this "I"? *All there is is God*. That is the whole point. *If* you truly accept this from your personal experience—even this is not in your control—and not because I say it, that whatever happens just happens and is not Nina's action—it is a reaction of the brain to an impulse over which you have no control—if this experience is repeatedly there, *then* at some point the mind-intellect which is Nina begins to ask itself, "If there is no action which is 'mine' then 'who' is this Nina that I'm so concerned about? Is there a Nina at all?" That's when the *real* seeking begins. And this, I think, is what St. John of the Cross called the dark night of the soul—then the ego is really in its corner. It repeatedly says, "If 'I' don't do anything, then what is this 'I' that 'I' am concerned about?" It repeats this until there is the sudden realization that there never was an "I." All there is is God, or Consciousness, and this "I" is merely a creation of the mind. Then the dark night of the soul ends in dawn—the dawn of Wisdom.

(To two visitors) Your names are?

MARKUS *Markus and Matt.*

RAMESH   So Markus, you have been listening to my concepts. Tell me, do you truly accept that nothing happens unless it is God's will or the will of the Source? Is it possible to accept that?

MARKUS   *I have a problem with the definition of God's will. What is "God's will"?*

RAMESH   God's will is the will of the Source. The manifestation has come from the Source. So whatever happens in the manifestation can only be what the Source wants.

MARKUS   *I can accept that, yet I don't know.*

RAMESH   Of *course* you don't know. I told you it's a concept.

MARKUS   *It's a concept, yes.*

RAMESH   It is a concept which points to the truth. If you don't want a concept, Markus, there's only one thing you can do.

MARKUS   *What is that?*

RAMESH   Sit still. Don't ask questions.

MARKUS   *Yes, I didn't want to.* (general laughter)

RAMESH   Why are you here, Markus? Somebody told you to come here?

MARKUS   *A friend of mine told me of you.*

RAMESH   Nobody twisted your arm.

MARKUS   *But I wanted to come here. It's good to be here.*

RAMESH   I see. Spiritual vitamins? *(the room fills with laughter)*

MARKUS   *No, I wouldn't put it like that...but actually I don't*

27

know what I want from you.

RAMESH   I Am knows everything. Markus knows nothing. So Markus saying, "'I' don't know anything" is the Truth. But the trouble is Markus wants to know his source, the Source. Is this possible for Markus? What does Markus really mean when he says "Markus"? It's mind-intellect, ego, me—and what is this "me"? The scientists say the "me" is really nothing but a combination of genes plus childhood conditioning. That's what the psychologists and scientists say. The "me," each "me," is nothing more than the genes plus childhood conditioning, all of which I call programming. You had no choice in being born to particular parents; therefore, you had no choice about your genes. You had no choice, for the same reason, in being born in a particular environment; therefore, you had no choice about the conditioning you received as a child in that environment.

MARKUS   *Is there a choice anywhere?*

RAMESH   *There is no choice anywhere* is correct. That is a concept. No individual has any choice because the individual doesn't exist as an individual. He is only a reflection in the I Am. Where is "me" really? It is only an idea. The "me" itself is a concept, an idea, a reflection in the I Am, in the Truth, in the Source. So a reflection in the Source cannot know the Source. You stand before a mirror, there is a reflection. Can the reflection know Markus?

MARKUS   *No.*

RAMESH   So that is what is happening here. Markus wants to know the Source. The Source has created this reflection within Itself. So take it tentatively that nothing happens unless it is the will of God, or the will of the Source. Everything happens only because the Source wants it. The Source, which has created this manifestation within Itself as a reflection, is making that manifestation function. So

the manifestation and its functioning, which we call life—all of it is a reflection in the Source.

MARKUS *But where does the programming come from?*

RAMESH   Markus, where could it have come from except from the Source?

MARKUS *How does it exist in the Source? It just is? It's just there?*

RAMESH   First, there is the Source. The Source creates a reflection. The reflection is I Am. You see? Have you heard of Ramana Maharshi?

MARKUS *Yes.*

RAMESH   To me, in phenomenality, there is nothing higher than Ramana Maharshi. Now, Ramana Maharshi says the Source is the I-I. He calls it I-I merely to separate It from I Am. I-I is the Potential Energy. The Potential Energy activates Itself as manifestation as I Am and becomes aware of the manifestation. The I Am is the impersonal Awareness of the manifestation and its functioning. Then, for the functioning of the manifestation to occur, the Source—or God, or I Am—creates these body-mind organisms, and thus individual "me's," by identifying Itself with these body-mind organisms. So the Universal Energy, the Potential Energy, activates Itself into this manifestation. I-I on actualization becomes I Am, and I Am becomes I am Markus. Why does I Am become Markus? Because without Markus and all the billions of other names, life as we know it would not happen. It is only because Markus considers himself a separate being, separate from someone else—me and you—that the interhuman relationships happen. What is life? It's all interhuman relationships which are based on love, hate, greed, satisfaction. That's what life is, isn't it? That is because the "me" is there.

MARKUS *But as soon as you don't identify yourself anymore*

with this Markus, or whatever, is there really a life possible?

RAMESH I'm sorry?

MARKUS *Is there really a life possible when you don't identify yourself anymore with this name?*

RAMESH You see, that is what is happening. I-I has become I Am. I Am has become I am Markus, and *if* it is the will of the Source, if it is the will of God, that seeking should begin in this body-mind organism called Markus, *then* seeking will happen through this body-mind organism as it is happening now. And what is the process? The process starts when Markus, who is really the identification of I Am as Markus, begins to think, "Is there really any Markus other than a name? Is there really any Markus?" Then the seeking has begun.

MARKUS *But the circle is...*

RAMESH We can talk of circles and squares later. *(laughter)* So my point is I-I, I Am, I am Markus. There are billions of human beings. Out of the billions of human beings how many do you suppose, Markus, are seeking their real nature, or whatever it is? There is a verse in the *Bhagavad Gita* in which Lord Krishna says: Among thousands, hardly one begins to seek. You have heard of the *Bhagavad Gita*?

MARKUS *Yes.*

RAMESH So Lord Krishna says: Out of thousands there is hardly one who seeks me, and among those who are seeking, hardly one knows me in principle. Now, who decides, Markus, who will do the seeking? In fact, the seeking itself is God's will, God's grace.

You think "you" are a seeker. Markus thinks "he" is a seeker seeking God, but the seeking was not Markus's choice. Markus is, you can say, lucky or fortunate that the

Source, or God, decided that the seeking would begin in this body-mind organism. So the seeking began not because Markus decided at some point, "From tomorrow I will seek the truth." In fact, the seeking has happened *in spite of Markus*. The seeking is really misery, isn't it? By and large?

MARKUS *The seeking itself—it is, yes.*

RAMESH The seeking itself is misery. Why should Markus choose to be miserable? So what I am saying is the seeking has begun. The seeking begins with a Markus thinking, "I am seeking God, or enlightenment, or peace," or whatever you call it. The seeking begins with Markus thinking "he" is doing the seeking, and the seeking can end *only* when there is the realization that there never was a seeker. The seeking is God's grace and the realization is God's grace, or the will of the Source.

So the seeking begins with an individual thinking "he" is the seeker and cannot end until there is the firm realization that there never was a seeker. The seeking is happening independently of the seeker. Truly, there is no Markus other than a name given to a body-mind organism. In other words, the seeking ends only when there is the realization: there never was a thinker, thinking was happening; there never was a doer, doing was happening; there never was an experiencer, experiencing was happening. Thinking, doing, experiencing are all part of the functioning of manifestation which can only happen through a body-mind organism.

Why did the seeking for God happen in this body-mind organism, whereas in some other body-mind organism the seeking is for money? He only seeks money, and he thinks that Markus is crazy looking for something in the air, that Markus would be much happier if he sought money or power or fame. Now, why is seeking money happening through one body-mind organism, and why is seeking God or Truth happening through this body-mind organism called Markus?

33

MARKUS *This is God's will.*

RAMESH   This is what I call God's will or the intention of the Source. It makes no difference to me whether you say intention of the Source or God's will. It's easier to talk in terms of God's will because for many this third person thing goes over their heads.

MARKUS *Is there something beyond, or before, or outside of the Source?*

RAMESH   You see, let me put it this way: I say God's will, again a concept. What I am saying is Consciousness, or the Source, *in action* is God.

MARKUS *Can you repeat that?*

RAMESH   The Source, or Consciousness, or Energy, or Totality, *in action* is God. That's why I prefer the word "God" when you understand it is *not* an entity, but the same as Source. So God's will started the seeking, and it is only God's will which will end the seeking. And the seeking will end only with the realization that Markus was never the seeker. Markus was never the thinker. Markus was never the doer.

I'll show you why you are not the doer, Markus. Whatever you call "your" action—if you analyze it, is it Markus's action? Any action, trivial or big, important or unimportant—any action which Markus thinks is "his" action—is nothing but the reaction of the brain, which is inert matter. The brain is part of the inert body-mind organism that cannot create anything. It can only receive and react. The brain is a reacting agent, an apparatus.

MARKUS *So this body-mind is receiving and doing?*

RAMESH   That's right. So what I'm saying is a thought comes, the brain reacts to that thought, and that reaction is what Markus calls "his" action. Markus sees something or hears something, the brain reacts to it, and that reaction is what

Markus calls "his" action. But Markus has no control over what will happen. Markus has no control over what thought will arise. Markus has no control over what he is going to see, or hear, or touch, or smell, or taste. Therefore, Markus has no control over what thought will arise or what he will see. The brain reacts to something over which Markus has no control, and how does the brain react? According to the programming—genes plus conditioning.

If you have a personal computer, you put in an input. What will be the output, Markus? Exactly according to the way it is programmed. What can a personal computer do except bring out an output strictly according to the way it is programmed? And who puts in the input? Not the computer. *You* put in the input. So in the body-mind organism which is a programmed instrument or computer, God puts in an input. He makes you hear something, see something. He sends a thought. That is the input.

MARKUS *What if there is a body-mind identifying with its name who doubts what he or she is going to do? Is it already clear what will happen?*

RAMESH Be mindful of what happens, Markus. Find out what happens from your personal experience, not because of a concept. From your own personal experience find out whether what you think is "your" action is really someone's action. Or is it merely the reaction of the brain to an input over which you have no control, according to the programming over which you have had no control?

MARKUS *I can accept that. What* is *the programming?*

RAMESH The programming is genes over which you had no control, and childhood environmental conditioning over which you had no control. You had no choice in being born to particular parents.You had no choice, therefore, in being born in a particular environment. The genes and the conditioning are what the programming is.

So the brain can only react according to this

35

programming over which you have had no control. And you can find this out from your own personal experience, which you should do. Today or tomorrow find out. You can sit even now and from the past find this out. Some important things have happened, good things and bad things. Think of them, even if it's only two, or three, or four things, and try to remember how much "you" had to do with it or how much it just happened. From your own personal experience you *will* find that everything Markus has thought was "his" action, has never been "his" action. It has been the reaction of the brain, over which "he" has no control.

As you put an input into your personal computer, so God puts in his input into each uniquely programmed body-mind organism. No two human beings are alike. The fingerprints are different, everything is different. So each body-mind organism is uniquely programmed by the Source or God so that those actions will happen through that body-mind organism precisely as God wants them to happen—not as "you" want them to happen.

So even if you tentatively accept that any action which you call "my" action is really not "my" action—it is just happening according to God's will—then something which you think "you" have done and therefore caused some harm or grief to someone else is not a reason to feel guilt. In fact, every human being carries an enormous load of guilt. Most of the thoughts that come are, "I wish I hadn't done this, then so-and-so wouldn't have suffered," or "I wouldn't have been frustrated."

MARKUS *Yeah, but there is no guilt...*

RAMESH So what I'm saying, Markus, is if you truly accept that it was not "your" action anyway, why should you feel guilt? If you truly accept that it was not "your" action and this action has been praised by others, then why should Markus feel proud? If it is not Markus's action at all, and it is *only* something which Markus *sees* as happening, then what I'm saying is there is no guilt, and there is no pride.

MARKUS   *There is no guilt. There is even no morality?*

RAMESH   Wait a minute, we'll come to that. There is no guilt, there is no pride, and more importantly, if Markus understands that nothing can happen unless it is God's will—it is not Markus's action—then Markus also knows that something which happens through another body-mind organism is not "their" action. Consequently, whatever action another body-mind organism might think is "his" action affecting you, *you* know that it is *not* "his" action. So how can you call anybody your enemy? How can you hate anybody? How can you envy anybody? Once you accept that no individual does *anything*—actions happen through each body-mind organism according to the way it is programmed by God—then four beautiful things happen: no guilt, no pride, no hate, no envy. Life becomes simple.

Now, that must raise some questions. The main question at this time being: "If I am not responsible for anything, and things just happen, why should I do anything at all? Why should I not remain in bed all day?"

MARKUS   *I was thinking this yesterday.*

RAMESH   *(laughing)* You see, that is a valid question which the mind-intellect must ask. Who is this "me"? It is the mind-intellect. The mind-intellect is the Markus. So the mind-intellect, the ego, says, "If I don't do anything, and I am not responsible for anything, why should I do anything at all? Why should I not lie in bed and do nothing?" The answer to that is very simple, Markus. Markus thought "he" was functioning, but what was really functioning?— the *Energy*, the Universal Energy functioning through this body-mind organism. That is the one which produces actions. So that Universal Energy functioning or operating through this body-mind organism will continue to operate, and that Energy will not let Markus remain idle for any length of time. Some action will happen through this body-mind organism because the Energy will bring it about—physical or mental. So the Universal Energy inside this body-mind organism will continue to bring about actions because that is its nature. It is the nature of the Universal Energy to produce.

MARKUS *It would also be a bit boring just to be in bed all day.*

RAMESH   That is what the mind-intellect says, and this is quite right. That is also another part of it. And what you have said, in fact, is exactly what I have said: it would be boring to lie in bed because of the energy inside—you can't keep that energy suppressed, controlled all the time. You see? So you cannot remain idle. That is one aspect. The second aspect is responsibility. Markus's mind-intellect asks, "If I am not responsible for what I do, why should I not take a machine gun and go out and kill twenty people? If I am not responsible and everything that happens is God's will, why should I not take a machine gun and go out and kill people?"

MARKUS   *Yeah, but why should I do it?*

RAMESH   No, why should you *not*? Why should you not do it since you are not responsible? The point is if you are not responsible for "your" actions, why should you *not* do this? I'm taking an extreme case. You see, the answer to that, again, is that the basic misconception is you are saying why should "you" not do this and kill people? But what actually happens is that there is *no* "you" to do anything.

MARKUS   *If there is someone who is shooting twenty people, is this also then God's will?*

RAMESH   It *is*, Markus, that is what I am saying. And therefore, what I am also saying is "you" cannot do it because this body-mind organism is not programmed to kill twenty innocent people. So how can this body-mind

38

do such a thing simply because the brain hears that "you" are not responsible?

MARKUS *So there is no question actually of you just sitting in bed and doing nothing, because anyway you can't do anything against God's will.*

RAMESH That's right. So what remains is the question of responsibility. A murderer can say, "Yes, the murder happened, but this teaching tells me that 'I' have not committed the murder, God has committed the murder. Why should I be punished?" That is the next question. You see? The answer to that is very simple—God's will in respect of each body-mind organism is what I call the destiny of that body-mind organism, stamped at the moment of conception. At the moment of conception the destiny of that conception is stamped.

MARKUS *So you can switch these words, God's will and destiny?*

RAMESH They are the same thing. God's will in respect of each body-mind organism is the destiny. The destiny of a body-mind organism is God's will.

MARKUS *So this says actually "you" can't do anything, just accept.*

RAMESH That is correct, Markus. That is indeed what I am saying. So if a conception is not destined to fructify into a baby, then that conception will be aborted. The mother may decide to abort the conception. If it is born, how long that organism will live is part of the destiny, and during that lifespan, what will happen is also part of the destiny, which is God's will.

So if a murder happens, what has happened really, Markus? What has happened is that one body-mind organism has been killed and another body-mind organism is the instrument through which this killing has happened.

The one which was killed—it was the destiny of that body-mind organism to be killed by a particular body-mind organism; that is destiny. Nobody knows how one is going to die. It may be a natural death, it may be an accident, it may be murder, it may be suicide. So which of these four ways will apply to a particular body-mind organism is its destiny, stamped at the moment of conception. If it is the destiny of a body-mind organism to be murdered, that body-mind organism will be murdered. That will be the way that body-mind organism is supposed to die. What happens to the body-mind organism which committed the murder will subsequently also be the destiny of that body-mind organism. Not all crimes are detected. Not all crimes detected are punished. So whether that body-mind organism will be punished or not for the murder which happened through it will be its destiny and the will of God.

You had a body-mind organism called Mother Teresa which was so programmed that only wonderful things happened. Those wonderful things which happened brought a lot of rewards: Noble Peace Prize, many other awards and any number of acknowledgments. So what has happened? What I am saying is there was no Mother Teresa who received all those awards. Mother Teresa was only the name of the body-mind organism whose destiny it was to receive them.

On the other hand there is a psychopathic organism. The psychopath didn't choose to be a psychopath. But the psychopath has been programmed to do what society and the law calls evil acts, perverted acts. So those acts will happen through that body-mind organism which is programmed to commit such acts. That will be the destiny of that body-mind organism of the psychopath. And the psychopathic organism may or may not be punished, according to its destiny. But my main point is that whether it is the body-mind organism of a Mother Teresa or the body-mind organism of a psychopath, both have been

40

produced by the same Source. We can only accept God's will. We cannot try to understand God's will. Why can we not?

MARKUS *We cannot try to understand God's will?*

RAMESH You cannot even begin to try, Markus, for this reason: our intelligence is very limited, our intellect is very limited, whereas God's intellect is all eternity. So how can we, who can only see in a limited way, understand God's will? We cannot.

MARKUS *Nobody can?*

RAMESH Nobody can, because everybody is merely a small part of the total manifestation which is a reflection of the Source. All you can do, as you just said a little while ago, is to accept things as they are. This is it!

MARKUS *As soon as you accept this, there are no questions anymore.*

RAMESH That is the point. Whether you call it acceptance or surrender makes no difference to me. People who are happier to think in terms of God prefer the word "surrender." Those who are more intellectual and prefer to use the word Energy or Source will say "acceptance." It means the same thing. And what is the acceptance and the surrender? What is the *basis* of this acceptance and surrender?—That there is truly no "me" who can do anything. What is the final bottom line of acceptance and surrender?—That there is truly no "me" who *can* do anything. There is really, truly no "me."

NINA *Then these man-made structures of good and bad, wrong and right, that we spend our whole lives battling—if it is God's will then there is nothing right and there is nothing wrong. The psychopath is doing what is his destiny.*

RAMESH That is correct.

NINA *The right and the wrong is imposed by us on ourselves.*

RAMESH That is correct. That is quite correct. And that imposition of right and wrong for a particular body-mind organism is God's will in respect of that body-mind organism—*not* an individual but a body-mind organism. You see? It is the destiny of that body-mind organism we call a psychopath for certain things to happen. It was the destiny of a body-mind organism called Mother Teresa for those kinds of actions to happen.

NINA *And the way of a psychopath or a murderer, according to our rules, is to be put into prison or given the death sentence. That is in his destiny?*

RAMESH That is the destiny of that body-mind organism. Quite correct. That is indeed what I am saying. The act that happens is the destiny. The consequences of that act are also destiny.

NINA *So the one that gets away with a heinous crime or the one who gets penalized by his peers for the crime, that is also in his destiny?*

RAMESH And why do you forget the innocent man who gets punished? See, that is also destiny. And how many crimes have there been where innocent people were executed and then later it was realized that they were wrongly executed? That was the destiny of the man to be wrongly accused and executed.

So, Markus, is there any particular reason you came here to India? As a tourist?

MARKUS *Well, I wanted to do some meditation, and I wanted to see you. I wanted to see Papaji also but that's not possible anymore.*

RAMESH Yes. Now what started it, Markus? When did it start?

42

MARKUS   *What?*

RAMESH   This wanting to do meditation or whatever.

MARKUS   *This started very early.*

RAMESH   That's right. That is exactly the answer I was expecting, Markus. You'd be amazed how many people say that. "Oh, when did I start? I don't remember. Ever since I can remember." You'd be surprised at the number of answers, "Ever since I can remember." As a child? "Yes, as a child." So again my question is: if the seeking began as a child what did "you" have to do with it?

MARKUS   *Nothing.*

RAMESH   *Nothing.* I go deeper, Markus. What I'm saying is it is not only this seeking for God which is *just happening* without a seeker—whatever the seeking there never has been a seeker. Ever since a baby is born and seeks its mother's breast intuitively, life is nothing but seeking.

MARKUS   *But the question I would ask is why is this all happening?*

RAMESH   *Yes.* Why is there a manifestation and its functioning? Is that your question?

MARKUS   *Yes, why all this?*

RAMESH   You see, the answer is very simple, because what is this manifestation? It is the activization of the Potential Energy. So the usual answer given to Why? is because that is Its Nature. So *Its* Nature—meaning the Nature of the Source—is to activize Itself. My concept which makes it easier to understand this is that Potential Energy activates Itself. Why? Because it is the Nature of the Potential to activize, otherwise It would be dead matter, It wouldn't be Potential Energy. If the Potential Energy didn't

43

sometimes activize Itself, It would be dead matter. So it is the Nature of the Potential to activize Itself—the Big Bang. And when that tremendous energy of the Big Bang exhausts itself after billions of years, all this activization goes back into the Potential until the process starts again.

MARKUS *So it's actually just a game of Energy.*

RAMESH It is a game of Energy. You are quite right, Markus, that is precisely what I mean. It is the game of Energy. Or some people call it God's game. But it is a game of this Energy.

    Any questions Markus? *(silence)* So let what you have heard today sink in and perhaps you can bring up questions tomorrow. *(laughter)* What do you want to do in life, Markus?

MARKUS *To be a teacher.*

RAMESH A teacher? Yes, I see. Do you think you will be a good teacher.

MARKUS (laughing) *I don't know.*

RAMESH But you want to be a teacher?

MARKUS *Yes, I can imagine myself to be one.*

RAMESH Ah, well, that's the whole point. I have a nephew, who at the age of 40, is right at the top of his profession. He is a pediatrician. Since the age of six or seven he said, "I am going to be a doctor." So someone asked him, "Why? Because you want to make a lot of money?" He said, "No, no. I want to cure people." So he became a doctor. He is curing people. He gets night calls almost every other night, and he goes willingly. So he is a good doctor. Why Markus? *(laughing)* Because he is programmed to be a good doctor.

▣ ▣ ▣

Gurur Bramha, Gurur Vishnu /
Gurur Devo Maheshwara / /
Gurur Saakshaath Parabramha /
Tasmai Shri Guruvenamaha / /

My Guru is Lord Brahma, Lord Vishnu,
   and Lord Maheshwara (Lord Shiva).
My Guru is the Supreme Self Incarnate.
I salute my Guru who is God Incarnate.

॥

Namo aadiroopaa omkaara swaroopaa /
Viswaachiya roopaa maayabaapaa / /
Tuziyaa saattene tuze guna gaavoo /
Tene sukhi raahu sarvakaala / /
Toochi shrotaa toochi vaktaa jnaanaasi anjana /
Sarva hone jaane tuzyaa haati / /
Tukaa mhane yethe naahi mee too pana /
Stavaave te kavana kavanaalaagi / /

My salutations to You, Who is beyond all forms.
My salutations to You, Who is the core of my Being.
My salutations to the all-pervading Consciousness
   which is the Source of the entire manifestation.
By Your grace I will sing hymns praising You
   and remain happy all the time.
I am totally convinced that both the talking and the listening
   happen by Your will.
Nothing can happen unless it is Your will.
Tukaram says:
   There is no sense of being separate from You.
   Whom do I praise, and for whose sake?

SCENE 2

Do you want a good laugh? Then consider this: nothing is real, everything is an apparition; everything is exactly as it is supposed to be; there is nothing good or bad; there is nothing to accept or reject.

You are Now—Here. Other than that, all knowledge is ignorance.

The trouble with spiritual seeking is that one is supposed to take it so seriously, so earnestly. That makes it difficult to "let go"— which is its essence...

MURLIDHARAN *The mind is a collection of thoughts, but the brain is a reacting agent. It has become an over-reacting agent to anything and everything that goes on.*

RAMESH That's its job! That's why it has been created.

MURLIDHARAN *But it causes a lot of disturbance!*

RAMESH Yes! So? Do you want to get rid of your brain?

MURLIDHARAN *I want to get rid of the habit of the brain. Quiet it down. Calm it down.*

RAMESH *(laughs)* The point is the brain is inert matter created to respond to something.

MURLIDHARAN *Over-respond!*

RAMESH You say it is over-responding. It merely responds! So if you don't go out anywhere and you sit quietly—you don't see anything, you don't hear anything—then how can the brain respond?

MURLIDHARAN *The thought* !

RAMESH All right. A thought comes and the brain responds to it. But if you sit quietly in meditation and the thought doesn't come, then how can the brain respond?

MURLIDHARAN *But as soon as a thought arises the brain overreacts to it.*

RAMESH The brain reacts.

MURLIDHARAN *It overreacts to it!*

RAMESH But what do "you" have to do with it? Let the brain react! What does Murlidharan have to do with the reaction of the brain? Murlidharan reacts to the reaction of the brain. That's the problem! The problem is not the brain. The problem is Murlidharan!

What is the ego? The mind-intellect is the ego. The problem is not the brain. The brain merely does its job. The brain merely reacts. The reaction of the brain is a natural reaction. So, if Murlidharan or the ego or the mind-intellect—same thing—reacts to the brain's reaction, what can the brain do? If Murlidharan does not react to it, where is the problem?

48

MURLIDHARAN *To quiet down.*

RAMESH What quiet down? The brain doesn't quiet down, the brain continues to do what it is created to do. It is a reactive apparatus, it is created to react to something which is seen or heard or thought. The brain is not overreactive. What is overreactive is the ego or the mind-intellect which gets involved in the natural reaction.

The brain reacts and anger arises. So if Murlidharan gets involved in that anger and says, "I should not have gotten angry, I must control my temper," how can you hold the brain responsible? Who is responsible for getting involved in the natural reaction of the brain? The brain is not responsible.

If you have an electric light, you put on the switch, the light is there and too bright. You don't say to the bulb that the light is too much. You can't hold the bulb responsible for the light it produces, and likewise you can't blame the brain for reacting to something for which it is created, for which it is made. But your mind-intellect, the ego, reacting to that natural reaction is involvement. It is possible not to get involved in the reaction of the brain.

MURLIDHARAN *Involvement happens unconsciously.*

RAMESH Yes!

MURLIDHARAN *Not consciously. You realize it and you find it's wrong...*

RAMESH Yes, I know. That is why I say involvement happens all the time because the ego has been conditioned—not for fifty or sixty years that Murlidharan has been living, but for thousands of years. The ego has been conditioned to react to the natural reaction of the brain and gets involved. That is what the ego does, you see? So the ego does what it is supposed to do. It has been conditioned for thousands of years. And the ego will continue to get involved so long as it is the destiny of that body-mind organism to get involved! But with the understanding it is possible not to get involved. The understanding is that the brain reacts according to its natural programming. You see? So if anger arises, you need not necessarily get involved in it. But if the involvement happens then, further, you don't need to get involved with that involvement.

Only that person who is involved with the involvement and does not want that involvement—who is concerned with spirituality—is who comes here. There is a certain amount of understanding, but in the ordinary person involvement goes on until another involvement comes. Only the seeker is concerned about getting involved. There is some understanding for every seeker, and depending on the understanding, there is the sudden realization: "I have been involved unnecessarily. Why should I get involved?" This sudden realization you don't produce out of your memory. You may think so. The sudden realization "I've been unnecessarily involved" is created by the understanding. The understanding produces the sudden realization. If the understanding is superficial—on the surface and intellectual—it does not get cut off until nine on a conceptual scale of zero to ten. For a while it may not even get cut off. But as the understanding goes deeper, the involvement gets cut off at seven, six, five—and, when the understanding is really deep, then involvement may happen and the cutting off may occur almost simultaneously. That depends on the intensity of the understanding—the degree of the understanding—over which you have no control! Why do you want the involvement not to be there, Murlidharan?

MURLIDHARAN *Because I realize the futility of that involvement.*

RAMESH   That's right. In other words, it's suffering! Involvement means suffering and you don't want suffering. That's why you don't want the involvement. The point is, if you are destined to suffer, if this body-mind organism is destined to suffer from involvement, it will happen until it is the destiny of this body-mind organism to come and listen to something, or read something, and then the understanding begins.

How quickly the involvement gets cut off will depend upon the degree of the understanding. Over none of these do you have any control. That is why I say, "If involvement happens, let it happen." If you let the involvement happen, you are really not involved with the involvement, then that involvement does not bring about any suffering. The *acceptance* of whatever happens excludes the suffering. So just wait and see what happens.

What is the basic problem? The basic problem is *expectation*. There is an expectation in this body-mind organism, the ego's expectation not to be involved, isn't it? The basis is the ego does not want to be involved, so there is an expectation. This expectation is the basis of everything. If there is no expectation then there is no problem! And whether the expectation gets erased will depend on the ego, and as long as the ego is there, which is not in your control, expectation will happen!

Again, the expectation happens and then there is a sudden realization produced by the understanding saying, "There is no use my expecting anything. I could expect something if I could do something about it, but if I can do nothing about it, what's the use of expecting something, wanting something? I can do nothing about it!" So why keep on wanting? That is the understanding!

As Ramana Maharshi says: A seeker has his head in the tiger's mouth. That is the consolation which Ramana Maharshi offers to the seeker who is frustrated and impatient. Ramana says: Your head is already in the tiger's mouth. There is no escape!

So there is no escape, your head is already in the tiger's mouth. What he says is—why be impatient? Wait until the tiger snaps its jaws! When the tiger snaps its jaws is not in your hands! In the meantime what does Murlidharan do? Murlidharan enjoys life as it happens. Instead of

51

getting involved in the involvement, Murlidharan just enjoys life as it happens. When you enjoy life as it happens, that means you accept whatever happens, and when you get into the habit of accepting whatever happens, expectations become less.

FRED   *The bigger the expectation, the bigger the frustration.*

RAMESH   That is correct. The bigger the expectation, the deeper the frustration. That is quite correct! So your next question is, "How can I get rid of the expectation?" The answer is it's not in your control! If it is God's will, at some point he'll put your head in the tiger's mouth. *(silence)* You can't go and put your head in the tiger's mouth! *(laughter)* Your head being in the tiger's mouth has happened because it is God's will and the destiny of this body-mind organism.

Why are the heads of only certain people in the tiger's mouth? Because it is the destiny of that body-mind organism. The programming in that body-mind organism is such that this kind of seeking happens. If the programming is to seek money, that's what will be happening—money will be sought. Expectation arises because there is an individual seeker who says, "I want power. I want money. I want enlightenment." The basic understanding which will arise—if it is God's will and the destiny of a body-mind organism—is that there has never been a seeker! Life is nothing but *seeking*! Therefore I keep repeating, "Ever since a baby is born it seeks its mother's breast intuitively." The baby does not consider itself a seeker of the mother's breast. The *seeking* after the mother's breast happens intuitively.

The problem arises, the expectation arises, because a seeker comes into being and says, "I want this." The expectation is there! So whether the seeker is seeking money, or whether the seeker is seeking power, or whether the seeker is seeking enlightenment, *there is truly no seeker!* A particular kind of seeking happens in a body-mind organism because it is programmed for that kind of seeking to happen. *(silence)*

52

So, you've heard something and the brain reacts to what is heard. How does the brain react to what is heard now, Mauna?

MAUNA *Ah...*

RAMESH What is the reaction of the brain to what has just been heard?

MAUNA (silence)

RAMESH That's right! Silence! "Who" asks any question? There is *no one* to ask any question. Quite right. So, what happens? Silence!

MARKUS *Is it correct that there never was a thinker, there never was a perceiver, there were never entities which perceive things?*

RAMESH What you say is correct. I repeat again, and again, and again, "This is a concept!" What the mind says is, "How do I know it is the Truth, how do I know what Ramesh is saying is the Truth?" It is not! It is only a concept! Whether that concept is acceptable to this body-mind organism or not depends on the programming. You see?

MARKUS *I want to get clear about "I" and "ego," like what the concepts are about "I" and "ego."*

RAMESH So, the ego is the "me"!

MARKUS *It's the illusion that there is a perceiver?*

RAMESH What you say is there's really no thinker! That is quite correct. My concept is *thinking happens* but there is *no thinker, doing happens* but there is *no doer.* Seeking is part of the doing! There is doing but no doer, seeking is part of the doing; therefore, there is *seeking* but *no seeker.* Experiencing happens, but no experiencer.

MARKUS *So, the ego is the illusion that there is...*

Ramesh   A thinker, a doer, a seeker, an experiencer. Quite right! *(silence)* But *it is there*! It is there, isn't it? The ego is still there, the thinker is still there, the doer is still there, the seeker is still there, the experiencer is still there which says, "I experience pain or pleasure." It is still there. So what does this ego do, Markus?

Markus   *Whatever God acts through it.*

Ramesh   That is correct. So what this listening produces is the understanding that the doing will happen, the thinking will lead to the doing, and the doing will lead to consequences. The thinking or seeing or hearing or any of the senses will lead to some doing, and the doing will lead to consequences. The doing happens through a body-mind organism because it is God's will, the consequences also happen because it is the destiny of that body-mind organism and God's will. So the mind-intellect at this point says, "Why has God created the psychopath at all? Why has God not created all body-mind organisms of a Mother Teresa or a Father Teresa?" *(laughing)* You see, this is what the mind-intellect says, which means asking God why he's doing some things. So "who" is this "I" asking God why he's doing one thing and not another?

Markus   *God asking himself.*

Ramesh   God will ask himself, quite right, until there is the realization that the "me" cannot ask questions, then the asking questions will stop! *Only* if it is God's will. The questioning stops because the understanding happens that there is truly no answer to the questions that the mind raises. Then the questioner gets absorbed in God.

Mita   *Ramesh, it might be a silly question, but at night when we go to sleep, we dream. But is it really God dreaming within a dream?*

Ramesh   That is correct.

MITA *And if that is so, then the dreams have no significance in terms of our understanding of what they mean, what a dream means?*

RAMESH No. But the personal dream may have significance on the body-mind organism. You see, there is a famous homeopath, Mr. Shankara. One of his main points is that he deals in dreams. So he asks the patient what kind of dreams he has. What he means is among the dreams that happen, there is often one basic point. It may be fear. It may be losing the way. You see? So that helps him to indicate the medicine.

MITA *Yes, because we therapists, you know, we are taught to examine your dream and...*

RAMESH *Sure!* That's why I'm saying it!

MITA *So all of that is still, would you say, valid to do, or would you just throw it all out?*

RAMESH Wait a minute, wait a minute! The validity refers to phenomenality. The validity remains for this life. You see? There is disease; therefore there is the physician, and the physician gives you medicine. Whether the medicine works or not—it's God's will! So these therapists examine the patient's dreams and make some suggestions. Whether the suggestions work or not will again depend on the destiny of that patient and the will of God. But all of it— the disease, the medicine, the dream and its analysis— refers to phenomenality. It happens in the phenomenality of this life. It really has nothing to do with the spiritual part!

But as far as the spiritual part of it is concerned, the personal dream and the living dream are basically not different. In the living dream there are rivers and mountains thousands of years old, babies being born, people dying. Same thing happens in a personal dream. In other words, in this living dream the basis of the living

dream is space and time, and the basis of your personal dream is also space and time; therefore, essentially both dreams are very much alike.

WOLFGANG *What is the meaning of the Guru? Does the Guru know the disciple through the impersonal? Does the Guru feel love for the disciple?*

RAMESH Does the Guru feel love for the disciple? "He" doesn't feel love for the disciple, Love between the Guru and disciple happens. Does the Guru love the disciple? No. Is there Love between the Guru and disciple? *Yes.*

ESTRELLA *It's impersonal?*

RAMESH Depends on how you look at it. That's why if your question is "Does the Guru love the disciple?", then no. "Is there Love between the Guru and disciple?" Yes.

ESTRELLA *Love is not personal? Love is impersonal?*

RAMESH Love is impersonal, correct.

ESTRELLA *Always?*

RAMESH No not always. Love can be personal. If there is a man and woman and they love each other, is not that love personal?

ESTRELLA *Yes. I think there is a difference between Love and personal love. Love is for everybody.*

RAMESH Yes. So what you are talking about is personal love and impersonal Love. Sure, there is impersonal Love and there is love.

ESTRELLA *No, but when love is personal...*

RAMESH You see, if somebody says, "I love this," then that is personal love. If the Love happens, then it is impersonal Love. "I love this person" or "I love this object" is personal love, which love can change to hate.

ESTRELLA *Yeah.*

RAMESH So that love which can change to hate is not the Love that I am talking about.

ESTRELLA *Yeah. The personal love can change to hate, but the impersonal Love, no.*

RAMESH The Impersonal cannot change to anything because It is Impersonal.

VERA *Personal love is attachment.*

RAMESH Personal love is attachment. Quite correct.

WOLFGANG *When the disciple is away from the physical presence of the Guru, does the Guru remain inside ?*

RAMESH Inside what?

ESTRELLA *Because I think the love is recognized outside...*

RAMESH Then it means the love of the disciple for the Guru is personal. If the Love which the disciple feels for the Guru is impersonal, distance cannot matter. You see? So if the love is personal, then the love which the disciple feels is for the Guru as a personal object which he sees. If the disciple feels the physical presence of somebody and *needs* it, that is not the impersonal Love that you are talking about. If it is real Love which the disciple feels for the Guru, it will remain even ten thousand miles away.

INES *I have another point. The physical presence of the Guru is not necessary. So the impersonal feeling of Love for the Guru—this is for me not on the level of time and space. You can understand?*

RAMESH Yes. And yet the physical presence of the Guru does bring about a feeling, and that feeling can itself be bondage. If a disciple feels that he *has* to be near or in the physical presence of the Guru, it is a bondage.

Swami Nityananda—he was Swami Muktananda's Guru—had another disciple who he thought was very close to enlightenment. So he told him to leave the ashram and go and live somewhere else, because Nityananda realized that was the disciple's bondage. The disciple's last vestige of bondage was the *need* of the physical presence of the Guru. So he sent him away. You see?

BRENT *Can you talk a little bit more about the Guru-disciple relationship? When I read the book about how Mark came and saw you and just felt special. There was like a connection. And then he went away for a long time and knew that it was pointless to seek, but still, internally, the seeking went on. Basically, he said something like you were always there for him even though in physical presence you weren't there. But you were there. Can you explain?*

RAMESH What's there to explain?

BRENT *I don't understand it.*

RAMESH What don't you understand? What he said was that he was five thousand miles away, but the presence was there.

BRENT *And this is important for the transformation of the heart? The actual devotion to you or just the teaching ?*

RAMESH You see, the Guru-disciple relationship is essentially an Eastern concept, an Indian concept. It is a totally foreign concept to the Western mind. The Western mind says, "teacher and pupil." The pupil pays something to the teacher and that's the end of that. But the Guru-disciple relationship is essentially spiritual. The same thing persists in art and music in India. The Guru is considered as God, even in art and music.

BRENT *It seems like, often at night, before I go to sleep, there will be questions that come up or small doubts. But when I sit here in the morning they seem irrelevant. I'm just saying it's like why did I even think that last night. Do you know what I mean?*

RAMESH Sure.

BRENT *For example, Alana asked you about rebirth, which was a bit much for me. There is a resistance. Even now, intellectually, there is absolutely no substance to it. But when I sit here there doesn't seem to be any point in asking a question. However, when I go home and I'm away from you...*

RAMESH There is a certain atmosphere in this room. You don't have this atmosphere just anywhere. What happens in this atmosphere is the mind is subdued. That is part of What Is.

BRENT *So in that sense, for the deeper understanding...*

RAMESH You see, it is part of this concept of Guru-disciple relationship that the more devotion the disciple has the quicker the process will happen. That is the basis of this concept. The Guru-disciple relationship is a concept.

BRENT *And to actually be sitting in the presence of the Guru...*

RAMESH Yes.

BRENT *That's what I'm trying. For two months I've come back and you've told me nothing different from what you told me last time, but at some level it has gone deeper. And this is the benefit of sitting with the Guru. So to actually be in the presence of the Guru is better for the teaching to grow stronger than to sit at home reading books.* (everyone laughs) *I know why I can't go home.*

INDRANI *Ramesh, it's good what he's saying because I experienced the same thing when we went back in February after we were here for twelve days. I had this atmosphere which continued a long time, and then suddenly it dropped because I felt jealousy popping up and then something else would pop up. I thought, "Gosh, it's all ended again. It's all coming back again. Why? Why?" And now I'm back here and it's all gone again. It's funny, I'm glad that he asked you this, because...*

RAMESH   Yes.

BRENT   *When I went home last year, I was going to go back to school. I was thinking, "What are you doing with your life? Get on with your life." All that sort of thing. Follow the dreams. But within a week of getting back home, my life had changed. All the things that had made me happy didn't make me happy anymore. But I knew my programming was such that I had no other way of living life. So within a week I knew that I was coming back here. And then when I got back here I thought, "What am I doing here? Why aren't I getting on with my life?" So it's a different feeling to actually be sitting here.*

RAMESH   Sure.

MARTA   *How necessary do you think, do you believe it is to have a Guru to become enlightened?*

RAMESH   You see, it is part of the Indian tradition. According to the Indian tradition it is necessary to have a Guru.

MARTA   *Okay, tradition. That is a tradition. But what is your concept about this?*

RAMESH   My own feeling is that a living Guru is necessary. But I'm not saying that a transformation *cannot* happen unless you have a Guru. But it is helpful to have a Guru to guide you.

BRENT   *So when you were translating for Maharaj, intellectually you had a very strong grasp?*

RAMESH   No. On the contrary, I went practically bare.

BRENT   *No. I mean after six months of translating, you had a good solid understanding of what his concepts were?*

RAMESH   Oh, yes indeed!

BRENT   *After that six-month period when you had an intellectual understanding, were many doubts still coming up for you, before the final understanding?*

RAMESH   No.

BRENT   *No?*

RAMESH   It became less and less and less and less until they disappeared.

INDRANI   *Ramesh, didn't Ramana Maharshi say that a Guru is not necessary, that Self-enquiry alone would help?*

RAMESH   No. He repeatedly said a Guru is necessary.

INDRANI   *Then I misunderstood.*

RAMESH   Yes. He said he himself did not have a physical Guru, but he always said a Guru is necessary.

INDRANI   *I see. So he didn't have a Guru.*

RAMESH   *He* didn't have a Guru. But he was one in a billion.

HANS   *There is an introductory word in one of the books which states that the Guru gives up his oneness for the sake of the Guru-disciple relationship.*

RAMESH   Yes.

HANS   *And that the Guru is absorbing the feeling, the sense of duality from the disciples. I mean, there is much more than just listening to the talk here. Did I understand correctly that the Guru is somehow taking on himself this duality that each of us is feeling, the sense of being split or separate? How is it that the Guru is taking this away from the disciple?*

RAMESH   God's will. God's will. So the Guru-disciple relationship is the mechanism through which the seeking is happening. You see? The Guru-disciple relationship is merely the mechanism—phenomenal mechanism—through which the seeking is happening.

HANS *But there is much more than only words being exchanged. The teaching in words is just a little part of it.*

RAMESH How do you mean?

HANS *I mean, you give intellectual explanations of how it works, how our ego is set up, the whole teaching. This is an intellectual process at one level.*

RAMESH Indeed, yes.

HANS *But other processes are going on at a much deeper level at the same time.*

RAMESH Yes. It goes on. That is correct. But unless the understanding is there, then in most cases it has to be at an intellectual level.

HANS *As a starting, for a start.*

RAMESH Yes, that's right. Because "who" is seeking? The seeking is happening through the mind-intellect which is part of the programming of the particular body-mind organism through which the seeking is happening. So this mind-intellect is the seeker, and the seeking is happening through the mind-intellect until there is the realization in the mind-intellect that what is being sought is *beyond* its understanding. You see? The seeking goes on until there is the realization by the mind-intellect that what is being sought is impossible for the mind-intellect to understand. And then the mind-intellect surrenders. You see? The mind-intellect can surrender only when it comes to the conclusion, again intellectually, that what is being sought is truly beyond it. Why, Hans? Why? How can the mind-intellect come to the conclusion that what is being sought is beyond it?

HANS *To me it's an experience that the mind stops. That there*

63

is this state of awareness where there is no thinking. At the same time, I'm sitting here having heard your words over and over again. Intellectually I understand, but I'm being drawn here every day. I come from far away just to sit here. Even though I've heard your words so many times, it feels like a moth being drawn into the candle's light, into the candle's flame. I don't understand why, it just happens.

RAMESH   That is part of the phenomenal mechanism of the seeking. The process of seeking also happens through the body-mind organism of the Guru. You see? It is part of the Indian tradition and later on of the broader Eastern tradition that in the presence of the Guru there is something intangible to help bring about the understanding. And the "presence" of the Guru may continue even after the Guru is no longer physically present. What that "presence" is, is not necessarily physical. You go to Ramanasramam, Ramana has been dead for 47 years, but his "presence" is very much there.

JEAN   *His presence?*

RAMESH   Yes.

JEAN   *In the sense of...*

RAMESH   Pardon?

JEAN   *In what sense do you mean this?*

RAMESH   His presence as Consciousness. Got it?

JEAN   *Yes.*

RAMESH   Good.

INDRANI   *So this is again God's grace acting, that I'm here.*

RAMESH   Absolutely. At this moment, Indrani, *none* of us could have been anywhere but in this room. At the present moment, I repeat, *none* of us could have been anywhere other than in this room.

INDRANI *So you are God's grace that is being busy now* ?

RAMESH Yes, sure. Yes.

MARTA *Does the Guru have to be a living master* ?

RAMESH Yes, that is what the Indian tradition says.

MARTA *I mean, it has to be actually in the physical presence* ?

RAMESH That is what the Indian tradition says.

VINCENT *How is it determined that this or that person is my Guru?*

RAMESH Ramana Maharshi said you would *feel* it. You would feel it.

VINCENT *I've been with Poonjaji and felt very blessed to be with him, and I felt very much respect for him, but I didn't feel he was my Guru, so...*

RAMESH So?

VINCENT *My question is, actually, "Are you my Guru ?"*

RAMESH You tell me. Are *you* my disciple?

VINCENT *Yes.*

RAMESH Then I'm your Guru.

MARTIN *But you were saying it has to be a physical Guru, or can it also be spiritual? Nisargadatta Maharaj, for instance, can he be my Guru?*

RAMESH They say anything can be your Guru, but a living Guru is better than merely a concept of it. You could say Ramana Maharshi is my Guru, but what the tradition says... Make no mistake. Never forget that whatever is there between a Guru and disciple, it is a concept. It is a concept. Never forget that.

65

PADMA *When you say it is a concept, am I right to understand that there is something basically irrelevant, because what happens anyway is the will of God?*

RAMESH   That is correct.

PADMA *So this concept has no consequence at all.*

RAMESH   That is correct. Quite right.

PADMA *So a concept...*

RAMESH   It's pure intellect to help you. You use a concept to get rid of another concept. So you use a concept of God's will to get rid of the concept that you are a separate individual.

PADMA *Would you call it an illusion of the mind or something like it? Something like a play of the mind is the concept?*

RAMESH   Yes, sure. Quite correct.

PADMA *Of no real importance.*

RAMESH   That is correct. A concept, as you say, is a play of the mind.

PADMA *So, also when you say a Guru is a concept?*

RAMESH   Yes. That's right. I say it's a concept. The Guru-disciple relationship is a concept.

瓦 瓦 瓦

*Tuja saguna mhano ki nirguna re / *
*Saguna nirguna eku Govindu re / / *
*Anumaanenaa, Anumaanenaa / *
*Shruti neti neti mhanati eku Govindu re / / *
*Tuja sthoola mhano ki sookshma re / *
*Sthoola sookshma eku Govindu re / / *
*Tuja aakaaru mhano ki niraakaaru re / *
*Aakaaru niraakaaru eku Govindu re / / *
*Tuja drishya mhano ki adrishya re / *
*Drishya adrishya eku Govindu re / / *
*Nivritti prasaade Jnaanadeva bole / *
*Baaparakhumaadevivaru Viththalu re / / *

Govinda! (Lord Krishna)
Can I praise You by giving You attributes,
  or are You beyond all attributes?
You alone *are*, with and without attributes.
Do not doubt these words, my friends.
The *shruti* says, "Not this, not that"
  and arrives at the I Am,
  the impersonal Awareness of Being,
  the One who is my Govinda.
Govinda!
Are You the gross or the subtle?
In phenomenality Govinda is all there is—gross and subtle.
Govinda!
Are You with form or without?
You alone *are*, in all the forms and beyond.
Do I call You manifest or unmanifest?
Govinda, You are the source of all manifestation.
The Source alone is.
By the grace and authorization from my Guru Nivritti,
  Jnanadev says: All there is is Vitthala (Lord Krishna).

回

*Lahaanapana degaa devaa / mungee saakharechaa ravaa / / *
*Airaawata ratna thora / tyaasi ankushaachaa maara / / *

67

Jyaache angi mothepana / tayaa yaatanaa katheena / /
Tukaa mhane jaana / vhaave lahaanaahuni lahaana / /

God, please make my ego small.
The humble ant is contented with a particle of sugar.
The proud elephant Airawat, a jewel among elephants,
   has to bear the pain of being speared.
He who has a strong ego,
   who believes that his will prevails,
   undergoes a lot of misery.
He can never be Home.
Tukaram says:
   Please understand that for happiness to be,
   the ego has to become smaller than the smallest.

SCENE 3

Neils Bohr said it all when he declared that "A great truth is a truth whose opposite is also a great truth." Alternatively, we could accept the statement of Alfred North Whitehead that "All truths are only half truths." The fact of the matter is that in phenomenality there is no such thing as "truth."

Life is misery and then you die, and we keep on asking why.

A sage has moved away from the reptilian and mammalian brains and is living primarily in what is now known as the new brain—which does not ask why.

INES *I feel that this is very important, that it has an effect in my normal life.*

RAMESH Quite right. In fact, if any teaching that any Guru gives you has no practical effect on your life, then that teaching is no good. It's only a theoretical teaching.

INES *Yes.*

RAMESH A teaching must have some effect on your attitude or on your life, otherwise it's of no use. So what kind of an effect do you think this teaching has on your life?

INES *There are so many effects on so many...*

RAMESH Levels.

INES *So many levels.*

RAMESH How?

INES *For example, in the last weeks the search stopped, and I saw the stupidity of trying to destroy this ego, for example...*

RAMESH Yes.

INES *I saw what kind of motivations were there for becoming enlightened. There is still this identification, but I have no problem with it.*

RAMESH It depends on what you mean by ego, Ines. What do you mean by ego? Do you mean identification with the body-mind organism?

INES *I think that I am someone.*

RAMESH Yes, you are someone. You see, that identification continues after enlightenment. That's why I say whether it is Jesus Christ, Ramana Maharshi, or whoever, if he was called by name he would have responded. Would he not?

INES *Yes.*

RAMESH If he were called by *name*, that means there is identification with the name, and there is identification with the body. So identification with the name and form continues to be there even after enlightenment.

INES *So the main thing is that there's not the idea that there is someone who acts?*

RAMESH Yes. As long as there is a feeling that nobody acts, that there is no *one* to act.

INES *So, it's a feeling to be like a puppet?*

RAMESH Yes, to accept that you are merely a puppet.

INES *And, as I told you, in my case this is switching. There is no longing to feel like a puppet. But this was not the point.*

RAMESH Yes.

INES *Now I see there were quite funny and stupid motivations, like having a good father who says, "Well done!" But there are other effects of your teaching. For example, life feels the same as it felt before, but at the same time there's another view of it. An example of this is sometimes I'm sitting here with you and the view changes. I have the feeling there is only this one Consciousness. I don't feel this as an object, but there is just one, and this whole scene is within It.*

RAMESH Just one event that is happening?

INES *Yes. It is one event which is happening. And you are this, the same as me—an object in this Consciousness.*

RAMESH That's right. And the talking and the listening *is* happening.

INES *Yeah.*

RAMESH Isn't it? The talking and the listening *is* happening.

INES *Yeah, that's true.*

RAMESH That's all that is happening.

INES *It's very different because this Consciousness is always the same, and in the last few weeks this has given me a very separate feeling, you can say. There's no strong emotional movements. It's like...*

RAMESH   Wait a minute. There is no strong emotional movement, you are saying?

INES *No. Yeah. In the beginning when I came here there were strong...*

RAMESH   Emotions. Yes, but now, even now, surely emotions must arise?

INES *Yes. The emotions sometimes come and disappear.*

RAMESH   I understand. Yes.

INES *But there is...*

RAMESH   There is no horizontal involvement in time. That is what you are saying.

INES *Yes, something is always the same.*

RAMESH   Oh, I see.

INES *So emotions can come...*

RAMESH   And go...

INES *... and go. Or situations arise where I feel uncomfortable, and then I feel comfortable. Doesn't matter, something happens. But there is something very...*

RAMESH   I understand. Something there is a *basic*.

INES *There is a* basic.

RAMESH   Which continues changeless.

INES *Yes.*

RAMESH   I see.

INES *And sometimes I'm sitting here and that there is a feeling there is only something going on in this oneness.*

RAMESH   Yes.

INES   *Then I have a thought. Last week I had the thought that I wanted to ask you if you would accept me as your disciple. And then I was sitting here and there was only this oneness. You and I were sitting here, both as objects, and there was no "you" I could ask.*

RAMESH   Yes. And if I accept you as disciple, what will you do, Ines?

INES   *It's so stupid.* (Ramesh laughs) *So I drop this question. You know? I speak about it but...*

RAMESH   Yes. A bit late in the day isn't it, to ask whether I accept you as my disciple? (*laughing fondly as he speaks*) After how many years? (*everyone laughs*)

INES   *It was because you said that Ramana didn't have any, didn't accept any disciples.*

RAMESH   Yes.

INES   *So this question comes up.*

RAMESH   Ramana is the only Guru that I know who stated quite explicitly he had no disciples. You see? And he also said he had no Guru. He had no living human Guru, and he had no living disciples. He made that perfectly clear. Why, I don't know. There need not be any reason, but the fact remains that he said he had no disciples. Therefore, if somebody traces the lineage of his teaching to Ramana Maharshi, that is a lie. That is not true, because the lineage could not have started from Ramana Maharshi since he did not have any disciples. No disciples, no lineage. *No* lineage can start from Ramana Maharshi. That is the point.

RAGHUNATH   *Yesterday you said that the lifespan of human beings and all living things is programmed already.*

RAMESH   Yes, is destined.

73

RAGHUNATH *That means no one can increase it, no one can.*

RAMESH That is what I say and that is a concept.

RAGHUNATH *But modern medical science has succeeded in increasing the average lifespan of the human being.*

RAMESH Yes.

RAGHUNATH *How are you going to explain that?*

RAMESH Do you think this medical research is not part of what Consciousness is doing? You think this medical research that is going on is not part of God's will? Then what makes you think that God, in determining the destiny of a particular body-mind organism, does not take into account the medical research?

RAGHUNATH *The average span of the life has increased.*

RAMESH Average is only statistics.

RAGHUNATH *Then what does it suggest* ?

RAMESH It only suggests that God *knows* what is going to happen. Therefore, in fixing the destiny of certain body-mind organisms, God always takes into account medical research. *(pause)* I still don't see the problem. *(pause)* You are talking of someone's destiny being formed and medical research taking place later? Is that your problem?

RAGHUNATH *I'm coming back to the original question. The medical research that is taking place—is it not the result of perseverance on the part of mankind* ?

RAMESH Where did this perseverance *come* from? Where did mankind buy that perseverance from?

RAGHUNATH *Individuals, you know.*

RAMESH Yes, I know, but where did that individual buy this perseverance from? Is that perseverance of those particular individuals not part of their programming? The patience of certain people, the perseverance of others, the genius of a few individuals—are these qualities not part of the programming of body-mind organisms? And that programming—who has fixed that programming? God has fixed that programming. Isn't it? So where is the problem? I still don't see the problem.

RAGHUNATH *The problem is we find we are making progress.*

RAMESH "Who" is making "what" progress? There is progress. *Yes.* There is evolution and there is progress. "Who" is making that progress, and is that progress independent of God's will? The progress that is being made by human beings—individuals with tremendous perseverance, tremendous patience—is that independent of God's will? Is that patience and perseverance not part of the programming of those individuals?

RAGHUNATH *That is so.*

RAMESH If that is so, then obviously God has programmed those body-mind organisms with such patience and perseverance so that they will pursue this medical enquiry. Isn't it?

ESTRELLA *The identification becomes lost.*

RAMESH Becomes lost. That is because it is God's will.

ESTRELLA *Destiny?*

RAMESH Destiny. God's will for that to happen through a body-mind organism.

ESTRELLA *But a body-mind organism doesn't do anything? That is what's happening?*

RAMESH That is happening. That is correct. The body-mind organism does nothing. That is the whole point.

ESTRELLA *If I will it or not will it?*

75

RAMESH   You cannot will it and you cannot not will it. If this body-mind organism has been programmed to will it, it will will it. But whether that willing it happens or not depends not on the one who wills, but on God's will. I mean, nothing can stop you from willing. Willing means wanting. Doesn't it? So wanting happens. Wanting happens if it is supposed to happen. Expectation happens if it is supposed to happen, but whether that expectation turns into what is expected is not in your hands. I mean expectation cannot stop because that is part of God's hypnosis. It is part of the Divine hypnosis that the individual who thinks he or she is an individual will expect something. That is natural. That is part of the *maya*. But whether what is expected will happen or not will depend on your destiny or God's will, which is the same thing.

ESTRELLA   *That means the ego is stupidity* ?

RAMESH   *Yes!* But still it is there, isn't it? I mean, having understood that the ego is stupidity, will the ego go away?

ESTRELLA   *I cannot do* nothing.

RAMESH   You cannot do nothing. You cannot do anything at all about anything. You see? Yet you have to do something. So what can you do? Just wait and watch whatever happens. What else can you do? Just watch what happens without judging it as good or bad. You see? Other than that what can you do?

WOLFGANG   (reading Estrella's questions) *Okay. So Consciousness chooses a particular thinking mind, ego, to eliminate, and then the Impersonal flows through that body-mind organism which continues as an object.*

RAMESH   Yes. Quite right, even if enlightenment happens quite early as in Ramana Maharshi. He lived almost fifty years after that. How did Ramana Maharshi live for fifty years? He was doing whatever anyone thought he was doing. The doing happened. There was no Ramana

Maharshi who thought "he" was doing anything. But the doing continued to happen because there was a body-mind organism through which Energy continued to function according to the way it was programmed, and according to the way that body-mind organism was destined. That body-mind organism was destined to die of cancer, therefore cancer happened. (*pause*) You see?

So you can say, "How could he have been enlightened if he was not able to avoid cancer? If there is a 'me' who is enlightened, then that 'me' should probably be able to stop cancer." But enlightenment means that there is no "me." So the "me" cannot care how the body-mind organism is dying. The body-mind organism dies according to the way it is destined to die and in the circumstances in which it is destined to die. There is no "me" to care.

WOLFGANG *Inside the body-mind organism where enlightenment has happened, there is the apperception of being an instrument. The sense of one's own will is lost.*

RAMESH That is correct. The sense of one's personal will is lost. That is correct. In fact that is enlightenment. Enlightenment means there is no "me" with a sense of personal doership. "I" can do nothing. Everything that happens is God's will. One-hundred percent acceptance of that—which is surrender to God's will— *is* enlightenment. That does not lead to enlightenment, that *is* itself enlightenment.

NANDA *I was feeling frustrated the last few days with my high expectations, like I thought I should be able to fulfill them. And then I realized, because you've said over and over again, that I couldn't do anything.*

RAMESH Yes.

NANDA *Then at some point I decided that maybe I should drop my expectations and just accept the good things which come along, with whatever understanding is there now.*

RAMESH   Sure. Quite right. There's a sense of satisfaction that arises when there is some acceptance. Acceptance is not in "your" control. If there is nothing in "your" control, then there is nothing for "you" to do.

NANDA   *Every time I know this I "go out" again, I project something outward again because it's such a nice feeling.*

RAMESH   Yes. So you see, the point is there is no objection, Nanda, to feeling that you are doing something. At the turn of the century a German genius called Hans Veihinger wrote a book called *The Philosophy of As If*. In it he says that if you truly understand and accept that you have no free will, that you have no control over anything, then having accepted it you go about your business in life *as if* you have free will. He used the sun as an example. You *know* that the sun is not moving anywhere, yet you use the words "sunrise" and "sunset" as if the sun is moving. So use your "free will," *assume* that you have free will, and continue to use the word, and continue to *act as if* you have free will.

 Since this is so, that is why I say, "How do you act, how do you live your life, how do you make your decisions?" And the answer is very simple: do whatever you like to do by any standards of social justice, morality, and responsibility *as if* you have free will—knowing deep down that you have no free will. Then what happens is the weight of those decisions does not hang on. You know deep down that you have no control. Nothing can happen unless it is the will of God. So with that understanding, what happens is you make your decisions, you act as if you have acted, but the weight of responsibility, including any possible guilt or regret, does not remain. You see?

BILL   *Can we apply that to* sadhana*, spiritual practices, actions in the world, business relations? What of practice or effort? I've read quite a bit of Ramana Maharshi and he says that as long as there's a sense of other or separation...*

RAMESH So what does he say? He says to find out Who am I? Doesn't he? And he says you expect something. Then what is the answer? "Who" expects it? You want something. "Who" wants it? You want to know something. "Who" wants to know? So when this question is asked there is a subtle reminder that there is no "me." Therefore, he says when you ask this question the "me" drops into its Source. The Source is Consciousness. Where has the "me" come from? The "me" has come from Consciousness, or God. So when you ask this question the "me" drops into Consciousness, or God, becomes merged in God. That is truly *japa* practice,something which you keep repeating. You see? Which practice are you referring to? You said "*sadhana*."

BILL *That's the only one that I'm aware of.*

RAMESH You're not aware of any practice of meditation or yoga?

BILL *I dropped that stuff.*

RAMESH Oh, I see. You are not aware of any process of *kundalini*-arousing?

BILL *Thousands of techniques and processes, yes.*

RAMESH So you said you have dropped them?

BILL *Yes.*

RAMESH Did *you drop* them or did they *get dropped* in the process of seeking?

BILL *They got dropped.*

RAMESH They got dropped as part of the evolution, as part of the process of seeking. They began, let them begin. They have dropped off, let them drop off. So accept whatever is happening. Therefore I repeat again: perhaps you like to meditate and the question is should you or should you not

79

meditate. The answer is simple—meditate! If you feel like meditating, meditate. If you like salmon, eat salmon!

BILL *So I have a choice of whether to make the effort of enquiry, or I can just watch TV? It seems like this ego has a choice.*

RAMESH   No, what I'm saying is whatever will happen, will happen according to the destiny of this body-mind organism. If the destiny of this body-mind organism is to watch TV, watching TV will happen. If the destiny of this body-mind organism is to practice Self-enquiry, the practice of Self-enquiry will happen. It does not depend on Bill's wishes. So it is truly not Bill's choice whether to watch TV or whether to practice Self-equiry. That is my whole basis. It is not under Bill's control. Bill doesn't even have the control to raise his arm. Bill doesn't even have the control to scratch. Why do you scratch? Because there's an itch. If the itch wasn't there you wouldn't have scratched. So apparently you did the scratching because the itch happened. Ramana Maharshi told a man this basic that everything is destined, no individual has free will. Have you read that?

BILL   *Yes.*

RAMESH   So this man raised his arm and said, "By raising my arm, is that also part of the destiny, not my free will?" And Ramana Maharshi confirmed it. Now why did Ramana Maharshi confirm it? There was no further questioning. If the man had insisted on further questioning I don't know whether Ramana Maharshi would have answered it. Ramana Maharshi had a trick of looking over somebody's shoulder and sitting silent if they persisted with stupid questions. (*laughter*)
  So what he would have said I don't know, but there is a very simple answer. Why did this man raise his arm, Bill? He thought "he" had raised his arm. He raised his arm because he heard Ramana Maharshi say that he had no free will. The brain reacted and then "he," the thinking

mind, thought, "What does he mean I have no free will? I can raise my arm." So the man raised his arm. The man raising his arm was primarily a reaction of the brain to something that was heard. You see? And to that extent, therefore, it was not out of his free will that he raised his arm. Raising of the arm was merely the reaction of the brain and then the involvement of the thinking mind to being told that he had no free will.

BILL *But the* maya *reflects back to the ego that I am doing this. So it sure does seem like I have a choice to touch a person. It seems that way.*

RAMESH And that *is maya.*

BILL *Ah ha!*

RAMESH Your thinking that you have the choice as a separate individual to do what you like is itself *maya,* or Divine hypnosis.

INES *There is always an interpretation going on.*

RAMESH Which is the thinking mind.

INES *For example, where our hotel is, there is a fair and puppets.*

RAMESH On Sundays?

INES *Yes. And we are the same like those puppets.*

RAMESH You are indeed.

INES *And there's always the mind interpreting it and playing with images and making a story out of it. All the time.*

RAMESH Yes, but the children watching the puppets, do you think the children think they're mere puppets?

INES *No. For the children they are real.*

RAMESH They think they are real. So the children are "hypnotized" into thinking that the puppets are real. You see? So that is how Divine hypnosis has hypnotized us into thinking that all these objects that we see in the manifestation, all the human beings, are real.

INES *And also if I see someone, I don't see him as he is. I interpret: I like him or...*

RAMESH Quite right.

INES *This fits in my system and this not. He has a meaning in my life or he has not. So it's always only my story in this film.*

RAMESH As Ramana Maharshi says, "All thinking begins with the 'I' thought" which is the ego, which is the sense of personal doership. You see? But the sense of personal doership will lead to involvement. That is natural. But the important thing to understand is that if something leads to involvement all is not lost. Being involved all is not lost.

The involvement continues horizontally in time, there is a sudden realization that you have been involved, and then the involvement gets cut off. Does it not? In the beginning involvement may not get cut off at all, but when there is some understanding, that understanding produces the sudden realization that there has been involvement. So in a presumed scale of zero to ten, involvement may begin and get cut off at 9. As the understanding goes deeper, the sudden realization of involvement happens quicker and quicker. Thus it gets cut off at 9, 8, 7, 6 until finally when the involvement happens there is a sudden realization and the involvement gets cut off immediately. But this sudden realization is not produced by "you," it is produced by the *understanding*. That is what is to be understood. The sudden realization of involvement is not something which "you" can produce out of "your" control. It is the understanding that produces the realization.

INES *Two days ago you said it's not like you have the choice, but there is still the opportunity to suffer and to be bored. This I understood because if there's no involvement there is always the same...*

RAMESH   There is no suffering.

INES   *There is no suffering, but also no longing so much.*

RAMESH   Quite right.

INES   *And no enjoyment, and it's like...*

RAMESH   It's like being bored.

INES   *Yeah, it's like being bored.*

RAMESH   You see, so what you want out of life is only excitement and not unhappiness.

INES   *No, I don't feel bored; I feel very peaceful.*

RAMESH   Peaceful. Wonderful. Then there is no problem. If you interpret that as a sense of peace, that's all you're looking for, Ines. What you are really looking for is peace. Peace means absence of unhappiness *and* absence of excitement.

INES   *But so often we want the excitement also. We want the peace together with the excitement.*

COLIN   *Enlightenment must be the greatest excitement, many people seem to think.*

RAMESH   *Many people* seem to *think.* That is correct. *(laughter)* And that is why they want enlightenment. Bliss. Great bliss. So the word "bliss" is really most misleading. It raises expectations. The word "bliss," related to enlightenment, raises expectations. You see?

COLIN   *So where does the word "bliss," in connection with enlightenment, arise?*

RAMESH   I don't know. I'm not a historian of Vedanta.

COLIN   *I thought that Ramana Maharshi...*

RAMESH   Ramana Maharshi did not speak English. Ramana

83

Maharshi must have used the word *ananda*. Nisargadatta Maharaj did not speak English. So all the books that have said "bliss" are translations for the word *ananda*, and to me *ananda* means peace.

COLIN *Oh, right. Okay.*

KAVITA *Is the experience of ananda, even in an enlightened person, colored by the body-mind organism's...*

RAMESH You see, you have a sense of happiness. Something good happens, then the feeling of happiness arises. What happens after that? Until another expectation arises there is the brief interval between the sense of happiness and another expectation. Is that not peace? So when expectations are not there, what exists is peace.

KAVITA *I was just wondering because I've been reading your translation of Jnaneshwar in* Experience of Immortality *. In parts it is very lyrical and effusive and poetic. It reminds me of bliss and the way we usually think of bliss—a very expansive, joyful state. So I'm just wondering, does it depend on the* jnani's *own...*

RAMESH You see, Jnaneshwar didn't speak English either, and the usual word *Sat-Chit-Ananda*—Being-Consciousness-Bliss—has become a traditional label which gets repeated.

KAVITA *What I mean is, do the different jnanis have different temperaments?*

RAMESH Quite right.

KAVITA *You talk about Nisargadatta Maharaj being different from Ramana Maharshi. So if the jnani has a body-mind organism that has, say, a poetic temperament from nature...*

RAMESH Sure, sure. Then poems will happen. Then poetry will happen.

84

KAVITA *So it colors the expression.*

RAMESH Of course it does.

INES *So my experience is sometimes there is such a strong love, and all this, and then I can make some poetic expression.*

RAMESH Quite right.

INES *But what I understand now is this What Is is always the same. This is where it's happening. It's not this strong fire.*

RAMESH Therefore, my point is *That* exists, what we are. What is the Consciousness? What is the I Am? I Am is that interval between two expectations, one expectation is satisfied, another one hasn't arisen yet, in-between is what is called *ananda.*

INES *But those are not only expectations.*

EVE *So a desire arises and immediately it is satisfied. For instance, I long to have a certain type of watch, and then suddenly it happens that somebody gives it to me. Now there are two things in the desire, I also feel happy.*

RAMESH Yes.

EVE *I feel happy, and I think this watch brought happiness.*

RAMESH Yes.

EVE *Which is wrong.*

RAMESH Quite right. That is wrong. Wrong is correct.

EVE *It is wrong because this feeling of happiness is the release of the tension created by the desire.*

RAMESH Quite correct.

EVE *So that's, in a certain way, to understand that external material things are not going to give us happiness.*

85

RAMESH   Correct, because that doesn't last.

EVE   *Despite the fact we always think, in the material sense, that the more I have the more I will be happy.*

RAMESH   Quite right.

EVE   *And this for me is cutting the root of this realization of a desire because, simply, the tension and the energy which are gone is a feeling of relief.*

RAMESH   Quite right. That is correct.

EVE   *Of course, as you said, ten days later there is another item I see in the catalogue and think, "Oh such beautiful..."*

RAMESH   Quite right.

HELEN   *What you've said looks so simple, but in our daily life, to keep this thing in mind...*

RAMESH   But have I asked you to keep anything in mind? Then, why keep it in mind? Why try to keep anything in mind? Do you always keep in mind that the sun doesn't go anywhere, that the sun is fixed and all the planets revolve? Do you keep *that* in mind?

HELEN   *No.*

RAMESH   *Why* don't you keep it in mind? Shouldn't you keep that in mind? I mean, it's an important fact. *(laughter)* Why don't you have to keep it in mind? You accepted it! All right, so you accept the teaching. That's it. So after that, is your problem what do you do in life? Is that your problem?

HELEN   *Yes.*

RAMESH   How do you make your decisions?

HELEN   *I make decisions and tackle the situation.*

RAMESH   Yes, then you tackle the situation. Make your

decisions according to your standards of morality, responsibility, social justice, and whatever norms you have according to your spiritual disciplines and what your religion tells you to do. Do whatever you want to do according to what you think you should do. In other words, what I'm saying is, do whatever you think you should do. Is that not simple enough?

HELEN *But what I* think *I should do is the programming.*

RAMESH *Yes!* Therefore, why bother? (*laughter*)

HELEN *It is not in my hands.*

RAMESH It is not! Quite right. It is destined. So by whatever standards you make your decision, then that decision was supposed to be made by you according to God's will and your destiny. But that doesn't prevent you, or shouldn't prevent you, from using your discretion *as if* you have free will. You see? Use your standards—"My religion tells me I shouldn't do this, my feeling of social justice tells me I should do that, I should help someone."

Somebody else's religion may tell him to do something else. But by and large most religions will tell you to do the same thing. Social justice will tell you to do the same thing. The only understanding is that what you decide to do will not happen unless it is destiny and the will of God. So make your decisions. Try to put those decisions into effect. Where is the problem? So the teaching is still simple. Isn't it?

EVE *Yesterday Isabelle and I were talking, and unexpectedly one of us said, "If we had done that." Suddenly laughing we looked at each other.* (Ramesh laughs) *But who is there to think? I mean, there is no point going into the past and saying that we should have done something, because it was not in our hands.*

RAMESH No. There is a more direct answer, Eve. And that is: "*If* we had done that. But we *didn't* !" *(laughter)* You see? "But we didn't!" That is the whole point—you didn't!

EVE *We didn't. But why didn't we? Because it was not in our hands. So the laughter.*

RAMESH *Yes*! You didn't. That is all. So what is this sudden laughing? That is the sudden realization that you were involved. You were about to be involved. "Why did we not do that?" was an involvement. Suddenly there was a realization, and that realization is *not* what "you" produced, but that sudden realization is what the *understanding* produced.

EVE *So no more brooding about...*

RAMESH That is the point—no more brooding. Quite right. No more brooding is correct.

DANIEL *Thoughts keep coming.*

RAMESH Do "you" make them happen? You just said "thoughts keep coming." So what do you want to do about it? What *can* "you" do about it?

DANIEL *I start brooding over it.*

RAMESH Yes. So what?

DANIEL *So I should stop.*

RAMESH "Who" should stop? You see? The stopping or involvement will not be there if it is your destiny not to get involved any longer. If it is your destiny to get involved still longer, then it will happen. So let the thoughts come, let the thoughts bring about involvement, let the involvement be there. And if the destiny is for the involvement to be cut off, it will be cut off. And what will cut off the involvement? The understanding. You *have* come here. God *has* sent you here. You *have* been listening. You *have* been under-standing. So now let that understanding *function*. But what "you" want to do is to use that understanding to produce something.

DANIEL *Use understanding to tackle the situation.*

RAMESH   I know. "You" want to use the understanding to "tackle" the situation. Isn't it? That is the whole problem. What I am saying is let the understanding do it. What "you" want to do is to *use* that understanding to tackle the situation, and it can't be done. So if the situation gets tackled, and you think "you" have been able to do it, a sense of pride will arise—"I" tackled the situation. But if you truly understand that the situation *got* tackled, then gradually this sense of doership will become less and less.

◫◫◫

Jethe jaato tethe tu maazaa saangaati /
  Chaala visi haati dharuniyaa / /
Chaalo vaate aamhi tuzaachi aadhaara /
  Chaala visi bhaar save maazaa / /
Bolo jaataa barala karisi te neeta /
  Neli laaja dheeta kelo devaa / /
A vaghe jana maja zaale lokapaala /
  Soire sakal praanasakhe / /
Tukaa mhane aataa khelato kavatuke /
  Zaale tuze sukha antarbaahi / /

Wherever I go, You are with me, my Lord.
You hold my hand and we walk together.
I sought You purely by Your grace.
You took away the misconception of individual doership
  and what remains is peace and freedom.
The thinking mind gets involved and talks stupidly.
  Your grace intervenes and cuts it off.
I was feeling guilty about the ego.
In Your compassion, You gave me the knowledge
  that everything happens by Your will.

You took away my thinking mind.
The working mind is thoroughly enjoying the freedom.
I look at all the people as Your manifestation.
They remain close to my heart.
Tukaram says:
  I now dance in wonder.
  I have realized the peace
  of Your presence within and without.

SCENE 4

If you keep looking at the moon in the water you will miss seeing the moon in the sky. If you keep focusing on the finger pointing to the moon, you will miss the moon. Also, don't forget that today's moon will not be tomorrow's moon!

That prayer is true prayer which is not based on fear and hope.

Consider yourself dead—and you can do whatever you like.

RAMESH   Your name is? What can I do for you?

VISITOR   *My spiritual name is Rishi. My Finnish name is Taavi. We've been to several ashrams. Most of the people there are spiritual seekers, so I believe they want to know themselves or they want to find some peace.*

RAMESH   So, they want to find some peace. That is what they really want. Why is the peace not there?

TAAVI *Because of the mind.*

RAMESH   And you can't get rid of the mind, can you?

TAAVI *Even though we have tried quite a long time, we haven't succeeded totally.*

RAMESH   No! *(laughs)* "You" haven't succeeded—totally or not! Why is that? Because "you" didn't *create* the mind.

TAAVI *No, it was there from the beginning.*

RAMESH   It was there from the beginning. So what you are trying to do is to control the mind and the mind cannot be controlled. The mind has a nature of its own and the nature of the mind is to go out.

TAAVI *Yes, it seems to be working on its own, not asking our permission to do so.*

RAMESH   Quite correct. So, Taavi, my point is your group is on a pilgrimage, seeking peace?

TAAVI *Or God, or the Self, or whatever you call it.*

RAMESH   Yes, and you haven't found it.

TAAVI *I believe we are carrying it with us.* (laughter) *But there seems to be some filters between. So the point might be how to remove these filters.*

RAMESH   That's right. The point is how to remove the filters. So, did you create the filters, Taavi?

TAAVI *I don't know whether I created them or the world created them, but they seem to be there.*

RAMESH   And you didn't create the filters or the screen or the obstruction.

TAAVI *Right.*

RAMESH   So if you didn't create the obstruction, what makes you think you can remove it? You want to remove it by some action which you call "your" action?

TAAVI *Or inaction.*

RAMESH All right. Is that inaction in your control?

TAAVI *So far it seems not to be.*

RAMESH Not to be. What you call "your" action or inaction, positive action or negative action—is it "your" action? My point is, is it Taavi's action? If you watch that, then you will come to the basic. My point is that Taavi can create no action. All that exists, really exists, is a body-mind organism, and an action happens through that body-mind organism.

TAAVI *There seems to be a strong identification with this action or inaction.*

RAMESH Identification? "Whose" identification? You see, there is a "me." There is a Taavi who says, "It is 'my' action." So my suggestion is, if you understand what that action is, then Taavi may accept that it is not "his" action. And if there is no Taavi's action, can there be a Taavi? So my point is try to understand if there is any action which Taavi can call "his" action. What I'm saying is: any action that happens, happens through a body-mind organism.

Make no mistake, whatever I am saying—whatever any sage has said at any time, whatever any scripture of any religion has ever said at any time—is a concept. A concept being something which some people may accept, some people may not accept. So the answer is that whatever I say is not knowledge, it is not truth, it is a concept created by the mind.

TAAVI *If I understand correctly, you want us to question whether our actions are our actions.*

RAMESH That is correct. So my suggestion is that what you

call "your" action is merely the reaction of the brain to an outside event over which you have no control. How does any action happen? Any action happens through a body-mind organism because the brain reacts to a thought which comes from outside. You cannot create a thought. The brain can only react to a thought. The brain is a reactive agent. So a thought which comes is not in "your" control. What you see is not in "your" control. What you hear is not in "your" control. The brain reacts to this thought or something you see or hear or taste or smell or touch.

TAAVI *If I understand correctly, this means that this identification with our actions or our thinking is a spontaneous process which only takes place. And you want that to be changed—is that it?*

RAMESH No! "You" cannot change anything. "Your" changing anything would be "your" act, would it not, Taavi?

TAAVI *Yeah, it would.*

RAMESH It would, and we are still at the point where I am asking Taavi to tell me what is Taavi's action.

TAAVI *As far as I understand, what I call my actions is that I identify myself with the thinking and with the actions which happen here.*

RAMESH So the actions happen?

TAAVI *Yes.*

RAMESH And you say they are "your" actions. But if the actions happen, how can they be "your" actions, Taavi? If they are "your" actions, you must have control over those actions. And what I am saying is that you have no control over "your" actions. Whatever you think are "your" actions are merely the reactions of the brain to a thought or something you see or something you hear or touch or smell—any of the senses. The same thought occurs to three people or thirty people. The same thing is seen by three people, the same thing is heard by three people—yet the brain will react in a different way.

TAAVI *According to the conditioning.*

RAMESH   You are quite right. The brain reacting to an event is out of "your" control, according to a programming that is also out of "your" control.

TAAVI *So it looks like this action or reaction is like a happening which is outside our choice.*

RAMESH   That is precisely what I am saying. An action that happens, happens without "your" control over it, and if an action happens without "your" control, how can you call it "your" action?

TAAVI *I see the point. There must be some reason which has caused that individual to identify himself with this condition and action.*

RAMESH   Quite right. Why does an individual identify himself or herself with actions? Because he or she thinks he or she is a separate individual. But there is no separate individual. All that exists is a body-mind organism. The individual simply does not exist. But it is still there. Taavi may not exist, but he is there. It is Taavi who has to live his life. It is Taavi who has to make decisions. So Taavi to that extent does exist. What I am saying is an action happens and Taavi thinks it is "his" action. So if it is not Taavi's action, then you can have a concept of God, and you can say they are God's actions through a particular body-mind organism.

Every individual body-mind organism is a programmed instrument created by God. Every human being is a uniquely programmed organism. No two individuals are alike. God has these billions of body-mind organisms through which he brings about an output according to the way he wants it. He makes you see or hear or touch something, and the brain reacts and brings out an output. *Any* event is an output according to God's choice. Any action that happens is really God's action.

TAAVI *Life's totalities acting this way.*

RAMESH Certainly. Whether you call it the Universal Law or Consciousness or Totality, you can say that any act that happens is God's act through this body-mind organism or part of the impersonal functioning of Totality, or Consciousness. So all actions which happen through all body-mind organisms at any particular moment—the total of that is *What Is* at the Present Moment.

If you truly understand and accept that all actions which happen are God's actions through a body-mind organism, then you understand that God's will with respect to a particular body-mind organism is what I call the destiny of that body-mind organism—not of an individual—because truly, *the individual does not exist at all*. All that exists is billions of programmed computers through which God, or Consciousness, produces such actions as are supposed to happen.

TAAVI *But as long as an individual feels that he is an individual or that he is an ego, then he has the feeling that "I want to get rid of this problem."*

RAMESH So the problem arises only if you identify that action as "your" action. The mind says, "I did something yesterday or the day before or a year ago, and it hurt certain people." Therefore, you have a sense of guilt. You have a sense of frustration if "your" action does not produce a result which "you" wanted to produce. So if you truly accept that it cannot be your action, then it has to be God's action or an action of Consciousness.

TAAVI *But can it be said this way—that since this conditioning or identification with the actions and thinking process has taken*

96

perhaps millions of years, it is a very strong inclination and therefore it is very hard to get rid of it?

RAMESH   Of course it is. Why is it so hard to get rid of? Because you are trying to get rid of something which you have not created. Who has created this separation? What has brought about this feeling of separation which means unhappiness? "You" didn't create it, so who has created this separation? God has created this separation through what I call Divine hypnosis or what Hinduism calls *maya*. The basis of *maya* is that everyone thinks "he" is separate. Everyone thinks it is "his" action. Therefore, if the action is successful, he feels pride. If the action is not successful, he feels guilt or frustration.

TAAVI   *Does it mean that* maya *means the power of identification?*

RAMESH   *Maya* means false identification with the body-mind organism as a separate individual. *Maya* means separation. If a capable hypnotist can make two thousand people believe that something exists when it doesn't exist, or nothing exists when something exists, would it be impossible for the Divine Hypnotist to make every human being feel that he is separate? So if God has created this hypnosis, my suggestion is that it is only God who can remove it.

TAAVI   *So being under this Divine hypnosis, I believe all the truth-seekers are humbly praying "Please remove this" because it creates so many problems.*

RAMESH   That is all you can do. Pray that he removes this hypnosis. But the seeker doesn't do that. The seeker says, "I can remove the hypnosis by *sadhana*. If I do this *sadhana*, that hypnosis will disappear." What I say is that if you do the *sadhana* it will not disappear unless it is the will of God that the hypnosis disappears. So why is it that one seeker out of thousands is seeking the removal of the hypnosis?

The other thousands are not seeking this, they are seeking something else: money, power, what they call happiness, worldly goods, worldly happiness.

TAAVI *I understand that the amount of suffering and perhaps Divine grace slowly make it so that the veil is removed a little bit and that one starts to find the final removal.*

RAMESH Out of thousands of people there is only one seeker who seeks the removal of the *maya*. The others are happy or unhappy with their identification with this hypnosis.

TAAVI *It must be grace.*

RAMESH You are quite right. Therefore, even the *seeking* of the removal of this hypnosis is God's grace, not because of "your" will or wanting. Therefore, who is the real seeker, Taavi? Is Taavi the seeker or is the seeking happening through a body-mind organism to which the name Taavi is given?

TAAVI *I think that this seeking will not stop even if I would decide that I would stop it. It will continue. I cannot stop it.*

RAMESH You are quite right. So why has the seeking begun in *this* body-mind organism and not in thousands of others?

TAAVI *That's the grace.*

RAMESH I know, but why does grace happen in *this* body-mind organism?

TAAVI *How can I know that?*

RAMESH You can know by understanding that for seeking to happen through this body-mind organism, God has created this body-mind organism with such programming that seeking will happen. If God has produced a body-mind organism with a programming which can only seek money, that body-mind organism will seek money! So it is no use saying, "He is only seeking money. I am seeking enlightenment."

The moment the ego or the individual thinks he is seeking enlightenment, that "he" is a seeker, he consciously or subconsciously places himself in a higher position than someone who is seeking money. That itself strengthens the ego! When will this ego not get strengthened? When you truly understand that there is no seeker after enlightenment. Seeking happens as a matter of grace through a body-mind organism which God has programmed in such a way that this kind of seeking will happen. Therefore, how can Taavi say, "'I' want to hasten this process of seeking"? The process will go on strictly according to the will of God.

TAAVI *The desire to hasten the process is also part of the programming.*

RAMESH Quite correct. But not merely part of the programming, but part of the separation which is the Divine hypnosis. So it is this hypnosis which creates an individual and that individual wants to hasten that process.

TAAVI *But that's quite natural because this Divine hypnosis is quite painful. So it is very natural that the individual who feels himself to be an individual would want to get rid of this hypnosis.*

RAMESH I know. So, you want to get rid of the hypnosis. Someone else wants money, someone else wants power. Where's the difference? No qualitative difference. There is an individual and there is wanting. Whether the wanting is for money, power, or enlightenment truly makes no difference so long as he thinks he is a seeker.

So my point, Taavi, is if you truly understand that there is absolutely no seeker seeking enlightenment but that the seeking is happening, then will there not be some understanding that if "you" did not start the seeking, "you" will have no control over the seeking? Seeking will take its own course. Then will you not sit and at least be relaxed and say, "All right, let the seeking take its own course according to God's will." Then if you let the seeking take its own course, there won't be the unhappiness!

TAAVI *This seems to be leading to the acceptance of seeking as some sort of very natural process.*

RAMESH   Quite correct. You are quite right. Seeking *is* a natural process which is made unnatural by Taavi saying that "he" is a seeker.

TAAVI *I agree that this Taavi is a very unnatural entity, and whatever this ego is trying to do, it creates problems.*

RAMESH   It creates problems. So how can the problems disappear? The problems will disappear only when the seeker understands that "he" is not the seeker. Seeking is an impersonal process at God's will.

TAAVI *This seems to be very understandable. I mean, the ego, "me," cannot reach there by its own efforts.*

RAMESH   The ego cannot reach *what*, Taavi? *What* is the object of the seeking?

TAAVI *Clarity. Situations where the problems created by the mind cease.*

RAMESH   When will they cease, Taavi? They will cease only when there is a total acceptance, a total understanding that there is truly no Taavi as a seeker. *Seeking* is an *impersonal process*. If that is accepted, then only will the seeker disappear. Unhappiness will cease only when the seeker disappears, and even the disappearing of the seeker is not in the control of the seeker.

TAAVI *If I have understood correctly, there seems to be a mental process where there is an understanding that one is impersonal, but then at certain points when there is greater stimuli, the ego comes back again, which makes things very hard.*

100

RAMESH   Certainly. But when that happens, what does Taavi do? Taavi again accepts that he did not create the ego. The ego was created by God. So if the ego comes up again and again and Taavi understands that that is not in his control, why is Taavi unhappy? Because Taavi thinks that "he" should be able to do something about it! But if Taavi truly understands that the arising of the ego is part of that natural process, then let it happen, let the ego come.

TAAVI   *It seems to be unavoidable. One cannot avoid the ego taking form again. If somebody says "You are stupid!" or "You stole my money!" I would say, "No, I didn't!" and the ego is there.*

RAMESH   Quite right. The answer to that is to accept the ego as part of the natural process. Where is the unhappiness, Taavi? The unhappiness arises in "your" trying to control "your" ego. But if you accept the ego instead of fighting it, then the whole attitude is different. What most teachings tell you is that you must fight the ego. You must kill the ego. My point is that "you" are the ego! How can you kill the ego? All that can happen is you accept the ego which is there. It is there because God created it, and it is only God who can remove it.

So when you accept the ego, then you surrender yourself to that Power which has created the ego. When you have surrendered to that Power which has created the ego, what have you really surrendered, Taavi? You have surrendered the ego itself! When you have truly surrendered to that Power which is in control, then what do you say to yourself? You say, "All right, God, do whatever you like. It is your will and your power. If you want the ego to come back again and again, let it come up. I'm not going to fight it."

So the final understanding is *acceptance*, total acceptance or total surrender which means the same thing. You accept that nothing is in "your" control, that there is truly no Taavi. Taavi is merely the name given to a body-mind organism. That is the understanding. But until the understanding becomes total, the ego is bound to come up again and again. Let it come up.

TAAVI *It is true one cannot avoid it coming up. And as I understand it the ego is this energy which keeps coming again and again.*

RAMESH It keeps coming again and again because it is the will of God and the destiny of that body-mind organism.

TAAVI *So this process of surrendering oneself or the process of acceptance—even that is in the hands of God.*

RAMESH That is a good understanding, and it takes you a lot forward when you truly understand that even this acceptance, even this surrender, is not in your control. This surrender or acceptance will happen only when God wants it to happen. But the encouragement in this state of helplessness or hopelessness is that this body-mind organism, so long as it thinks it is an individual, can take encouragement from the fact that he or she is one in thousands who is a seeker after enlightenment—what Ramana Maharshi calls your head is already in the tiger's mouth. So it is an encouragement to the supposed individual so long as he thinks he is an individual and if he is frustrated. This statement says: Don't feel discouraged; your head is already in the tiger's mouth. You are one of the few chosen people through whom the seeking is happening. Let the seeking continue to happen. Let it take its own course. Don't bother with it.

TAAVI *The ego makes this process unnatural, whereas it should be natural.*

RAMESH Yes. Even the arising of the ego is a natural process. And when you even accept the ego, it is a very big thing. When you do not consider it necessary to fight it, it is a big step forward in the understanding. How does this teaching help you in your life? The basic teaching is:

nothing happens unless it is the will of God or the impersonal functioning of Consciousness.

TAAVI *So this means that this living becomes very natural and then God will be guiding this process towards the right end.*

RAMESH   And how does this affect your life? It makes life simpler when you say you are not in control of your life. Any action that happens is not Taavi's action. Any action which happens is God's action through this body-mind organism to which Taavi is a name given. If that is accepted, then you won't have a feeling of guilt. If something has happened which has hurt people, I am not saying you will not try to help them. You will try to help them but without a sense of guilt. If whatever happens turns out to be good, then Taavi will not have a sense of pride because Taavi knows that it is not "his" action. There may be a feeling of satisfaction, certainly. Why not? But there won't be a feeling of pride. So no feeling of guilt or frustration or pride.

   And more important, Taavi, when you understand that anything which happens through this body-mind organism is not Taavi's action, you also understand that something which happens through some other body-mind organism is not his or her action. So someone else may think he or she has hurt you, but you know that action could not have happened unless it was God's will. Therefore if you are hurt, it is not because that other body-mind organism wanted to hurt you, but because the hurt is part of your destiny. You were destined to feel hurt therefore you felt hurt.

TAAVI *Let me raise one question and that's the ethical choice. There are certain points, whether they are part of the programming or not, where one is consciously thinking whether to do this action or that action. And one is naturally thinking that these ethical decisions are part of his spiritual approach. So what is the point of this?*

RAMESH   I will tell you. This is the same question, I think, which Hope had yesterday. *(to Hope)* Have you got your piece of paper?

HOPE   *Yes. But I think I know the answer.*

RAMESH   (*laughing*) Yes. But anyway, let us hear the question.

HOPE   *Well, it was, "If I give up responsibility, can I count on my programming to take over the responsibility?"*

RAMESH   You see, the question of "responsibility," and you are saying "ethics." What it boils down to is: "If nothing is in my control, how can I be responsible? And if I am not to be held responsible, do I act irresponsibly? Am I to act irresponsibly?" The answer is that "you" don't act responsibly or irresponsibly. Whatever happens is according to the will of God. But the practical question still remains, which is your question.

TAAVI   *But there is a possibility for misunderstanding that one would start to follow one's lower instincts and say that this is a spontaneous thing, and it is the will of God.*

RAMESH   Quite right. So, you try to follow your baser instincts. My point is, Taavi, that your following your lower instincts is exactly what God wants you to like. What you like to do is precisely what God wants you to like to do. But what happens? How often does what happen, happen according to what you want? Sometimes it happens according to what you want, and sometimes it happens according to what you do not want. So whatever happens is the will of God. If what has happened is what you wanted, it simply means that it has happened not because you wanted it but because it has tallied with God's will! So if your will does not coincide with God's will, what "you" will, will not happen. Even if you try to follow your baser instincts, if that is not to happen it will not happen.

104

TAAVI *That's true.*

RAMESH So your question is, "What do I do? How do I live my life?" The answer is extremely simple, Taavi. Do whatever you think you should do by any standards of ethics or morality or responsibility.

TAAVI *Let's say that a chain smoker wants to quit smoking. His addiction may say to continue smoking, but he knows that it's good to try to overcome this addiction and get rid of smoking.*

RAMESH So, what I am saying is: what is to prevent him from trying? If the trying is to happen, then it is the destiny of that body-mind organism. If the trying is not to happen, it will not happen. Ten smokers decide to give it up. So how many actually try and how many don't will depend on their respective destinies; and among those who try, who succeeds and who won't will also depend on their respective destinies.

In fact, a colleague of mine in the bank, we used to sit next to each other, used to be a fairly heavy smoker. He said, "Ramesh, I am not going to smoke from tomorrow." He had a tin of fifty cigarettes, he finished the cigarettes, crumpled the tin, and put it into the waste paper basket and said, "I am not going to smoke." And he didn't. Yet smokers have been trying to give up smoking for ages. The American humorist Mark Twain said, "Giving up smoking is easy. I have done it many times."

BRUCE *And what about prayer?*

RAMESH An ordinary man's prayer is really a begging. When a car stops at the traffic light, two beggars come to the car and you decide. When I say you decide, I mean a thought occurs. The scientist says that a thought occurs a fraction of a second before the brain says it is "my" thought. The thought occurs: "This one is a strong man; he can work; I shall not give anything to him." And for the second beggar the thought arises: "He is an old man; he needs help." You decide to give him money. You put your hand in your pocket, and by the time you take out your purse the light has changed and the car goes. So in these two cases it is not the destiny of either of the beggars to receive any money. Whether the beggars receive any money or not does not really depend on what "you" want to do, but on whether it is in the destinies of the beggars to receive the money or not. A third case is a beggar comes, you decide to pay him, you take out your purse, and there is enough time to give him the money. In the three cases it was the destiny of two beggars not to receive money, and the destiny of the third beggar to receive the money. So whether the beggar gets what he wants depends on his destiny.

Whether God answers your prayers or not will depend on your destiny. So we have created a God as a concept because he is more powerful than we are. We are not able to get what we want, and therefore we pray to God. What I am saying is: "By all means pray, but don't expect your prayer to be answered."

BRUCE *Isn't prayer part of the* maya?

RAMESH Yes.

SINGH *But you said that praying is the only thing you can do in order to get enlightened.*

RAMESH No! What I am saying is that praying is the only thing which can happen. When you feel totally helpless— "Nothing is in my control. What can I do?"—pray or hope that that Power will bring about something quicker. But it is not in your control. So the very fact that you pray to God to hasten the process means you accept that it is not in your hands. The fact of accepting that it is not in your control is a big step forward. But the true prayer is that prayer when there is no "one" praying. Gratitude is a true prayer. The thought suddenly occurs, "Considering everything in the world, I am in such a happy position." A sense of gratitude arises. That is the genuine prayer— prayer in which there is no one praying for anything.

SYDNEY *So actually, if there is this longing to pray to someone, it's okay to localize Consciousness, or the Source, in a manifestation such as one's Guru or a Divine manifestation?*

RAMESH Sure! I mean, if it is easier to pray by "localizing" Consciousness, or the Source—why not?! You see, if you feel the Source is too impersonal, then localize It on Ramana Maharshi, Jesus Christ, Mary, Buddha, Krishna, Kuan Yin, or whomever.

BRUCE *Ramesh, can you say something about the Gayatri mantra?*

RAMESH It is a mantra and every sacred mantra is supposed to have a certain power, a certain energy. The basis is that the mantra will release certain energy, and whether that energy produces what is expected will again depend on the destiny of the body-mind organism concerned.

TAAVI *God is searching for himself through me?*

RAMESH God is searching for himself through a body-mind organism—not through "you," not through Taavi! Taavi is not concerned. Let the seeking take its own course. When the seeker takes the attitude of letting seeking take its own course, more and more it doesn't matter.

TAAVI *I believe this would mean that since the seeking has started already by the will of God, then because of the will of God it will continue to its end.*

RAMESH That is correct—in its own time, in its own process. And when this is accepted more and more deeply, the seeker goes more and more into the background and the seeking happens more and more quickly; because it is the seeker, the individual, who is the obstruction. So that final acceptance is when the seeking happens and there is no seeker.

TAAVI *It is nice that you say that there is the obstructer to the seeking.*

RAMESH Yes, the seeker is the obstruction.

TAAVI *For the seeking to take place.*

RAMESH You see, seeking begins with a seeker seeking enlightenment with the objective that it will give him great happiness or peace—that is, it will give him something. And the seeking will disappear only when you understand that there is truly no seeker. The seeker surrenders himself, and then the enlightenment is likely to happen. When the seeker truly comes to the conclusion that it is not in "his" hands, why should "he" bother?

TAAVI *Is the seeker witnessing the seeking taking place?*

RAMESH *Which* seeker? The individual? No!

TAAVI *But there seems to be awareness.*

RAMESH Yes. So when the seeker goes further and further into the background there is more and more awareness of impersonal seeking.

BRUCE *Do all kinds of rituals and those kinds of things help the seeker to come quicker to...*

RAMESH You see, some body-mind organisms will go in for rituals, some will not. Why will some body-mind organisms go in for rituals? Because it is the destiny of that body-mind organism, for the seeking to happen, to pass through the stage of ritual!

BRUCE *So it is not for everybody.*

RAMESH It is not for everybody. If some body-mind organism is programmed for *bhakti*, devotion, that body-mind organism will not react easily if the teaching is *jnana,* knowledge. It may be that a body-mind organism is programmed in such a way that both *bhakti* and *jnana* are there. But a body-mind organism may be programmed in such a way that both money and spirituality be sought! It is not that the programming excludes one from the other. The only thing is to accept whatever happens as God's will. So if God sends you to a place where there is *bhakti,* accept it. Then a thought may occur, God will send the thought: "It is enough, now you go somewhere else." So the body-mind organism goes somewhere else.

LINDA *Have you ever considered or heard of collective seeking* ?

RAMESH   Sure. You have heard of this Maharishi Mahesh Yogi? He is quite well known.

LINDA *Oh! TM, yes!*

RAMESH   Oh! TM! Yes! *(laughing)* When my daughter went in for Transcendental Meditation some years ago, her son was six years old at the time. She used to tell him, "Look, I am now doing my TM. Don't disturb me for twenty minutes. Make sure nobody disturbs me for twenty minutes." So he told my wife, "Mummy practices TM. Do you know what TM means?" My wife said, "No." He said, "Twenty Minutes." *(everyone laughs)*

So, Maharishi tried an experiment. He had, I think, two thousand people doing this TM twice a day for fixed periods for three months in a small place somewhere in the States. And the police commissioner reported that the crime rate had gone down substantially for no apparent reason. So, *something* happens!

LINDA *What I'm talking about isn't silent meditation. I'm talking about conversation where the group is actually practicing seeking together through questioning.*

RAMESH   Certainly! There is energy producing meditation in one case, energy producing conversation in the other.

It is still energy functioning collectively. Energy functioning collectively will produce something.

SINGH *I have a hard time with this thing about experience. For instance enjoyment, and how you say there is no one to enjoy but there is enjoyment.*

RAMESH Certainly! Sure.

SINGH *So this I don't understand. You, this body-mind organism that is Ramesh, experience this enjoyment which is out there.*

RAMESH Yes. Enjoyment will arise, fear may arise, anger may arise, gratitude may arise, compassion may arise, satisfaction may arise. Satisfaction is enjoyment! So what arises is a reaction of the brain to an outside event. You eat something which, according to your programming, you like. There is satisfaction, there is enjoyment!

SINGH *Without anybody to be satisfied or have satisfaction.*

RAMESH That's right. Therefore, I am saying—anger happens, there is no one to be angry; gratitude arises, there is no one to be grateful; compassion arises, there is no one to be compassionate; fear arises, there is no one to be afraid.

SINGH *I think I can mouth those words, but how can I be sure there is actually no one?*

RAMESH You can't! Unless it happens to you. When it happens to you, you will understand.

SINGH *Maybe it would help if one keeps saying "There is no one who is actually experiencing; this is just happening."*

RAMESH Ho! In any experience—whether it is sheer terror or sheer ecstasy—when it happens there is no experiencer. *All* experience is impersonal experience. The personal experiencer comes later and says, "'I' had a horrible experience." Or, "'I' had a wonderful experience."

SINGH *When experiencing is happening, the person is out of the way, like enjoying food.*

RAMESH   That's right. That is correct. So the person says, "'I' had an excellent meal." But that will not happen. The enjoyment will happen. You see, that is why the sage is supposed to be a *maha bhogi*, a super-enjoyer. The sage is eating a meal, there is great satisfaction. Why is he a super-enjoyer? Because he doesn't compare that satisfaction with something he had earlier, or he doesn't wonder, "When am I going to have a meal like this again?" So when he is not bothered about the future, the enjoyment is direct. That is why he is called a *maha bhogi* because there is no individual enjoyer. Also, he is called a *maha tyagi*, a renouncer or super-giver, because there is no individual who gives up anything. So there is only giving up.

SINGH *The thinking mind is not processing.*

RAMESH   The thinking mind is not concerned. Quite right.

BRUCE *Ramesh, I have a question about the concept of destiny. When you refer to destiny, is it the destiny of the body-mind organism?*

RAMESH   Yes. Indeed!

SINGH *Does that include or is that similar to the destiny of the ego?*

RAMESH   No. The ego has nothing to do with it. It is the destiny of the body-mind organism. The destiny is always of the body-mind organism. The ego, frankly, doesn't exist! The ego does not have a destiny.

BRUCE *Does the body-mind organism exist?*

RAMESH   The body-mind organism exists as part of the manifestation.

SINGH *What is the ego?*

RAMESH The ego is the Divine hypnosis, the ego considering itself as a separation. Divine hypnosis creates separation and that separation is an ego, the identification with a body-mind organism as a separate individual. So when the ego is removed, the hypnosis is removed. Who can remove the hypnosis? Only that Power which created the hypnosis can remove it.

SINGH *The mind is a collection of thoughts.*

RAMESH Ramana Maharshi said, "Mind is a collection of thoughts." He must have been speaking in Tamil. In my case the concepts of a working mind and thinking mind arose which people have found very useful for understanding. When Ramana Maharshi referred to the mind he was referring to the thinking mind. The thinking mind is a series of thoughts and what I call horizontal thinking. Ramana Maharshi said "collection of thoughts," which is involvement in both cases. Horizontal thinking is involvement.

BRENDAN *But Ramesh, Nisargadatta Maharaj said, "Mind is the content of the Consciousness."*

RAMESH Yes. That is to say Consciousness is the source of the mind. Where does the mind arise? Where does thinking arise? Only if you are conscious.

BRENDAN *How can you differentiate between ego and mind?*

RAMESH You can't. They are the same. The thinking mind and the ego are the same. They are synonyms.

BRENDAN *Then why isn't it the ego that has the destiny? This, the body-mind organism, is just a mechanical...*

RAMESH I know. So what happens to the body-mind organism is the destiny of the body-mind organism. Whatever happens in life to that body-mind organism happens only to the body-mind organism—it does not happen to the ego. The ego, because of this hypnosis, thinks, "It is happening to me."

BRENDAN *I thought you said mind and ego are synonymous.*

RAMESH Yes! The thinking mind and the ego are the same.

SINGH *So when you say body-mind organism, you include mind.*

RAMESH No! Body-mind organism, mind can be both. In the ordinary case it is working mind and the thinking mind. In the case of a sage it is only the working mind.

SINGH *Is the body-mind organism like the program in a data machine which produces thinking?*

RAMESH The thinking happens according to the way that the body-mind organism has been programmed. The thought will arise as God's input into a particular body-mind organism. Why does a thought occur? Because that is supposed to produce an output. So the equation $E=MC^2$ was there all the time, but it was only that body-mind organism named Einstein which was programmed to receive the equation that got that thought.

BRENDAN *When you use the term "body-mind organism," you don't mean mind?*

RAMESH The term "body-mind organism" means body and, in the case of an ordinary person, both the working mind and the thinking mind, but only the working mind in the case of a sage.

TAAVI *Doesn't this mean that this destiny when it happens to the body-mind is factual, but what happens to the ego is fiction?*

RAMESH That is correct, Taavi. Because the ego is merely a fiction! But what happens in life happens only to the body-mind organism. It is the body-mind organism which is sick, it is the body-mind organism which succeeds, an act happens which is called successful or not.

SINGH *Isn't that a fiction too? The body is a fiction too?*

RAMESH How do you mean, the body is a fiction too?

SINGH *It doesn't exist.*

RAMESH If it doesn't exist, then who is talking now?

SINGH *Because of the* maya.

RAMESH Yes. So the *maya* has created this body-mind organism. The body is part of the manifestation. If you truly accept that the entire manifestation is illusory, then is this not also illusory? If this is illusory, who is talking? If you truly accept that the manifestation is illusory, there can be no more questions!

SINGH *That's correct.*

TAAVI *You very beautifully presented that the ego has really nothing to do with the truth-seeking, there is nothing the ego can do. You were also saying it is God's grace. But it also looks like the grace is flowing through Gurus.*

RAMESH The Guru is merely a mechanism in phenomenality for this to happen. For the grace to flow, the Guru is the mechanism.

TAAVI *Then being in the presence of a Guru or a saint is very good for the seeking to take place.*

RAMESH For the seeking to *progress*. When the seeking begins, the Guru is not necessary. For the seeking to progress the Guru is necessary, and whether you get a Guru or a suitable Guru will depend on the destiny of the body-mind organism. If the destiny is for a process to be long-winded, then the process will take you first to a place where rituals are done, then to some other place where something else is done, then to a third place where you are told what to do and what not to do, until gradually you move on. The knowledge becomes deeper that "this cannot be what I am seeking." Or, it may be your destiny that you go to the final place directly. Some people who have come here have come after twenty years of seeking, while some others have come directly here.

TAAVI *The seeking or the opening seems to be very natural in the presence of the Guru.*

RAMESH That is the traditional Eastern concept. It is still a concept. But what happens is, as Linda said, the collective thing happens. It is part of the phenomenality. So the Guru's grace happening is still a part of phenomenality. It is part of the process. It is part of the Energy functioning. But the traditional Eastern way is to say that for the seeking to progress substantially, the Guru and his grace are necessary. Whether it happens or not, again depends on the destiny of each body-mind organism.

SINGH *But even coming here, what you get is still not in your control.*

RAMESH No! Even coming here is not in your control or what you get out of it. Coming here was in your destiny and what you get out of it is also your destiny.

HENRY *Ramesh, the actual physical manifestation one might call a brain-body, but you are using the term "mind-body" as a larger thing. In other words, mind is more than just the brain.*

RAMESH In the ordinary case it is both the working mind and the thinking mind. In the case of a sage the working mind is still there.

HENRY *But that's more than just a brain.*

RAMESH It's a matter of interpretation.

BRUCE *Ramesh, when we go away from here, there may be people who I would like to tell about these kind of experiences*

115

who will have difficulties with certain aspects of it. I wonder if you've found a gentle way to share this knowledge with people. How can we tell people without scaring them? I cannot just walk up to somebody and say, "You're a fiction, buddy!"

RAMESH *(laughing)* The whole point is that if the talking happens, let it happen, and the effect of that talking will depend on the destiny of the hearer! So people sometimes ask me, "Should I talk to them?" and my answer is, "Don't talk to them, but if talking happens, let it happen." If you want to talk to them, there is a "me" wanting to talk. But whether the talking happens or not is again not in your hands.

SINGH *What about free will?*

RAMESH The whole basis of this teaching is that you have no free will. Everything that happens is part of God's will through this body-mind organism. If there is no "your" act at all, how can there be "your" freedom? My point is that the human being truly has no free will. It must be that either "your" will prevails, or some *other* will prevails, or some other power. Is it your experience that "your" will has always prevailed?

BRUCE *No.*

SINGH *There isn't some other power also with evil ?*

RAMESH Sure. Therefore life as we know it has always been opposites—good and evil.

BRUCE *Do we have a choice between bad and good?*

RAMESH "You" don't. That is my whole point. You see, there was Mother Teresa, an organism programmed to do only good deeds. There is another organism which is a psychopath which didn't choose to become a psychopath. So only evil things happen through that organism. The organism of a Mother Teresa and of a psychopath were created by the same Power for those things to happen!

BRUCE *The distinction between the two is only in the mind.*

RAMESH That is correct.

SINGH *Ramesh, what about the story in Buddhism of the Eightfold Path and right effort and things like that? What about effort?*

RAMESH Effort will happen if it is destined to happen. Effort will not happen if it is not supposed to happen.

BRUCE *So what's this about the Eightfold Path, the training and so on?*

RAMESH I have no idea. I am not a Buddhist. That is a teaching, you see. If someone goes to Buddhism, it is the destiny of that organism to go through that path of Buddhism, and some people stick there.

BOB *Which is another concept.*

RAMESH You are quite right, Bob!

BRUCE *But listening to you, Ramesh, the story about the Eightfold Path and so on sounds like, you know, bullshit.*

RAMESH So it's all bullshit. So leave it, don't touch it!

TAAVI *But isn't it so that it might be the best thing for some body-minds organism to go to liberation through that path?*

RAMESH Sure. As Ramana Maharshi said, "You can reach the top of the mountain in various ways." You can walk, but if somebody tells you that you get more merit if you crawl, then you can crawl. Or, you can go in a bullock cart or you can go in a car or helicopter. And you have no choice!

JOHN *One thing I have found really helpful was what Nisargadatta Maharaj said, "Anything that you believe will take you to the truth."*

117

RAMESH "Who" is to guarantee it? It will take you to the truth if that is the destiny. First, the way itself is the destiny. Whether it will take you to the goal is, again, destiny.

TAAVI *That seems to take us to an inner silence.*

RAMESH That is correct. That is absolutely correct.

◫◫◫

Deha devaache mandira / Aata aatmaa parameshwara / /
Jashi usaata ho saakhara / Tasaa dehaata ho Ishwara / /
Jase dudhaamadhe loni / Tasaa dehi chakrapaani / /
Deva dehaata dehaata / Kaaho jaataa devalaata / /
Tukaa mhane moodhajanaa / Deva dehi kaa pahaanaa / /

The body is the temple of Consciousness.
Parameshwara (Consciousness) resides in the body, not "you."
Like the sweet juice in sugarcane,
    Ishwara (Consciousness-in-action) is the essence
    of the body-mind organism.
Chakrapani (Lord Krishna) is always present in the body
    just like butter is in the milk.
God is within the body.
Why do you go to the temple to see Him?
Tukaram says:
    My dear fools, can't you see
    that God is always present within you?

◫

Jaavoo devaachiyaa gaavaa / Ghevu tetechi visaawaa / /
Devaa saangoo sukhaa dukkhaa / Deva niwaareela bhooka / /
Ghaalu devaasicha bhaar / Devaa sukhaachaa saagar / /
Raaho jawali dewaapaashi / Aataa jadoni paayaasi / /
Tukaa mhane aamhi baale / Yaa devaachi ladiwaale / /

Let us go to the village where God lives.
He will give us rest and peace.
All our happiness and unhappiness come from Consciousness.
Only God can make our wants disappear,
  and give peace to the heart.
Let us surrender the ego at His feet
  and remain close to the God within us.
Tukaram says:
  We who have accepted His will,
  are His favorite children, the apple of His eye.

SCENE 5

*There is a theory that if a certain number of
a species learn something new, then the
entire species will understand it
spontaneously through a vibratory process
called "morphic resonance." Well then, why
not just wait patiently for enlightenment to
happen?! Why bother to seek?*

*It is only man's sense of morality which
makes him commit a sin—otherwise he
would be as moral as the higher animal.*

*Does life have a meaning, a purpose?
Perhaps only, "Go forth and multiply" until
some cosmic catastrophe ends it all!*

*There is a Serbian saying: "Be humble
because you are created out of dung; be noble
because you are created out of stars." But
this "you" that is "created" is only a body-
mind organism.*

RAMESH   So, what was said yesterday—any questions?

PADMA   *What is Consciousness?*

RAMESH   What is Consciousness? You know you exist, do you not? There is awareness of existence, isn't there? You could not have been aware of existence without Consciousness.

PADMA   *Is it my consciousness, or is it a Universal Consciousness?*

RAMESH   *Consciousness is all there is* . Consciousness is the Source of everything. There has to be one Source of everything.

PADMA   *Is your teaching that God and Consciousness are the same?*

RAMESH   Yes. To me Consciousness and God are the same thing. For some people it is easier to listen to whatever is said in terms of God. You see, someone says, "I have a very simple intellect. You talk of impersonal Consciousness and the functioning of impersonal Consciousness, and it goes over my head."

PADMA   *Is the material world a reflection in Consciousness ?*

RAMESH   That is correct. That is exactly correct. The material world is merely a reflection *in* Consciousness.

PADMA   *So what is a reflection?*

RAMESH   You go and stand before the mirror. What do you see? What you see in the mirror is the reflection.

PADMA   *Would Consciousness be there if human beings were not there?*

RAMESH   Yes. Consciousness would be there, is there, It

has been there and will always be there. Consciousness is all there is, whether the manifestation is there or not. The movie may or may not be there. The moving pictures may or may not be there, but the screen is always there.

PADMA *So there is nothing, nobody whatsoever, that has Consciousness?*

RAMESH Correct.

PADMA *Consciousness is like spirit?*

RAMESH Consciousness is the impersonal feeling of Awareness.

PADMA *There is the necessity of somebody who feels?*

RAMESH No, *not somebody* who feels, but the impersonal *feeling* of Awareness is Consciousness, *not* awareness of I am so-and-so. I Am is the same feeling which every human being has. On that there is superimposed I am so-and-so. You see? So-and-so is what hides the I Am. It is the ego that hides the I Am, and it is the ego which is looking for the I Am. The seeker is the so-and-so who is looking for the I Am. And until there is realization that the seeker is what hides the I Am, I Am cannot be seen.

PADMA *Would you link the idea of Consciousness with the question of what is Reality?*

RAMESH Consciousness is the only Reality, Reality being something which is there of Its own accord. A reflection cannot be there of its own accord. You go into the sun, there is the shadow. The shadow does not have an independent existence. So Reality is that which has an independent existence, and the only thing which has an independent existence is Consciousness. Got it?

123

PADMA   *Got it.*

RAMESH   Good!

INDRANI   *There is confusion in my mind, Ramesh. Could you please help me? Now, if you say this world is a reflection in Consciousness...*

RAMESH   Yes.

INDRANI   *Yes, but something can only reflect if there is something...*

RAMESH   Yes, Consciousness is all there is.

INDRANI   *Yes, but how come It reflects a world then ?*

RAMESH   Consciousness creates the reflection *within* Itself.

INDRANI   *Oh! An illusory world is that which is being reflected.*

RAMESH   That is correct. When you stand before the mirror, what is seen in the mirror is illusion. It's not there. It can be there only if *you* are there. So this illusory world as manifestation cannot be there in the absence of Consciousness. The moving pictures cannot be there in the absence of the screen. So, the screen is real. The moving pictures are not real. Consciousness is Reality. Everything is the manifestation, the human beings are part of the manifestation. The functioning of the manifestation is like a dream.

ANAND   *How do I get in touch with my consciousness and maintain that contact?*

RAMESH   Now, I guess we've just said it is not "your" Consciousness.

ANAND   *It is not mine.*

RAMESH   It is not "your" Consciousness. Anand wants to get in touch with "his" Consciousness. What is Anand?

To me it is merely the name given to a body-mind organism. So what I see is a body-mind organism which is an object, which is part of the totality of manifestation. You see? And this body-mind organism, this object as part of the manifestation, is an instrument through which the impersonal Consciousness, or Energy, functions. There are various gadgets—fans, lamps, kitchen gadgets—through which electricity functions. So all human beings are merely programmed instruments through which Consciousness, or impersonal Energy, or God, functions.

ANAND *How do I get in touch with Consciousness?*

RAMESH "Who" gets in touch with Consciousness? Consciousness is all there is. If Consciousness is all there is, can there be anything else that can get in touch with Consciousness? Consciousness is the Source of the manifestation, and this body-mind organism which considers itself Anand is part of the manifestation.

ANAND *Intellectually I'm getting that. But then how can I experience a level of...*

RAMESH Is it not your experience that you *exist*, Anand? Is it intellectual? Is it not your experience, actual experience, that you *are*, that you *exist*, not as Anand, but that there is existence? You *exist*, I Am. So, I Am is the experience. It's not intellectual. In fact, "I'm Anand" is intellectual. I Am is Reality. I Am is experience. "I am Anand" is a thought which arises only when you are awake.

ANAND *Is the ego also intellectual?*

RAMESH Ego *is* intellectual. Your mind-intellect and the ego are the same. Me, the ego, and the mind-intellect are the same. They are various names for the same thing which arises in the body-mind organism and creates a feeling of separation, and that feeling of separation causes misery. In deep sleep this feeling of Anand and the mind-intellect

126

does not exist. In sleep there is no Anand, there is no Anand's mind; therefore, there is no misery.

MARTIN *How come things feel so solid and so enduring and material?*

RAMESH Yes. Now, a clever hypnotist can make two thousand people believe something which is not there is there as a solid entity, can he not? So if a clever hypnotist can make two thousand people believe there is something solid when there isn't, then is it difficult for the Divine through hypnosis to make each individual mind-body organism think that the world is real, solid?

MARTIN *It is easy to imagine that it is possible. Can this hypnosis be removed?*

RAMESH Sure. Certainly. How? Only that Power that created the hypnosis can remove the hypnosis. The hypnotized being cannot get rid of the hypnosis. (*everyone exclaiming "Ohhh!"*) And that is what the seeking is all about. The seeking is the hypnotized being wanting to remove the hypnosis and wanting to know how he or she can do it.

MARTIN *And it's pointless trying?*

RAMESH That is correct. That is precisely what I am saying. And yet the trying is happening, is it not, Martin?

MARTIN *Yes.*

RAMESH So why is the trying happening?

MARTIN *Because Divine hypnosis is also creating the trying.*

RAMESH That is correct. That is precisely correct. That Power which has created the hypnosis is creating this effort to get rid of the hypnosis. That is why I keep saying that there is *no individual seeker seeking enlightenment.*

MARTIN *Still it feels so much as if I was real. I continue getting involved with all this and...*

RAMESH   That is itself the hypnosis. "I" am Martin, "I" am a separate being, "I" am in control of my life, "I" want to achieve enlightenment. That *is* the hypnosis.

ANAND *How does the hypnosis go away? I mean, how does it cease to be?*

RAMESH   Who can remove it? That is the question. Only that Power which created the hypnosis can get rid of the hypnosis. What brought you here, Anand? Have you heard about me?

ANAND *Well, it so happened that I have been teaching reiki, and one of my students, Alana, mentioned that she was coming here today, and so that's how I came. And it is definitely a thing that had to be; of that I am clear. This was meant to be.*

RAMESH   Yes, but what are your interests?

ANAND *My interests? To realize myself.*

RAMESH   Why? When did it begin?

ANAND *Well, actively it began seven years ago.*

RAMESH   What happened seven years ago, Anand?

ANAND *Things were going all right from the material point of view, but I felt some kind of emptiness, something missing.*

RAMESH   Quite correct. That is quite correct. So what you are saying is that this feeling of emptiness arose. You didn't like that feeling of emptiness, did you?

ANAND *No.*

RAMESH   So you didn't *create* that feeling of emptiness. The feeling of emptiness *arose*. You see? Why did the feeling of emptiness arise? Because that was the beginning of the *wanting* to remove the hypnosis.

ANAND   *And in which I had no part.*

RAMESH   In which "you" had no part. That is my point. You see? So the seeking which began seven years ago did not begin by Anand saying, "I want to find out what life is all about." It began by itself, as part of God's will or as part of the impersonal functioning of Consciousness.

ANAND   *Isn't there some kind of passivity about all this?*

RAMESH   Certainly, certainly. Isn't there some kind of passivity in deep sleep?

ANAND   *And a total absence of free choice also.*

RAMESH   Yes. That is what I mean. Everything happens by God's will. Nothing has happened unless it was God's will.

ANAND   *And how do you hold a chap responsible for his actions?*

RAMESH   Who? You tell me. I mean, what is your question: "How do you hold someone responsible for his actions?"

ANAND   *Yeah.*

RAMESH   "You" *don't* hold someone responsible for his actions. In fact, what I'm telling you, Anand, is that "you" are not responsible for your actions because they are not "your" actions. Whatever happens through this body-mind organism is *an* action which happens through this body-mind organism. And with the happening of that action, Anand, who doesn't really exist, says, "It is my action."

Now, whatever your action is, have you thought of what that action is? How does any action happen? How does any action in any body-mind organism happen? Any action in any body-mind organism is the reaction of the brain to an outside event over which it has no control. The outside event, being a thought, occurs—you see something, you hear something—and "you" have no control over what "you" thought might happen. You have no control over what you are going to see or hear or touch or smell or taste. The brain reacts to this over which you have no control. And that reaction of the brain, according to the programming in this body-mind organism, is what you call "your" action.

ANAND *Yet...*

RAMESH So your question is, "If truly everything that happens is not 'my' action, it is part of the impersonal functioning of Consciousness, how do I live my life? How do I act in society? Do I not have to act responsibly?" That is your question, isn't it?

ANAND *Yes.*

RAMESH The answer to that is extraordinarily simple. What you have been doing so far, continue to do exactly the same thing. Have you not been living responsibly all your life?

ANAND *Yes, but I just thought it doesn't work. I mean...*

RAMESH No, what we are analyzing is your living responsibly, and what I'm saying is you continue to do the same thing in the future. What I'm saying is you continue to live your life responsibly, which means according to certain standards of morality which you have, which each one has. So, what does anyone do? He or she continues to live according to that standard of morality and responsibility which he or she has.

ANAND *Technically one is not living, he or she is* being lived, *you can say.*

RAMESH That is precisely what I'm saying. "Technically,"

as you put it, a human being does not live his or her life. Life is being lived *through* that body-mind organism according to the destiny of that body-mind organism that was stamped at the moment of conception, which is the will of God. So the will of God in respect of each individual body-mind organism is the destiny of each individual body-mind organism stamped at the moment of conception.

MARTIN   *Shall I continue to live responsibly as if there is no choice and this body-mind organism is just lived? It does not matter that I live responsibly or...*

RAMESH   Then *don't* live responsibly! Live irresponsibly if it is possible for you to live irresponsibly! If this body-mind organism has been programmed to live responsibly, can "you" decide to live irresponsibly? Not possible, is it?

MARTIN   *I actually don't have to bother at all.*

RAMESH   *(responding to Florence laughing)* It's funny, isn't it? It really is funny.

FLORENCE   *It's funny because one makes it so important to be good all the time...*

RAMESH   Yes, that is precisely it.

ANAND   *It's so significant that I'm doing so many things which actually do not work...*

RAMESH   Yes, Anand. You see, that is why I keep saying that nothing can happen unless it is God's will. Accepting that does not prevent you from living your life as you have lived so far in a responsible manner according to certain moral standards, which is part of the programming of this body-mind organism.

ANAND   *That again is just a program. Where does karma come in?*

RAMESH   Karma, what do you mean by karma?

131

ANAND *The law of cause and effect.*

RAMESH   That is correct. Karma means cause and effect. Karma means events happen, deeds are done, and they have their consequences.

ANAND *Over which I have no control.*

RAMESH   Over which you have no control.

MARTIN *I remember you were saying, Ramesh, that once it is realized that there is no doer, then there is no pride and no guilt. And still I have the experience that I feel guilt and pride, so it is not in my control then?*

RAMESH   You have truly not accepted that everything happens according to God's will. You have truly not accepted that Martin doesn't do anything. You have not truly accepted that Martin, as such, does not exist.

MARTIN *But if Martin is not existing, how shall he accept?*

RAMESH   Now what you are saying is what can you do about your acceptance?

MARTIN *Nothing.*

RAMESH   Nothing! So even the happening of the acceptance is not in your control! Even the acceptance of the concept that everything is God's will—even that is not in your hands. So the happening of the release from the feeling of pride and guilt and hate happens, *if* it happens, only if there is total acceptance. And the total acceptance may or may not happen according to God's will. So if it is not God's will that there should be total acceptance, there will not be this total freedom from guilt and pride and hate.

This feeling that it is not really "my" action may come and go. It is a flip-flop. Sometimes the mind accepts that "yes, truly there is nothing which is my action" and other times it says "it is my action." So this flip-flop is part of the destiny of this body-mind organism.

MARTIN *And the flip-flop can also end?*

RAMESH The flip-flop ends when it is supposed to end—according to God's will. So until it's God's will, this flip-flop will continue to bother you.

HANS *Ramesh, is there no development? Can one say that the flip-flop is a stage of development, a state in time ?*

RAMESH Hans, "whose" development? Hans's development? There is no Hans, so "whose" development?

HANS *If there is flip, there is Hans. If there is flop, there is not.*

RAMESH That is right. Hans comes and goes.

INDRANI *Ramesh? I was reading your book* Experiencing the Teaching. *There is something I didn't understand that I would like to ask you. When you say, "going backwards into the future."*

RAMESH Yes, "backwards into the future" is, say, you have done something which causes pain to someone else...

INDRANI *An action of mine causes...*

RAMESH That is, you are looking into the future, but you walk backwards into the future if you understand that that body-mind organism which was hurt or benefitted was living its destiny. Therefore, what happens through this body-mind organism named Indrani has to happen for the other body-mind organism's destiny, and it doesn't necessarily cause any effect for Indrani. For the destined effect, there was the necessary cause. You see? One thing impersonally leads to another—no guilt, no pride.

Why would the first thing happen? A leads to B. My point is that A had to happen because B had to happen. By saying you "walk backwards into the future," you have no problem in the present. You can then accept the present as part of what you have to do.

PAUL *So the Consciousness of each one is not only one part of the whole Consciousness, because when I feel that I Am, then I feel all.*

RAMESH That is correct. In deep sleep there is no separation because the individual is not there.

PAUL *There is only I Am.*

RAMESH Only I Am, which is also the only thing present in the waking state, but in the waking state the mind-intellect, the ego, takes over and covers the I Am. So when the individual ego is there, then the I Am gets covered. When the individual ego is *not* there, what shines is I Am. Therefore, there are certain moments when you feel extremely happy and content. Why? Because in those moments the individual ego is not there.

ANAND *Suppose, say, everybody bought into this notion— everybody in the world. What do you think would happen ?*

RAMESH What would you think would happen, Anand?

ANAND *This whole struggle for everybody, in any case, would end because there would be no difference since what would be, would be.*

RAMESH The struggle for everybody would end. There would be no misery for anybody. Can life as we know it exist without the opposites? Would you be interested in a movie in which everything is just happening wonderfully, everybody is quiet, everybody is nice to everybody? Who would be interested in that movie? So this movie of life *has* an interest only because life is a combination of opposites. There has never been beauty without ugliness. The very word "beauty" would have no meaning unless ugliness was there. The very word "goodness" would have no meaning unless evil was there. You see?

Any questions? Yes, Stephanie?

STEPHANIE *So somebody who is evil, who leads an evil life, is just living out their destiny?*

RAMESH Now, basically, there is nobody who leads an evil life. There is no "one" who leads an evil life. Take an extreme case of a psychopath.

STEPHANIE *Hitler.*

RAMESH All right, Hitler. Someone else may say Saddam Hussein or Napoleon or Stalin. I take an extreme case and say a psychopath. The body-mind organism of a psychopath has been so programmed so that only perverted and evil actions will happen. On the other hand, there was a body-mind organism called Mother Teresa who was so programmed that only good deeds would happen. Are there two powers which created the body-mind organisms? Or is it the same Consciousness, the same God which has created both body-mind organisms because life as we know it concerns opposites?

STEPHANIE *So what is the purpose of that?*

RAMESH Purpose? How can a little mind know the purpose of the entire Consciousness? This little mind is like one little screw in an enormous machine with billions of screws and nuts and bolts wanting to know the purpose of the entire enormous machine. How can one little screw understand the purpose of the enormous machine? So how can one little mind understand the purpose of the Creator? Not possible.

STEPHANIE *So, I've felt like I had choices. I felt like I could either sort of flow in God's will or choose something to go against God's will. But you're saying it's an illusion? Even if I'm thinking I'm really choosing against God's will, I'm choosing God's will? So, God gives us feelings with which to make those choices?*

RAMESH "You" don't make any choices. You think you

are making a choice, but the choice you are making is exactly the choice God wants you to make according to the destiny of that body-mind organism, whatever the consequences.

STEPHANIE *So does God use feelings to manipulate our choices?*

RAMESH   God, you can say, is manipulating the programming inside this body-mind organism. Each human being is a uniquely programmed instrument. No two humans are alike. Who has given each human being a unique programming? God has given the human being a unique programming. Why? So that he can bring about such actions through each uniquely programmed body-mind organism as he wishes.

ANAND *Puppet show?*

RAMESH   That is correct.

STEPHANIE *To what end?*

RAMESH   To what end? To God's end which you, as one screw, cannot understand.

STEPHANIE *So there is no way to understand that* ?

RAMESH   No way to understand that.

STEPHANIE *So you don't understand that?*

RAMESH   There is no way for the mind-intellect. All that can happen is to accept.

STEPHANIE   *There is no way into some sort of collective unconsciousness and have a feeling not necessarily intellectual, but a sense of understanding?*

RAMESH   For whom? "Who" is to have this understanding, Stephanie?

STEPHANIE *Sure!*

RAMESH   And what's "Stephanie"? It's just a name given to that body-mind organism. So how can a *name* understand anything? It's only the mind-intellect which wants to know and understand its Source! So is it possible for the mind-intellect to understand its Source? Not possible.

MARTIN   *For example, I landed last night in Bombay and I picked up my suitcase, went to the hotel, and noticed it was the wrong suitcase.*

RAMESH   Yes.

MARTIN   *So there was no choice? Now, I tell myself I should pay more attention to what I'm doing, but listening to what you say, I have no choice. It just happens.*

RAMESH   So what you are saying is that I am saying it was your destiny, because it was the destiny of that body-mind organism to pick up the wrong suitcase. Yes! Whatever the consequences.

MARTIN   *So I shouldn't worry about it?*

RAMESH   Whatever the consequences? Ahhh!— That is another matter! Why worry about it? Yes, quite right. But if this body-mind organism is programmed to worry, worrying will happen, won't it? But if another body-mind organism is programmed, "Who cares; what has happened has happened," then worrying will not arise for that body-mind organism.

MARTIN   *And even if sometimes it happens and sometimes it doesn't is only programming?*

RAMESH   That's right. Yes.

SERGIO   *So then the world with all the corruption, wars, and so on...*

RAMESH   Disease and poverty and wars...

SERGIO   *This is just needed.*

RAMESH   All are a part of life as we know it. All are part of What Is.

SERGIO   *Yeah, so all this trying to make the world better, to take care of the rubbish is also a part of God.*

RAMESH   That is the point.

SERGIO   *Right!* (laughter)

RAMESH   You see, what you are asking is that if disease has to be there, then what is the use of the medical profession? But the medical profession is part of the totality of manifestation. Thus, there is disease and there is cure.

ALANA   *Is it just a matter of maintaining the balance of all kinds, that is why the opposites exist?*

RAMESH   "Maintaining the balance," what do you mean?

ALANA   *Well, I'm assuming, I guess, that opposites exist for there to be balance.*

RAMESH   That is correct. But who maintains that balance? Do you know?

ALANA   *No. There is balance.*

RAMESH   "There *is* balance" is correct. But one thing— there is balance *where*? Where? There is balance in the *totality of manifestation* . I'm *not* saying there is balance in the *world.* I'm *not* saying there is balance in *every individual's life.*

ALANA   *But on the grand, grand scale.*

RAMESH   On the grand scale there *has* to be a balance, otherwise the world—the manifested universe—wouldn't exist. But the human being thinks only in terms of itself. The human being is proud that the smallpox germ has been eliminated. Wonderful!—The smallpox germ has been eliminated. The human being considers this a great achievement. But from the point of view of the smallpox germ is it supposed to be wonderful to be eliminated? So the smallpox germ was eliminated according to God's will. And if it is God's will to eliminate the human being, the human being will be eliminated. And *still* the balance will be maintained.

SERGIO *Ramesh? Is there a sense of balance because it seems like a sense of balance in the universe or is there just no point of reference?*

RAMESH There is no point of reference.

SERGIO *It's just balance, just a question of...*

RAMESH Let me make it perfectly clear what I'm talking about. The universe being in balance is just a concept.

SERGIO *Because who is there to say what is balance?*

RAMESH Let me go again to the bottom of the thing. Anything, any saying that has been said at any time from Jesus Christ to Ramana Maharshi, anything any scripture of any religion has said is a concept—a concept being something which some people accept and some people may not. So no concept can be the Truth. The only Truth is I Am. This Awareness of existence, this no one can deny. And an atheist may come and say, "I don't believe God exists." But if I ask him, "But you know you exist, do you not?" he can't deny that. So this Awareness of existence, this impersonal I Am is the only Truth. Everything else— any thought, any statement—is a concept. And it has to be understood that it is *only* a concept.

PADMA *So your teaching is that all effort to understand is only conceptual?*

RAMESH It is part of the functioning of Consciousness or part of God's will. And it is part of God's will to remove the hypnosis in certain body-mind organisms. So this teaching is a part of the process of the removal of the hypnosis accordingto God's will.

PADMA *So the small mind is not charged to understand Consciousness?*

RAMESH   That is correct.

PADMA *So what are we doing here for more than one hour ?*

RAMESH   "You" are doing nothing. (*general laughter*) You being here is part of the destiny of this body-mind organism. Your being here is only because it is God's will that you were to be here, otherwise, you wouldn't be here.

ALANA *So is there no cause and effect ?*

RAMESH   There is. Everything is cause and effect.

ALANA *But there's no worry about it.*

RAMESH   That is the point. No individual is responsible for any cause. Everything is cause and effect. Everything is causation. Some things happen, and they have their effects. Those effects become new causes that have their effects. That is what life is all about.

LIV *But they are all God's will. There is no individual.*

RAMESH   That is the point. That is my concept.

ANAND *Consciousness speaks through every living thing, not only human beings, right?*

RAMESH   Consciousness *thinks* through every human being. Consciousness *speaks* through every human being. Consciousness *acts* through every human being . Consciousness *experiences* through every human being.

ANAND *What about plants and animals and other living things?*

RAMESH   So, living is also happening through them.

ANAND *And there is no Consciousness?*

RAMESH Of course. It is Consciousness functioning through all of them.

ANAND *But they are not aware of that.*

RAMESH That is correct. That is the point. There is no individual awareness of the Consciousness.

ANAND *About the theory of evolution, then, whatever... Okay, I guess we get back to words.* (laughter)

RAMESH What do you do in life, Stephanie? Which part of America are you from?

STEPHANIE *California. I'm a lawyer.*

RAMESH What brings you to India? Is it your first visit?

STEPHANIE *Yes.*

RAMESH It must be terrible culture shock.

STEPHANIE *It's mind-boggling.*

RAMESH It really is mind-boggling culture shock. It is. You know, a doctor friend of mine, a gynecologist from New Jersey who met me in the States, wanted to come and see me. So he came. He checked into the Taj Mahal Hotel. Then he called me and I told him how to come here. So he came. He pressed the bell. I opened the door and he stood there literally white as a sheet. So I said, "What happened?" He couldn't talk. Finally he managed to say that he had gotten into a taxi and that it was a miracle he had ever arrived: the crowds, the way the taxi driver drove. (*everyone laughs*) That's why I say it's mind-boggling culture shock.

STEPHANIE *At every sensory level, it is.*

RAMESH In every sense. That is exactly it. So to this friend

141

of mine I gave advice, "The next time you travel in a taxi, make sure the driver knows where he is to take you. Then sit back and close your eyes, and you will arrive at the place if it's God's will. Or you won't." (*laughter*)

ALANA *Ramesh? So speaking of evolution, is it that man has evolved in a conscious way and therefore we live and think...*

RAMESH What do you mean when you say, "Has man evolved in a conscious way?"

ALANA *What I'm trying to ask is that we, out of all the creatures of the planet, think and speak and do all these things with consciousness, and we can just exist in Consciousness and are we humans...*

RAMESH There is no difference between a rock and an animal and a human being. The rock has no senses, therefore there is no need for the active Consciousness. The animal has senses and for the senses to work, Consciousness has to exist in its aspect of sentience. The human being has senses and therefore the human being has sentience, and in addition, the human being has been given the dubious gift of mind-intellect. Why? To make him unhappy! The animal doesn't think of the future; therefore, the animal is not concerned with the future and consequently is not unhappy. The human being is concerned with the future and therefore unhappy.

There have been photographs of a tiger lying under a tree and half a dozen deer moving about freely, grazing, not twenty yards from him. Why? Because there is an animal sense which tells the deer that the tiger is satisfied, he is not hungry. If the tiger is not hungry he is not going to kill. The tiger doesn't think of his next meal. The human being thinks of his next meal and the meals ten years later. Therefore he has to make provisions, and as a consequence there is greed and lust in the human being which is not there in the animal. But basically all are objects with different programming.

MARTIN *When you say "dubious gift" and everything is somehow perfect...*

RAMESH I'm not saying everything is perfect. What do you mean by perfect? Perfect means nothing is imperfect. And what I'm saying is life *is* imperfect. Life is not perfect. Life is full of contradictions. Life is full of opposites. So what do you mean by perfect? All I'm saying is that What Is is exactly what is supposed to be. I'm not saying it is perfect.

MARTIN *Why could it be "dubious" then?*

RAMESH "Dubious" because it makes you unhappy. The gift is dubious because the gift enables you to be unhappy.

MARTIN *If I'm supposed to be unhappy...*

RAMESH You will be unhappy. Quite right.

MARTIN *But still it doesn't...I said "dubious" then...*

RAMESH All right, Martin, *forget* the "dubious!" Now are you happy? (*laughter*)

WILLIAM *Is there enlightenment for animals?*

RAMESH Look! Is there enlightenment for *human beings*? You are asking, "Is there enlightenment for animals?" I'm asking you, "Is there enlightenment for 'you'?!"

WILLIAM *If there is no "me" then there is enlightenment.*

RAMESH If there is no "me" then there is *no need* of enlightenment! If there is no "me" thinking himself to be in bondage, where is the need for enlightenment? The animal doesn't consider itself to be in bondage.

ANAND *Okay, where do we go from here? After death what happens?*

RAMESH After death, what happens? After a kitchen gadget has gone totally out of order and is thrown into the wastebasket, what happens to the electricity? That is what your question is. After the death of a body, what happens to Consciousness? Nothing! Consciousness functions through other body-mind organisms. Electricity functions through other kitchen gadgets. You see? When this is totally understood, what is really happening, Anand? What has really happened? Consciousness was there as the manifestation and the functioning of the manifestation before the birth of this body-mind organism. And it will be the same after the death of this body-mind organism.

ANAND *What about heaven and stuff like that?*

RAMESH What about it? You tell me. For "whom" is the heaven? For Anand? And what I'm saying is there is no Anand, other than a name given to a body-mind organism.

ANAND *There is no heaven?*

RAMESH It is a concept. It is a concept which has a certain socio-economic purpose. The concept of heaven is a group concept to try to make a human being behave himself.

ANAND *Knowing full well that there is no choice anyway...*

RAMESH Ahh, you see! Similarly, the question of rebirth. The object is to try and make a human being behave, the basis of which is fear.

ALANA *But fear is not a gift, right?*

RAMESH Fear is part of life, and fear is part of the programming. One body-mind organism may be programmed to be timid. It's there. Another body-mind organism may be programmed to be physically courageous, but mentally not so or morally not so. Everything depends on the programming.
    (To a visitor) Are you here for the first time?

IRIS *Yes.*

RAMESH I see. No questions? There must be some questions.

IRIS *Nothing is bubbling inside, so...*

RAMESH Oh really! I'm glad. Your concepts are acceptable?

IRIS *Ninety percent.*

RAMESH Intellectually acceptable?

IRIS *All levels. All levels.*

RAMESH There is a certain logic in this. You know Adi Shankara, the Advaita master who started everything? He's supposed to have said that Advaita is sometimes only intellectual. And I keep repeating, "Do not discard intellectual understanding. It *has* to be intellectual understanding in the first place." So at the intellectual level, Adi Shankara said, "Whatever the concepts, do not accept them, or accept them only as you would accept a coin— see that it has the ring of truth." You see?

And Ramana Maharshi said, "You use a concept like a thorn to remove another thorn embedded in your foot." So you use this thorn of the concept that everything happens according to God's will to remove the thorn of the misconception that you have free will, that you are the master of your destiny. For that concept to be removed, you have this concept of God's will. But basically *both* are concepts. The only Truth is I Am.

Let us not misunderstand. I'm not saying these are concepts which you must accept. The other day someone came here and said, "But I cannot accept." And then I said, "Do you think I am concerned whether you accept it or not? Whether you accept it or not is your destiny."

IRIS *Even God's will is a concept?*

RAMESH Even God's will is a concept. God is a concept.

145

That's why all these people come and say, "I don't believe that God exists." They are entitled to say it. Why? Because God *is* a concept. Therefore, forget about God. God may not exist, but you exist, do you not? And this Awareness of existence, I Am, is precisely the God I am talking about.

ANAND   *I've been reading your book* Pointers from Nisargadatta Maharaj.

RAMESH   Oh yes, it makes sense?

ANAND   *Yes.*

RAMESH   What do you do in life apart from reiki?

ANAND   *I'm a reiki master and I teach reiki. By training I'm an engineer and an MBA. I've been working in things like advertising and marketing for fifteen years. Actually what happened is a year and a half ago I had a heart attack, and that was the major life-shift for me. It gave me the time and space to figure out what I wanted to do in life. So I got intensely into reiki, and today I don't take any medication. I teach reiki and also conduct workshops for companies.*

RAMESH   Oh, I see. Biggest source of "reiking" in money. (*laughter*) I am told being a reiki master is not as well paying as it used to be, that there are too many reiki masters and the price is going down because of competition.

ANAND   *No, I think what you say works. What work comes is the one to whom it was to come. So it really doesn't matter. And honestly, that's the way it's been with me. I guess the appropriate students come to the appropriate teacher.*

RAMESH   Quite correct. That is why people who come here who think *they* decided to come, I tell them that they haven't. God has decided that they come here. You have come here because it is God's will. You have been listening. That is because it is God's will. Yesterday there was someone who happened not to be interested, so he was not listening. It wasn't God's will that he should listen. If having listened, what happens *to* that listening, what effect that listening produces, is again God's will. There have been people who have been here just once, twice, three times, and there isn't resistance. And others have been coming day after day and the resistance continues.

🔲 🔲 🔲

Krishnaa maazi maataa Krishnaa maazaa pitaa /
Bahini bandhoo chulata Krishnaa maazaa / /
Krishnaa maazaa guru Krishnaa maaze taaroo /
Utari pailpaaru bhavanadi / /
Krishnaa maaze mana Krishnaa maaze jana /
Soiraa sajjan Krishnaa maazaa / /
Tukaa mhane maazaa Shri Krishnaa visaavaa /
Vaate na karavaa parataa jeevaa / /

Krishna is my mother and my father.
Krishna is my sister, brother, and cousin.
Krishna is my Master.
He will surely ferry me across
   the ocean of Divine hypnosis.
Krishna has become all the people around.
He has occupied my mind totally,
   leaving no room for any involvement.
My friend and the good man across the street
   are Krishna himself.
Tukaram says:
   Krishna is my home.
   Dear thinking mind, don't go in any other direction.

147

॥

Jnaaniyaanchaa raajaa guru mahaaraava /
  Mhanati Jnaanadeva tumhaa aise / /
Maja paamaraa he kaaya thorapana /
  Paayeechi vahaana payee bari / /
Brahmaadik jethe tumha volagane /
  Itara tulane kaaya pudhe / /
Tukaa mhane neno yuktichiyaa kholi /
  Mhanoni thevili payee doee / /

Your Master is the King of all Jnanis.
Jnanadeva says this:
  I am just a fool.
  What capacities do I have to impart wisdom?
  I am only the sandal beneath the feet.
  When Brahma and other Sages have extolled the Master,
  how can anyone judge Him or compare Him with others?
Tukaram says:
  No matter how much I strain my mind,
  I am not able to comprehend the Truth.
  Hence, I have kept my head at Your feet, O Master.

SCENE 6

*The believer is happy; the doubter miserable.
Both are deluded.*

*All you have to do—if you can!—is to give
up the belief that you are in control of your
life, and then there is nothing to achieve. In
other words, you do not have to reach the
Self: all you have to do is give up the mean
little false self.*

To know oneself is to forget oneself.

RAJAN *Basically I am a businessman. When I travel I like to carry a copy of the Bhagavad Gita with me, and I read it again and again and again. The little I understand, I try to build up on that.*

RAMESH Oh, I see. That's excellent.

RAJAN *Apart from my work I like to think about the Gita and*

149

make connections and understand things.

RAMESH So can you tell me what you understand from the *Bhagavad Gita*, in *essence*? There are seven hundred verses all spread out. In the core of the matter, what did Lord Krishna tell Arjuna?

RAJAN *In the core of the matter what really applies to me is basically to work without attachment and without seeking fruits of action. Usually businessmen always want to think in terms of a profit.*

RAMESH Naturally! That's what they are in business for.

RAJAN *Yeah, but they'll not enter into a commitment if they can't have their money.*

RAMESH That's correct!

RAJAN *Yes, but I'm beginning to look at it in a little different way: to enter into a commitment for the sake of beginning a relationship with a customer rather than first seeking immediate results. That is how the* Gita *applies also not to fear. For example Krishna advises Arjuna to get into the battle for the sake of fighting for the right and not to be weak-minded and run away from something.*

RAMESH Yes, but was Arjuna running away from something? He was not afraid, he was a brave warrior.

RAJAN *He was not willing to fight because he was fighting his own people.*

RAMESH Yes!

RAJAN *The point is what do you call your own people?*

RAMESH So about getting Arjuna to fight—what is the whole purpose of the *Bhagavad Gita*? The whole purpose was for Lord Krishna to *make* Arjuna fight. Isn't it? So in order to tell him that he must fight, what is the core of the matter that Krishna tells Arjuna? Why does Arjuna put down his bow and say: I don't want to fight because I see people before me who are my friends and cousins and even preceptors. I don't want to kill them. Basically this is what Arjuna says. So to that argument strictly, what is the core of Krishna's teachings? What does Krishna tell Arjuna in *essence* which makes him fight?

RAJAN   *Well, what I would think is: to follow one's own self and to realise one's self even in battle. That the Self is not destructible I mean It is indestructible. Death does not put an end to one's soul, you get reborn. So to perform one's duty is more important.*

RAMESH   Yes, but I mean why would Arjuna accept that? He'd say, "This is what *you* say, but how does it affect my not wanting to kill my friends and cousins? You tell me a lot of philosophy, but here are my friends and cousins, and I *don't* want to kill them."

MEERA   *What Krishna says is, "These are not your friends and cousins; they come and go."*

RAMESH   Oh yeah, "they come and go," but Arjuna wouldn't accept that. He'd say, "They *are* my cousins. What do you mean they are not my cousins?"

RAJAN   *So basically the present state is nothing but your own body which is temporary.*

RAMESH   That is what Krishna says, but it is philosophy just high in the air. Arjuna is a down to earth ordinary person who is a warrior. What Krishna says is: You are born a warrior, you are trained to be a warrior.

RAJAN   *"For a warrior to die in battle is itself an open door to heaven."*

RAMESH   Yes, but Arjuna does not care for heaven. He is not there to seek for heaven. Arjuna simply puts his bow down and says: I don't want to kill my friends and cousins and even preceptors. So Krishna *does* give him a very direct answer which is the final answer to all his doubts. You see, what does Krishna say? Krishna says: You think you are going to kill the people. I have already killed them as "Time," the destroyer of everything. I have already killed them. Who do you think you are to kill them? I have already killed them, you can only be the instrument for it happening now in the present moment, but I have already *killed* them.

You see, for that Arjuna has no answer, and Krishna says something further: You may decide not to fight them but it will be a useless decision. You are born a warrior. You have been trained to be a warrior. Your very *nature* is to be a warrior so even if you decide not to fight, your *prakriti*—your nature, what you are composed of, your programming—will make you fight. Your decision not to fight is useless. Nature will *make* you fight. In any case I have already killed them; therefore, fight, win the battle, enjoy the victory. You see he doesn't say, "Don't enjoy the fruits." He says: Win the battle, and enjoy the victory that will follow your fight. So you see, it is a very practical philosophy.

MEERA *Basically he is taking the responsibility away from us.*

RAMESH You are quite right. How does he take the responsibility?

MEERA *By saying he has done it, so it does not worry Arjuna.*

RAMESH So what does worry a person? Basically a person is concerned with guilt: "I have done something which I should not have done"—therefore he feels guilt. But if he truly understands that there is no action which he can do, that there is no action which any human being can do— where is the guilt? The human being is merely a programmed instrument through which God brings about such actions as he wants.

RAJAN (Incredulously surprised) *That means there is no free will?*

RAMESH "There is *no free will*" is correct. Now, having read the *Bhagavad Gita* are you prepared to accept that you have no free will?

RAJAN (embarrassed laughter) *No!*

RAMESH There it is you have read the *Gita*, concentrated on it.

RAJAN *But Krishna says there is a free will. You see for example...*

RAMESH Yes?

RAJAN *I can give it to you—there is a free will. For example he says...*

RAMESH For the moment, forget what Lord Krishna says. Is it your experience that your will prevails all the time? Is it your *own* experience?

RAJAN *Not all the time but very often.*

RAMESH Ah! Very often is no good. Very often may be ten percent or ninety percent. So my point is if your will does not prevail all the time, there must be some will which prevails all the time. If sometimes your will prevails, it prevails not because it is your will, but because your will corresponds with the will of that Supreme Power.

RAJAN *In other words it only brings about an understanding. One would say the instructions of the* Bhagavad Gita *only bring about in your mind a certain level with which you are able to understand.*

RAMESH You see—the *Bhagavad Gita*—you have to go behind the lines. What does Krishna say? Rajan reads the *Bhagavad Gita* from the point of view of Arjuna. What you have to do is to read it from the point of view of Lord Krishna. That is the point. So in effect what he says is: What you think is your action is really *not* your action, I have already done it. Whatever you think is your action has already been done in the totality of time.

MEERA *He has also brought the doubt in Arjuna's mind. But even that was programmed so that he could tell us the story.*

RAMESH   Yes, quite correct. So Arjuna has become an instrument for the *Bhagavad Gita* to be written so that millions of people can benefit by it. But those millions have to understand truth. In the *Bhagavad Gita* there is a verse— I don't know if you remember it—it says, "Among thousands of people hardly one seeks truth, and among those that seek truth hardly one knows me in principle." You see why? Because they merely read it, and they don't go behind the words.

What I'm saying is: what you call your actions are truly not your actions! What you are is merely a programmed computer through which the One who created the computer will bring about the output It wants. In order to bring about an output which It wants what does It have to do? Put in an input. If you have twenty computers, each programmed to bring about a particular output, then you'll first decide what output you want. Isn't it? And in order to get *that* output you'll use *that* computer which is programmed to bring about that output. So the billions of human beings are merely billions of uniquely programmed instruments through which God brings about such actions as he wants. You see? What input does he make? He sends you a thought. You cannot create a thought. The brain is inert matter, the brain cannot *create* a thought, the brain can only *react* to a thought. Or what else does he do? What are the different kinds of input? He makes you see something or hear something over which again you have no control. You see? The brain reacts to that input and you *think* it is "your" action. So is there truly any action which you can call "your" action other than the reaction of the brain to an outside event over which you have no control according to the programming of the body-mind organism over which you have had *no* control? What do I mean by programming

MEERA *But God has free will?*

RAMESH   There is no question of God having free will. If you say God has free will, you make him exactly what you are.

RAJAN *But one does have to exercise a certain control over oneself.*

RAMESH   Certainly!

RAJAN *Like you know, to control your greed, control your so many things. I mean you cannot say that's God's will.*

RAMESH   Therefore having understood this, your question is—how does Rajan live his life? If nothing is in Rajan's hands, if everything is God's will, Rajan still has to live his life in this world. How does Rajan live his life? The answer is extraordinarily simple—Rajan lives his life exactly as he lived before. He can't help it.

RAJAN *No, but there is a change. Suppose you take the time before I had read the* Bhagavad Gita*, I didn't have the understanding. Maybe I did a lot of things, and as you rightly said, I did feel guilty. I mean I thought it was the accepted thing, but today I don't think in that style.*

MEERA *It's created more guilt in you.*

RAMESH   (*laughs*)

RAJAN *You become more sensitive to the...*

RAMESH   No, you see, she is so right. You know what she is saying? This has created more guilt in you. Why has it created more guilt in you? Because you say, "I've read the *Bhagavad Gita*. I know what I should be doing but I'm not doing it." That causes more guilt, isn't it? "I know I should do something. The *Gita* tells me this and yet I'm not able to do it." More guilt, you see? So the answer is: do exactly what you've been doing before because why, Rajan? Because what you were doing before, even if you thought they were your acts, what was happening was *still* God's will. What you thought "you" were doing all your life was still God's will in respect to what you were doing. So what can you do other than let the body do what it is programmed to do? What else can you do?

RAJAN *I was not satisfied. That is the reason I am here today.*

RAMESH Yes, exactly! That is the reason you are here today, and having heard this will the final acceptance happen?— God's will. It will *not* happen unless it is God's will. God's will in respect of each body-mind organism is what I call the destiny of that body-mind organism which is stamped at the moment of conception, including the programming. You see? So when you truly accept that, then you continue to do whatever you were doing. You can't help it. What you thought were your acts before, were acts which were happening through the body-mind organism strictly according to God's will, and that position will continue to be. Only difference will be that earlier you thought they were *your* acts. Now you will have understood, if the understanding is to happen, that they are not your actions. Other than that, what was actually happening will not change. That is the problem since you think, "Having understood what Ramesh is saying, 'I' shall be a better person." I'm saying you will *not* be a better person— because the person was never there. All there is, is a conditioned body-mind organism—a programmed body-mind organism through which certain acts were happening before and through which new acts will keep on happening more or less the same way as before.

MEERA *Which is also required that way because other people and things are related to it. It is part of a whole.*

RAMESH Quite right. Everything is interconnected. So whatever act God brings about through a body-mind organism affects others. That is why a Zen master has said, "You pull out a blade of grass and you shake the universe." So what will Rajan say? "Oh, I must not pull out a blade of grass." But if the blade of grass is to be pulled, it will be pulled by whomever (*laughing*) is supposed to pull out the blade of grass. You see, basically the teaching is so simple. All this is based on just one thing—nothing can happen unless it is God's will. All this is based on just four words in the Bible—"Thy will be done." The important question is: having heard this will you understand it? Will the understanding be there? That understanding cannot be there unless it is the will of God. That understanding will be there *to the extent* that it is the will of God and your destiny. And when I say your destiny, I mean the destiny of this body-mind organism which was stamped at the moment of conception.

MEERA *Why is the moment of conception so important* ?

RAMESH Because that is when the body is created. That is when the body is there. That is when the *object* which later thinks he or she is an individual is created with the genes.

TOM *My hand is moving. It is moving according to the will of God, not because I want it to move* ?

RAMESH That is correct, not because you want it. In fact when Ramana Maharshi said categorically, "There is no free will," then somebody said, "How can you say I have no free will? I'm raising my right hand now. Is that also predestined?" And Ramana Maharshi said, "Yes!" He didn't pursue the matter and I really don't know what would have happened if he had, but if this matter is pursued with me I would say, "Why did you raise your hand? You raised your hand because the brain reacted to being told that you had no free will. So even your raising of the hand was merely a reaction of the brain to what was heard."

MEERA *Why is the impression created in all of us that we do have free will?*

RAMESH Because the freedom is concerned with the individual entity. Each one thinks he is a separate entity.

MEERA *But that is also created in us!*

RAMESH That is correct. Absolutely correct! You didn't create the separation. So who created the separation? God created the separation. That is why this feeling of separation. Each one thinking he is a separate being with free will is God's hypnosis—Divine hypnosis which has made everyone think he is a separate being.

RAJAN *But that causes a confused state of mind.*

RAMESH All right, if it is God's will to confuse you, why shouldn't he? And that is the whole point. Without every human being considering himself or herself as a separate human being with free will, how could life as we know it happen? So what I call free will is what the Hindu religion calls *maya*. Without *maya* life as we know it would not happen. So life as we know it to happen is *maya*—or God's will. He has created the feeling in every person that he is separate, and yet there is an instinct within which wants to find out, "Am I really an individual, or who am I?" And that instinct is also precisely what God has created so that "one in thousands will be seeking," and what he will be truly seeking—even though he may not know it— is to get rid of this separation. Basically what a seeker tries is to get rid of his separation, and when will that separation go?—only when it is the Divine will that the hypnosis will be removed. So whatever *sadhana* you do and whatever you think you are entitled to because of your severe *sadhana* is not in your control.

KAMAL *Can the functioning of the universe be understood by the mind? I'm not talking about the individual mind.*

RAMESH If you are not talking about the individual mind what mind *are* you talking about? You are talking of God's mind.

KAMAL *The functioning instrument.*

RAMESH The functioning instrument is just an object. It is inert matter. So what functions in the body-mind organism? Mind! How can the mind function unless there is Consciousness. Who created the mind? God created the mind. The source of the mind is Consciousness. How did the mind come into being? Only as a very pale reflection of Consciousness.

KAMAL *So the created cannot understand the Creator?*

RAMESH That is correct. That is precisely what I am saying. The created object *cannot* understand the Creator Subjectivity. Therefore you can only *accept* God's will— you cannot *understand* God's will. But you want to understand God's will, and what you are in effect doing is turning pure Subjectivity, or God, into an object. You usurp the subjectivity of Consciousness, or God, and say, "'I'want to understand That."

KAMAL *Which is impossible.*

RAMESH Which is impossible. Therefore all you can do is to accept God's will. You cannot know—you cannot even *try* to understand God's will.

MEERA *Is it impossible because you are a partial viewer?*

RAMESH No, because "you" are an object trying to understand Subjectivity. Basically there is *no you at all* other than as an object. And there are *no objects* other than the manifestation of Subjectivity—or God or Consciousness— *within* Itself!

KAMAL *We don't have the capability.*

RAMESH   That is the point. The created object cannot understand the Creator Subject.

ARUN *So Sir, the situation in the history of science in the last few hundred years will be treated as a stance which has no basis?*

RAMESH   Whatever the science has done, could it have happened unless it was God's will? Is it not part of the functioning of impersonal Consciousness? What makes you think what the science has done is separate from God's will?

ARUN *Science wants to comprehend and understand. It does not understand that It is incomprehensible.*

RAMESH   That's right. So only when the science truly comes to the point when it understands that *this* is impossible to penetrate will that science come to a stop—and the scientist will become a mystic.

RAVI *Actually that happens from time to time. It happens when science comes to something it can't understand and then it goes back. At that point it becomes...*

RAMESH   Quite right, it starts again.

RAVI *And that will go on forever.*

TOM *So Ramesh, an object can't be self-conscious, can it ?*

RAMESH   An object is an object! That power to be self-conscious is what? It is created by God. It is not part of the object. The idea of a "self" is a fiction created by God's hypnosis.

TOM *What I'm asking is: the idea of "I"...*

RAMESH   "The idea of 'I'" is the identity with the body as a separate being that is created so life as we know it can happen.

Tom *What I'm trying to say is: isn't it an apparent thing being seen by Consciousness?*

Ramesh Yes! So all that happens is that Consciousness is witnessing whatever is happening among the objects It has created. And that wanting to know Itself is something that is created by Consciousness. As the *Bhagavad Gita* says, "One in thousands "...

Tom *And the object itself cannot know Consciousness.*

Ramesh *And that is the final Understanding* ! So when that final Understanding happens, the object ceases to seek because the seeker is no longer there. The seeker understands that he is merely a created object. That is when the seeking stops, and *when* it happens does not depend on the fictitious will of the object.

Tom *The final Understanding is not like you understand a math problem, is it?*

Ramesh No. You see, "you" have got a solution to a mathematical problem, so there is a "he." There is a "me" who says, "'I' have understood that." This final Understanding is that Understanding in which there is no "I"—no "me"—to say, "'I' have understood." And when it happens—or whether it happens at all—is not in your control.

Eric *So that means we can never understand who we are. I think this is the misunderstanding where maybe other teachers are going wrong. For example, I heard from Poonjaji that there is something like a direct experience of the Self. People are having these experiences which could be called I Am experiences, or they call them experiences of Silence. Poonjaji said these are direct experiences of who you are. I think this is where we are going wrong because finally we cannot understand or experience...*

Ramesh When that experience happens *there is no*

experiencer. There is no "me" who has understood the Principle. The individual comes later and says, "'I' have understood." The same thing happens in an experience of utter terror. There is no individual there then. He comes later from memory and says, "'I' had a terrible experience." In the experience itself there is *truly no individual experiencer*. If this is truly and completely understood, then there will be no "me" craving for a repetition of that experience. It is the "me" which says, "I had a good experience," and there is a craving for a repetition of that experience—or a hope that a terrible experience will not happen again.

KAMAL   *In the* Bhagavad Gita *Krishna gives two paths...*

RAMESH   Four!

KAMAL   *Four? Okay, at least two I remember. One is through action and the other through* sankhya or...

RAMESH   What about *bhakti*? You see in fact, ultimately he says: When a man of *bhakti*—the devotion of a *bhakta*—reaches a certain intensity I give him the receptivity to understand, for Knowledge to happen. So what he says is that ultimately it is Knowledge.

MEERA   *But prior to that is "when I give him the intensity to ask for it."*

RAMESH   Quite correct. Indeed!

WOLFGANG   *On the other hand, when the understanding goes deeper... For example, in my case I was a more intellectual type, but I feel the more the teaching goes deeper the more devotion and love come up.*

RAMESH   Quite right, and that is why Ramana and others have said there is truly no difference between *bhakti* and *jnana*. Ramana says there are various ways of getting to the top of a hill.

ROHIT *But the* Gita *says* bhakti *can only happen when there is a certain level of intensity.*

RAMESH Yes, and who creates that intensity? The devotee? No! Even that intensity is created by God's will.

MEERA *Which means that in the whole world there is a certain number of people who have to be at a certain level in order to fulfill the order.*

RAMESH That is correct. That is the sense of balance which is the basis of the universe.

KAMAL *Then why are we all complaining about something or other all day?*

RAMESH Because you are supposed to!

KAMAL (laughs)

WOLFGANG *The more I can see everything is God's will the less I am complaining.*

RAMESH Yes!

WOLFGANG *Take the pollution in Bombay—I don't really complain about it. It is there. I mean the body doesn't like it, okay. But it is also part of What Is.*

RAMESH Quite right. You see, what happens, Wolfgang, is that the programming is accepted by the human mind where the physical part of it is concerned. The mind accepts that this body-mind organism was built to be a small man 5'5", 135 pounds. It can never ever, whatever effort it puts in, be 6'2" and 240 pounds. That, the mind accepts. The mind also accepts that the intellect is limited, that it can never be an Einstein. But the mind does not accept the rest. The mind says, "I can be a perfect being. I will make an effort and be the perfect man. I must meditate twenty hours a day." And it forgets its own temperamental limitations.

163

WOLFGANG *The Supreme Power that we can never know—in some ways we are That.*

RAMESH So if you are That—what questions can arise?

WOLFGANG *But exactly* because *we are That, we can't know It.*

RAMESH Absolutely correct, Wolfgang. You see, if you *are* That...

KAMAL *But that is what Krishna says are his divine forms. He gives us all his Divine forms in the* Gita: *" I am the water and I am the everything," even the cunning of the other person.*

RAMESH Quite right, everything. So when you accept that the cunning of the other person is not his fault, then you don't hate him. Anger may arise but you *will not* hate somebody for what they do.

MARY *We can know all the thousands and thousands of these aspects of phenomena, but the only thing we cannot know is ourselves?*

RAMESH That is correct. Why?

MARY *Well how can the "I" know Itself?*

RAMESH So Consciousness is not two. For something to know something else there has to be two—the knower and the known. If Consciousness is all there is—Pure Subjectivity—"who" is to know "what"?

YOUR HEAD IN THE TIGER'S MOUTH

Dalitaa kanditaa tuja gayeena Anantaa / /
Na visambe kshanabhari, tuze naam gaa Murari /
Nitya haachi kaarbhaara, muhki Hari nirantara / /
Maaya baapa bandhu bahina, toocha sakhaa chakrapaani /
Laksha laagale charanaashi, mhane Naamayaachi daasi / /

Ananta (Lord Krishna), I will go on singing Your name
   while grinding and pounding,
   and enjoy the feeling that "I am not the doer."
My darling Murari (Lord Krishna), I feel happy in remembering
   that You are present everywhere, all the time.
The working mind carries on with its work
   with Your name on the lips.
Chakrapani (Lord Krishna), You are my mother, my father,
   sister, brother and friend.
Namadev's servant Jani says:
   All my devotion is at Your feet.

回

Tuze roopa chitti raaho / mukhi tuze naama /
Deha prapanchaachaa daasa / sukhe karo kaama / /
Dehadhaari jo jo tyaache / vihita nitya karma /
Sadaachaara sanmaargaachaa / aagalaa na dharma /
Tulaa aavade te haati / ghado nitya karma / /
Tujhya padi vaahilaa mee / dehabhaava saaraa /
Ude antaraali aatmaa / soduni pasaaraa /
Naam tuze gheto Goraa / houni nishkaama / /

Paanduranga (Lord Krishna), Paanduranga, Paanduranga.

May Your form be in my heart
   and Your name on my lips.
The body is subject to the laws of phenomenality.
Let it do the work assigned to it by God or Nature.
Body-mind organisms react
   strictly according to the way they are programmed.
I truly understand that there is no good path

or good conduct for the instrument
other than the way it is designed and programmed.
Only those actions which You want,
  and for which You have uniquely programmed
  this body-mind organism, will happen.
Having understood this,
  I can only surrender at Your feet.
May the I Am in this body soar into the sky
  and not get involved with phenomenality.
Gora recites Your name with great feeling
  and without any expectation whatsoever.

SCENE 7

*It is a real joke that eating the apple in the
Garden of Eden separated us from the
universe through "knowledge." And it is the
"knowledge" acquired from splitting the
atom that proved to us that at the most
basic level—all things are "one"—that the
"ten thousand things" are actually "one."*

*By all means enjoy the movie of life—
participate in it—but never be unaware of
the screen of Consciousness on which it is
taking place.*

*The sage is not an achiever; he is not a
remarkable man. He is an ordinary man
without the ordinary man's wants, desires,
and frustrations. The sage is therefore
always as close to the Self as an ordinary
man is supposed to be.*

*Your true nature is that which exists in deep
sleep or in the interval between two
thoughts.*

MAHROUK *I was thinking that for years after I switched from searching in the materialistic world for answers—which I had been doing most of my life in psychotherapy, science and related areas—I then went into a psychic search in a sense. But there continued to be an interest in* facts. *I was fascinated in the esoteric sciences. I did a number of workshops in California on psychic healing and reincarnation therapy. I have had conversations with people who had died and whom I had known. And you know I find it very difficult to believe that this was imagination—they were so real.*

RAMESH Yes, so is this world that we live in.

MAHROUK *So I accept that they are as real as we are.*

RAMESH That's right. Sure.

MAHROUK *But what they seem to imply is that there is an existence without the body.*

RAMESH Sure. That's why they say if God can create beings with bodies...

MAHROUK *No, that I understand. But what they seem to imply is that the same being is in a spirit world.*

RAMESH So how does God create beings without bodies? We don't know! That's the answer! You see? So not every psychic being, every being without a body, had a body or was someone with a body, and not every being with a body becomes a being without a body.

MAHROUK *But some do*?

RAMESH Some may. That's why I say the mechanics of it we can't know.

MAHROUK *Yeah, well after five years I realized there was no point, and I didn't want any answers.*

RAMESH You see, also there is a friend of mine who has been attending here for many years. She has a master's degree in social work and that is her profession. She practiced for a while, but then some kind of psychic experience happened to her, and now she says she talks with angels. She makes a living, a good living, out of people who come to her with their difficulties. She talks with her angels, and just repeats what the angels say to her. I think there are many psychics in America.

BLAYNE *Yes, and Europe.*

RAMESH Yes, I believe there are many psychics there. So certain body-mind organisms are so programmed that a strong psychic element is part of the programming. Some body-mind organisms are programmed with the gift of seeing ahead. You see? So that is just one of the gifts—and often, I would say, it is a dubious gift.

BLAYNE AND MAHROUK *I agree. Absolutely.*

RAMESH You see, it's a dubious gift. But what I am saying is it is just a gift as part of the programming. When people ask me about Judy—that's her name who does the angel talk—because they see her here, I say, "One thing I can tell you: Judy is not a fraud. That is all I can tell you. Judy is not a fraud." And she talks sometimes for an hour, an hour and a quarter, to people she doesn't know who come to her. You see? To what extent her client benefits because of this angel talk is the destiny of that person.

BLAYNE *What about the ongoing relationship with a friend or a relative who has died? You can't always call them in, sometimes they don't come.*

RAMESH No. That's right.

BLAYNE *Depending on your relationship and whatever your gifts are, sometimes they almost always come, and then over a long period of time there is a fading out.*

RAMESH Sure.

BLAYNE   *But sometimes for years they can provide you information about your relationship with them which you didn't know about when you were having it.*

RAMESH   Sure.

BLAYNE   *And of course they can provide you with new information that's taking place in the future.*

RAMESH   Certainly, yes.

BLAYNE   *But it's not an incarnate—to use an incorrect word— it's not a body-mind organism who* is *looking into the future. Here it is a friend who is no longer, who is on the other side, continuing a relationship with you.*

RAMESH   Yes, that's right. So, that is part of God's will.

BLAYNE   *I agree, I agree.*

RAMESH   That's why I say not every being with a body becomes a being without body.

BLAYNE   *Oh.*

RAMESH   Not every being with body becomes a being without body. So which beings without bodies had bodies before, God knows. We can't know.

BLAYNE   *When I think of all the people I know in the States— because I spent eighteen years with this stuff, and like you said about Judy, some of them are absolutely not frauds and incredibly accurate. There are spirit guides and spirit teachers and people who have died and continued on in some course or...*

RAMESH   That's right. She calls it angels.

BLAYNE   *Yes, well, and there is quite a different energy from an angel realm compared to somebody who has died and continues to communicate.*

170

RAMESH   So what Judy is talking about may be different from what you are talking about.

BLAYNE   *Yes, it is.*

RAMESH   But it is still part of the psychic phenomena. So if you mean is there a psychic world, I see no reason why there shouldn't be. Why not? I say why not. Nothing is beyond God.

BLAYNE   *I know that world is there because I've experienced it.*

RAMESH   Why not?

ESTRELLA   *But I don't understand. If I die—finished! How can the ego exist in another world?*

RAMESH   Whether you call it ego, I don't know. All I am saying is, if it is God's will that there should be a connection between a being with a body and a being without a body, why should God not create that connection?

ESTRELLA   *Yes, but if, when we die, everybody goes to the pool of Consciousness, then...*

RAMESH   So, from that pool God creates a being without body which had a connection with the earlier body. What is to prevent God from doing anything that you don't understand, Estrella?

ESTRELLA   *Yes, but that seems strange.*

RAMESH   Yes, strange, of course. Things have happened. All of them have been recorded. All kinds of psychic phenomena have been recorded, Estrella. In fact there is a TV series called *X-Files*, and the whole thing is based on extraterrestrial and parapsychological phenomena.

BLAYNE   *You mentioned yesterday, which is interesting, the word "continuum." I mean, I know it's a concept and we have to use concepts to communicate, and frankly I'm getting tired of communicating. I'm sure you must be. Because what*

171

happens, once you have the realization and the appreciation that all is Consciousness and there is only the impersonal will of Consciousness, where can questions come from?

RAMESH   That is the point.

BLAYNE   *But the reason I keep indulging in this pool of questions is that as soon as I return to the "pool" that I came from—back in California or New York or wherever—I'm going to be deluged with questions for which I don't have answers. Now I've got two approaches: either be a fool and try to answer them, or else I can be like yourself and Ramana Maharshi and look over their left shoulder.*

RAMESH   Oh, no! Say that there are things which God can produce which no human being can understand. That's it. That is the answer to your question—God can do anything. We don't have the intellect to understand what he is doing. We cannot know the mechanics by which he does something. We cannot know the mechanics by which he produces the psychic world.

BLAYNE   *The Divine hypnotism—one of the mechanics of that hypnotism is that the mind-intellect continuously wants answers to questions, and it's a bloody loop.*

RAMESH   That's right. It is part of the Divine hypnotism. It is part of the Divine hypnosis. You see, a Zen master—he must have been some mischievous Zen master—said in a sentence of a few words with no explanation: "Awakening is always sudden. Deliverance may be gradual." He just left it at that. And the amount of discussion that has taken place...you see? My answer to this is very simple. When there has been the sudden awakening there is nobody left to be concerned about deliverance. There is no one left to be concerned about deliverance. "Who" cares? And if there is someone who cares about deliverance, awakening has not happened. You see? If there is someone concerned about deliverance, then awakening has not happened.

ROHIT *What is karma,* vikarma, akarma?

RAMESH I don't know about *vikarma* and *akarma*, but I can tell you, karma as far as I am concerned is action. Then you can make all kinds of combinations.

ROHIT *But karma in the line of causation?*

RAMESH Karma is an action which has its consequences. Those consequences become the karma for further consequences, and that is causation.

ROHIT *What are the causes of the karma?*

RAMESH Causes of the karma? Karma just happens because the Energy produces the karma.

ROHIT *Who is responsible?*

RAMESH No one; certainly not Rohit. And if Rohit is not responsible, why should Rohit bother about "who" is responsible?

LANCE In deep sleep nothing exists because there is no mind to observe anything?

RAMESH Yes, that's right.

LANCE *So the same thing...*

RAMESH In deep sleep there is no manifestation, and therefore there is no "me" to be involved in that manifestation. Consequently, in deep sleep there is peace. So the real problem is to experience that peace even when there is manifestation in the waking state. Isn't it? What is the object of seeking? The object of the seeking is to find that peace in the waking state, the manifestation, which is the same peace that exists in deep sleep without the manifestation. So what is the answer, Lance? How do you get the peace which exists in deep sleep in the waking state? Is it possible or is it not possible?

LANCE *If it is my destiny it's possible.*

RAMESH No. I mean in the case of the sage it has happened. A sage in the waking state finds the same peace that he finds in deep sleep. How does that happen? I am not speaking of the destiny of sitting in a cave for fifty years and then dying there. I'm talking about the person living in the world who has to live his life in this manifestation, and yet enjoys the peace which exists in deep sleep. And it *does* happen in the case of a sage.

Why does it happen in the case of a sage? What does he do in living and witnessing life as it happens which the average person does not do? That is the question, isn't it? The average person does not find the peace which exists in deep sleep during the waking state in a working life. The sage does. Why, Lance? Do you know why? And the sage is as much interested in this life as the ordinary person. I mean, it is not that he goes through life like a blind man. Oh, he sees, he's interested in what's happening. If there's something to laugh about, he laughs. If there's something which causes compassion to arise, he'll try to help. So he is deeply interested in life as it happens. But while he's interested, the main awareness is that this life which is happening is a movie which cannot happen without the screen of Consciousness behind it. So while he is interested in the movie, he is always aware of the screen of Consciousness. He is never unaware of the screen. He is interested in the movie with the full awareness that it is only a movie which cannot happen unless there is the screen of Consciousness on which the movie is happening.

DOUGLAS *Is he interested in it or disinterested in it?*

RAMESH No, he is interested. He is very much interested in it.

DOUGLAS *He doesn't get involved in it?*

RAMESH He doesn't get involved in it. Why does he not get

involved in it? Because he knows that this is only a movie and there is only the screen of Consciousness. All there is is Consciousness.

ROHIT *The movie, and the sage, and the Consciousness—are they not all Consciousness?*

RAMESH Consciousness is all there is. So what question can Rohit have?

ROHIT *Only the delusion of the movie being real.*

RAMESH "Who" has that delusion?

ROHIT *The deluded one.*

RAMESH Is there a deluded "one" when Consciousness is all there is?

ROHIT *No sir.*

RAMESH You started with "Consciousness is all there is." Wonderful. Then where does the delusion arise? For "whom" does the delusion arise? If Consciousness is all there is—you see, if you start from that point...

ROHIT *Yes, it arises for the one who deludes himself.*

RAMESH "Who" is this, if Consciousness is all there is? Who is this "who" which deludes itself? Consciousness is all there is. That is what you said. So if you accept that Consciousness is all there is—then? Then nothing!
    You see, this is what happens—theoretically you come with concepts: "Oh yes, Consciousness is all there is; $E=MC^2$; 'I' know all about the theory of relativity; 'I' know everything about everything; Consciousness is all there is."

ROHIT *Sir, you said that the sage is aware behind the movie, of the screen...*

RAMESH So what you are implying is if Consciousness is all there is, where is the sage?

175

ROHIT *No—where is the* movie?

RAMESH You *live* in this movie, do you not? Is this life not going on for you? Is this life not going on?

ROHIT *Is it apart from Consciousness?*

RAMESH Can *anything* be apart from That which is the Whole? The sage is aware that this movie cannot take place unless there is the screen of Consciousness. The average man is not. That is the only difference.

ROHIT *But then there is no movie.*

RAMESH Of course there is. The life goes on.

ROHIT *But it is not distinct from Consciousness.*

RAMESH If you truly understand that, then why are you interested in this life? Why are you interested in the problems in your office?

ROHIT *But that is a dynamic Consciousness, and that is a Consciousness which is static.*

RAMESH Oh, there are two Consciousnesses?!

ROHIT *It is a* nirguna *and a* saguna.

RAMESH Oh, so there are two?

ROHIT *No, they are not two.*

RAMESH If they are not two, then where is the question of this body-mind organism asking any questions? The only question you can ask is: if Consciousness is all there is, where does the sage come in? Where does the difference come in?

ROHIT *Then the sage is also not there?*

RAMESH The sage and the ordinary man are both characters in the movie. And the movie is happening on the screen of Consciousness.

ROHIT *Just as in the human movie there is a screen and the movie appears on the screen, then that movie is not real.*

RAMESH When that movie is over, what remains is the screen.

ROHIT *But then during the time that that movie is going on, is that movie real?*

RAMESH That movie is as much real as when you go out in the sun, your shadow is there. When you come in, the shadow is not there. Is your shadow real or not?

ROHIT *As a shadow it is real.*

RAMESH As a shadow it is real, so this movie is also real. A shadow as a shadow is real; therefore, this life as life is real.

ROHIT *Therefore the sage as a sage is real.*

RAMESH The sage and the ordinary man are both part of the reality that is life.

ROHIT *Can one say that it is a reflection of Consciousness?*

RAMESH Yes.

ROHIT *Just as in the sun there is a shadow, this is a reflection of Consciousness?*

RAMESH A reflection of this body. The shadow is a reflection of this body.

ROHIT *Then the sage and the ordinary individual are also reflections of Consciousness?*

RAMESH Part of the manifestation. The sage and the ordinary man are both *part* of the reflection. And the sage and the ordinary man are part—as two body-mind organisms—of the totality of manifestation.

ROHIT *Which is a reflection?*

RAMESH   Which is a reflection.

ROHIT   *Just as a shadow is?*

RAMESH   That is correct.

ROHIT   *Beautiful.*

RAMESH   Thank you. *(laughter fills the little room)*

IRENE   *But when the sage is witnessing the movie, what is witnessing—this consciousness or the impersonal Consciousness?*

RAMESH   The sage witnesses, as in anybody's case, with the mind, and the mind is not separate from Consciousness.

IRENE   *As long as ego is there?*

RAMESH   No. All observation—through the eyes, through the ears, through any of the senses—is happening because the mind is there. What sees? Your eyes don't see. It is the mind seeing the object through the mechanics of the eyes.

IRENE   *Through the instrument.*

RAMESH   That is right.

IRENE   *Ultimately there is some energy, the same as impersonal Energy?*

RAMESH   Yes, basically what is functioning is Energy.

IRENE   *The sage is also interested?*

RAMESH   That's right. He sees the manifestation. He doesn't say, "I'm not interested. It doesn't bother me. There is a fire, but I don't care. I'll go through the fire." No, he will avoid the fire if he doesn't want to get burnt. The sage is not disinterested in the movie. When he goes through the movie he gets interested in it, but that interest is strictly limited as part of the illusion. The awareness is never away

179

from what is Real. The awareness is *never* away from what is Real. And what is Real is Consciousness, the screen of Consciousness. Therefore, the sage witnesses the movie, is interested in the movie, but never unaware of the screen of Consciousness on which this movie is happening.

MAX *In other words, what you mean by always being aware of the screen on which this movie is taking place is that what is being seen is fictitious, and the sage doesn't get involved?*

RAMESH That is correct. He doesn't get involved, but there is awareness also. What is the awareness? The movie is both real and unreal, the shadow is both real and unreal. The shadow is real—you can see it. The shadow is unreal—it has no independent existence of its own. The movie, life, is real enough—you see it. You get involved in it. You react to what is happening. If a sage is watching a sad scene, tears may arise in his eyes. To that extent the movie is real. However, the awareness is that this is real but has no existence of its own. It owes its existence to the screen of Consciousness. Therefore, the screen of Consciousness is Real. The movie is unreal, and yet so long as it is there, it appears real.

Then, is the manifestation real? It is real and unreal. The question—Is the manifestation real or not?—is *misconceived*. The manifestation is both real and unreal: real to the extent that it can be observed, unreal on the basis that it has no independent existence of its own without Consciousness. So the only thing that has independent existence of its own is Reality, and that Reality is Consciousness. Consciousness is the only Reality. Everything else is a reflection of that Reality within Itself.

ROHIT *Sir, if manifestation is a reflection of Reality, then the mind is also a reflection of the Reality?*

RAMESH The mind is not separate from Consciousness. The mind is not different. The mind is part of the body-mind organism; the body-mind organism is part of the manifestation; and the manifestation is a reflection of Reality.

ROHIT *There is a view that the world is unreal, that it is only apparent to the mind. But even if an individual is not there, if there is no observer in the sense of the subjective-objective, even then does the manifestation remain?*

RAMESH No. If you are the only sentient being on Earth, and you are in deep sleep, "who" is there to say the manifestation exists? Does it exist?

ROHIT *But sir, the earth is there, the sun is there.*

RAMESH If "you" are the only sentient being on earth, and "you" are in deep sleep, how do "you" know the earth is there?

ROHIT *One will not know it.*

RAMESH Then "who" will know it? "You" are the only sentient being on Earth and in deep sleep.

ROHIT *But the world remains as Earth.*

RAMESH Even science today says that no object exists unless it is observed. The physicists say no object exists unless it is observed. An object exists because it is observed. And if there is only one sentient being on earth, and that only sentient being is in deep sleep, then "who" is to observe the manifestation?

ROHIT *But does the manifestation not remain?*

RAMESH No. There is no manifestation.

ROHIT *If I am in deep sleep...*

RAMESH If you are the only sentient being on earth what you are saying now is, "I may be in deep sleep, but the others..."

ROHIT *No, no, no. Rohit is in a deep sleep. His body will not be there?*

RAMESH If it is in deep sleep, is the body able to witness the manifestation?

ROHIT No.

RAMESH Then what are you talking about, Rohit?

ROHIT *Then this chair will remain, won't it? As a chair.*

RAMESH No, it won't.

ROHIT *Actually I feel, sir, one doesn't see the chair. One sees the appearance of a chair, and he gives reality to that appearance.*

RAMESH That's right, the mind gives it...

ROHIT *Any of your actions are part of the totality of the manifestation.*

RAMESH Correct.

ROHIT *Actually the whole cosmos, the whole existence itself, is supporting all your actions, and therefore you are the world...*

RAMESH But who is this "you" being talked about?

ROHIT *That "you" has finally...There is no "you."*

RAMESH The "you" *is* the Consciousness. And Ramana Maharshi, in one beautiful sentence he says, "Find out the 'I' in your 'my'"—my world, my family, my body. He says to find out the "I" in your "my."

ROHIT *Does the apparent world not remain?*

RAMESH The apparent world exists only so long as someone observes it, and that makes it *apparent*. What makes it *apparent* ? Because it is seen. It is observed.

ROHIT *Is then the world only apparent?*

182

RAMESH   The physicists say no object exists unless it is observed.

ROHIT   *It may not be as an object, but otherwise does it remain?*

RAMESH   If not as an object, then what else? As an idea in your mind?

ROHIT   *It will not be distinct. Objects are always distinct.*

RAMESH   And that which is now talking is an object in the totality of the manifestation. And the totality of manifestation is observed through a body-mind organism, of which and in which is Consciousness   Consciousness functioning as the mind. So in deep sleep the mind is not there.

ROHIT   *Mind as a subjectivity as in subject-object?*

RAMESH   Mind is the instrument which perceives things. The eyes don't see the world. The mind sees the world through the eyes. The mind hears the world through the ears. The eyes and the ears are merely the mechanical part of it.

ROHIT   *So what remains is only Consciousness?*

RAMESH   What remains is Consciousness, from which lofty angle you started to talk. From that lofty angle you started talking, and now you ask, "Does the manifestation exist if there is no one to observe it?" If all the sentient beings in the world are in deep sleep at the same moment, "who" is to say whether the world exists or not?

ROHIT   *If it does not exist as a manifestation, then how does it exist?*

RAMESH   It doesn't exist!

ROHIT   *Then it is only impersonal Consciousness.*

RAMESH   Yes, all there is is the impersonal Consciousness.

ROHIT *How can the mind know who is asking the question? Then what is the purpose of questions?* (*laughter*)

RAMESH Ask yourself.

ROHIT *That is what I am asking myself.*

RAMESH I'll tell you what the point in questioning is. The point in questioning by this body-mind organism is that this body-mind organism has been programmed to be a solicitor, and it is the solicitor who is asking questions. This body-mind organism is programmed to ask questions. So really you can't help it, Rohit.

ROHIT *Ordinarily, doesn't everybody function from the viewpoint of the mind, and everybody is enquiring?*

RAMESH You see, not everybody is. When you say "enquiring" you mean seeking. I'll repeat again: from the moment a baby is born and seeks its mother's breast intuitively, life is nothing but seeking. The baby does not say he or she seeks the mother's breast. But when you grow up and the ego comes into the picture, the ego says "'I' seek. 'I' do."

Basically, what I am saying is life is nothing but seeking, and there has never been any seeker. There never has been any thinker—thinking is happening. There has never been a doer—doing is happening as part of the impersonal functioning of Consciousness. There is no experiencer—experiencing happens. Later on in the experiencing there is no ego. If you are in ecstasy or real terror there is no individual; he comes later and says, "I had a wonderful experience. I would like to have more of those experiences." Or he says, "I had a terrible experience. I don't want any more of those." That is the ego which comes later. In the experiencing there is no ego. The ego comes later and assumes the role of the experiencer which it never was.

So the seeking happens. There has never been any

seeker. And that is the final understanding. The final understanding is that the seeking is happening. The seeking has taken its own course,and there never has been a seeker who started the seeking or who could control the seeking.

ROHIT *Is not the seeker the veil in seeking? Is there any independent seeking apart from the seeker which is the veil?*

RAMESH There is no seeker. All there is is the seeking. There *is no seeker.* That is my concept.

ROHIT *Then seeking from the point of view of a seeker is the veil...*

RAMESH You can call it what you like. All I am saying is that seeking begins with an individual *thinking* that he is seeking enlightenment. And enlightenment, or self-realization, or whatever you call it, cannot happen until there is the total, unconditional acceptance that there never was a seeker. Only then will the seeking stop.

ROHIT *Therefore seeking is only on account of the delusion of the seeker?*

RAMESH Seeking happens because the body-mind organism has been programmed for a specific kind of seeking to happen. If a body-mind organism has been programmed to seek money, seeking money will happen. If a body-mind organism has been programmed to seek fame, fame will be sought. If a body-mind organism has been programmed to seek power, then seeking power will happen.

ROHIT *So the common denominator is the seeker?*

RAMESH The common denominator is Consciousness which is doing the seeking according to the programming in the body-mind organism which It has created, which Consciousness has created.

ROHIT *You say that when the seeker ends, the seeking ends. Then how can the impersonal Consciousness be the seeker? Is*

185

it that the impersonal Consciousness is not the seeker, but It is programming the individual body-mind organism to seek?

RAMESH   When the "individual seeker" understands that he, the individual, is not the seeker, that the only seeker is God, or Consciousness, then the seeking stops. When there is total acceptance...

ROHIT   *Even then the seeking goes on?*

RAMESH   Then the seeking stops. This is the understanding. This is what the seeking is all about. The seeking is to understand that there never was a seeker.

TISHIA   *Does it start with just total acceptance of whatever comes?*

RAMESH   The end of it you mean?

TISHIA   *No, the start.*

RAMESH   The beginning is always the individual seeker thinking he is seeking enlightenment.

TISHIA   *Yes, but then if you accept that whether you get enlightened or not enlightened, it doesn't matter...*

RAMESH   That is the end of it.

TISHIA   Oh! (surprised laughter)

RAMESH   The beginning is the seeker saying, "I want enlightenment, and therefore I shall do this and that and this, whereby I shall get enlightenment." But when the final understanding is that there is no individual who can be enlightened—that there never was a seeker who could get the enlightenment which he thought he was seeking; that enlightenment is merely a happening; and that whether this happening happens through this body-mind organism or not is no longer of concern— *then the seeker is annihilated.* The seeker is fictitious. The final understanding is there never was a seeker—there was only seeking. And

186

the seeking was happening because it was part of the destiny of that body-mind organism.

So if the destiny of the body-mind organism is to be programmed to seek money, money will be sought. But if the destiny of a body-mind organism is to be programmed to seek God, seeking God will happen. But so long as there is a seeker, the seeker says, "I am seeking God; he or she is only seeking money. Therefore, I am superior to him or her." That is what the seeker does. The seeker says, "I meditate. I meditate two hours a day. He can hardly meditate for half an hour, therefore I am superior to him." So long as there is a seeker who keeps judging whether or not he is superior to someone else, he is concerned about "his" progress. "Am 'I' progressing?" The seeker is always interested in progress, "my" progress. So when the final understanding does happen—if it is God's will and the destiny of that body-mind organism—then the understanding is, "'I' have never really been the seeker. Why should 'I' be interested in how the seeking ends?"

TISHIA *I find when I sit here I become very quiet, but when I am away in the afternoon I only think of food, and getting things to buy, and sleep, and I read a bit. And at night I get a bit emotionally involved.*

RAMESH Emotionally involved? So, Tishia, what happens is there is interest in whatever is happening: food, buying, buying for friends. In all that, that is just happening. It is just happening. Later on, as you say, when you go back, Tishia says, "I have been involved with all that buying and I have not been thinking about seeking."

TISHIA *Yes.*

RAMESH You see? "I have been involved in eating and buying, and lots of things, but I have forgotten seeking." That is why Tishia *is*, but if Tishia says, "It has just been going on..."

TISHIA *Then I have no conflict anymore. Nice.*

RAMESH   That is the whole point. That is what I mean by no seeking.

TISHIA *Yeah, yeah.*

RAMESH   You see? So the real problem, as you say, is that at night, Tishia suddenly realizes that instead of seeking, she has been eating and buying. *(laughter)* "Instead of seeking I have only been eating and buying and talking with people, having a good time."

TISHIA *Just my program?*

RAMESH   So that is What Is. Whatever has happened is part of the impersonal functioning of Totality. Whatever has happened could not have happened, Tishia, unless it was the will of God. Whatever has been happening— whether you enjoy your eating, you enjoy your buying, you enjoy whatever—is happening and could not have been happening unless it is God's will. So why should Tishia be bothered with what has been happening according to God's will? But instead of accepting what is happening as God's will, Tishia says, "'I' have been buying, 'I' have been enjoying, instead 'I' should have been seeking." You see? That makes the problem.

So again my answer, Tishia, is do whatever you think you are doing, and whatever happens is not your doing. *Accept* whatever happens as God's will and have some sound sleep. *(everyone laughing)*

Bhaava tochi deva bhaava tochi deva /
  Ye arthi sandeha dharu nakaal / /
Bhaava bhakti fale bhaave deva mile /
  Nijabhaave sohaale swaanandaache / /
Bhaavachi kaaran bhaavachi kaaran /
  yaaparate saadhana naahi naahi / /
Ekaa Janaardani bhaavaachyaa aavadi /
  Manoratha kodi purati tethe / /

Love of the Guru is itself God.
Let there be no doubt about this.
Devotion ripens and God manifests Himself
  when there is pure unconditional Love
  or surrender to the Guru.
When this attitude becomes steady,
  the peace of I Am is experienced.
Love of the Guru is the penultimate step
  before the happening of enlightenment,
  and it remains in the heart forever.
No other *sadhana* is necessary.
Eka Janardan enjoys this love.
All my expectations got dissolved in it.

◻

Sukhaache he naama aavadine gaave /
  vaache aalaavaave Vithobaasi / /
Sansaara sukhaachaa hoeela nirdhaara /
  naamaachaa gajara sarva kaala / /
Kaamakrodhanche na chalechi kaahi /
  aashaa manashaa paahi doora hoti / /
Aavadi dharoni vaache mhane Hari Hari /
  mhanatase mahaari Chokhiyaachi / /

Sing the name of the Lord and spread happiness and peace.
Wail loudly for the Lord without any sense of shame.
Your family life will be simpler

189

if an acclamation of the Lord's name happens all the time.
Lust and greed will run away.
Chokha says:
  Let the singing of Hari (Lord Krishna) happen
  with deep feeling and affection.

SCENE 8

We are perpetually caught in a traffic jam of conceptual thinking. The only escape lies in jumping out of it—if we can do it!

回

Physicists keep telling us that solidity is an illusion and that everything is movement: everything is interacting or in process. What thinking and vocalizing into words do, is to pile up static "things" and thus make us forget that solidity is an illusion.

回

If you understand the theory of relativity, everything is exactly the way it is. If you cannot understand the theory of relativity, everything is exactly the way it is.

回

He says, "I am Edo and you are Udo: there is a big difference between Edo and Udo." But if there is a realization that they are just two names given to two body-mind organisms, then there is no entity involved and there is no difference between Edo and Udo.

RAMESH   Philippe, what do you do in life?

PHILIPPE   *I used to race cars—drive racing cars.*

RAMESH   Oh, wow!

PHILIPPE   *I stopped in 1991. It's a very good discipline .*

RAMESH   Total concentration, isn't it?

PHILIPPE   *Yes. You know top drivers know that there is no driver there when they perform...*

RAMESH   Quite right!

PHILIPPE   *That is the winning attitude. And there are a lot of common things to what we are talking about here. All these guys are very close to what we are talking about here, but they are only like that while in the car.*

RAMESH   That's right! So they live in the Present Moment only for a limited period.

PHILIPPE   *Yes. Their lives can be havoc.*

RAMESH   Yes. So in the car they enjoy that peace that they enjoy in deep sleep...

PHILIPPE   *Yes.*

RAMESH   There is no "me" then.

PHILIPPE   *And you know the body is tortured in those cars. It's very, very physically demanding.*

RAMESH   Oh, I sometimes watch them on the TV—a very hard life.

PHILIPPE   *And you go through all that crazy ordeal just for that state...*

RAMESH   How many years did you do that, Philippe?

PHILIPPE   *Ten, twelve years.*

RAMESH   Oh really. And you haven't had any accidents?

PHILIPPE   *Yes, plenty!* (Ramesh laughs) *But you know, also there is acceptance. You learn that when you see you are going crash. If you are very loose, if you accept the crash, you'll get less hurt than if you are all tense.*

RAMESH   And that is what I'm told is the basic instruction in the martial arts. When you fall, fall relaxed. You know, a friend of mine used to have bad eyes and was a very weak man, so his wife used to accompany him always and hold him by the arm. He had a tremendous sense of humor. Once they went to the movie house, and while they were climbing the stairs the husband lost the strength in his legs and he relaxed. He fell down the steps and his wife went with him. So he said, "What are *you* doing here?" *(everyone laughing)*

PHILIPPE   *The interesting thing with racing cars is that there is a very high level of perfection. So it is a very privileged activity because you work with professionals who are very committed. There are no loose ends. And because the body can die or get very badly hurt there is that commitment, you know, from the least mechanic to the top engineer. Also there is that sense of existence—mindfulness. The day one steps onto the track to prepare for the race, one enters a whole different universe of commitment and being in the Present Moment.*

RAMESH   Among those who are in the racing profession, really only a few make it to the top, isn't it? Very few, or am I wrong?

PHILIPPE   *No, no, very few. There are also some who try, and they don't have all the body-mind organism specifications.*

RAMESH   The programming is not good enough to perform well...

PHILIPPE   *Yes. The wish is there but it is not backed up by the right programming.*

RAMESH   So this spiritual seeking, how long has this been going on, Philippe?

PHILIPPE   *Long time. I think I was sixteen when I actually engaged. It started by not accepting what was given for truth around me. I was feeling there was something else behind...*

RAMESH   Quite right, yes. So seeing something behind that what happens is this: if I put an apple on my hand what do you see? You would say, "An apple." I remove that apple. What do you see now? "Nothing!" But in both instances the hand was there, you see? *(laughing)* The apple may be there, or the apple may not be there, but the hand is there all the time! *(both Ramesh and Philippe laughing)* How do you speak English so well?

PHILIPPE   *Because in racing the international language is English.*

RAMESH   I see. You have to communicate a lot?

PHILIPPE   *Yes. But it's tricky because I don't master it so well as it looks. But then again I feel English is a very good spiritual language. Better than French.*

RAMESH   I think so too. You know why? For one reason, in English you can differentiate between the "I" and the "me." "I" is the Self, "me" is the individual entity. I'm told you cannot do this in many languages. Therefore Ramana Maharshi speaking in Tamil was not able to use the language to differentiate between the two. You see? So he had to distinguish between them by saying "I-I" for the Self and "I" for the "me."

GABRIEL   *Bob Marley, the Jamaican reggae singer, used I-I to show the true essence.*

RAMESH   He probably read Ramana Maharshi! *(everyone laughs)* Unless the ego was doubly strong!

VISITOR   *So everything is a concept. And you say only one thing: the "isness" cannot be denied—but it cannot be confirmed either...*

RAMESH   If you don't deny it where is the question of confirmation, my friend? If you don't deny it, where is the question of confirmation? That is the whole point. The question of denying or confirming does not arise. You have been coming here for a few days now. Can you tell me something about yourself?

VISITOR   (silent)

RAMESH   Can you tell me something about this body-mind organism which thinks he still comes here? What is your name? You have a name?

VISITOR   *Edo.*

RAMESH   Edo, I see. He is Udo and you are Edo...

EDO   *Yeah, big difference...*

RAMESH   I know. *(laughing)* You see that is my point. You say there is a big difference. I say there is *no* difference! They're just two names given to two body-mind organisms. Where is the difference? But you say "big difference" because you say "'I' am Edo and 'he' is Udo."
    What is your specific question now, Gabriel?

GABRIEL   *Why is there no discipline for the beginner?*

RAMESH   What I'm saying to the beginner is to meditate—meditate on the fact you have no free will. What is the discipline? Find out from personal experience—from your past experience and your experience of today—whether any act that happens is your act or is it merely a mechanical reaction of the brain. Find out! Isn't that a discipline?

GABRIEL   *It is.*

RAMESH   So I'm saying—I'm telling you—that what you call "your" act does not exist! "You" cannot act! What you think is "your" action is merely a reaction of the brain to an outside event over which you have no control according to the programming over which you have had no control. Unless you find out from personal experience, it is no good.

GABRIEL *I live moment to moment. That is correct?*

RAMESH Quite right. What I'm telling you is to find out from moment to moment whether it was "your" action or was it merely reaction. Ramana Maharshi said to ask yourself from moment to moment, "Who wants that? Who am I? Who wants something?" That was his way. My way is to find out from moment to moment if anything that happens is your action or is it merely a reaction of the brain.

MARK *I can grasp that for a brief moment.*

RAMESH Why are you able to accept it only very briefly?

MARK *Because of the misidentification with body and mind.*

RAMESH How has that misidentification with body and mind happened? Did you create it? You didn't create it!

MARK *Yeah. Well, yesterday for the first time I heard about your idea or concept of programming and so forth and so on, and it makes sense to me.*

RAMESH So that sense—intellectual sense—can only be verified from personal experience. That is why I say from moment to moment find out. Ask yourself, "Have 'I' done it or has it just happened?" This is the only discipline— which Gabriel is asking about.

MARK *I think that's an excellent discipline, it's just I find it extremely difficult...*

RAMESH I know. I know. But whenever you remember—if you do it—that is good enough, Mark. You see? And then when you begin to remember, then that remembering will be brought about by this very intellectual understanding. So there will be a sudden realization that you have not been asking the question—then the question will happen. And so the understanding goes deeper.

The sudden realization that you have not been asking the question will happen more frequently until it happens moment to moment. Then at the end of the day you will say, "This whole day I have been watching myself. There is no action which is really my action." Then the mind-intellect says that if Mark has not been doing anything—is there a Mark at all? You see? And that is a big step in the understanding. The answer will come absolutely from personal experience—there is no Mark to do anything at all! That everything just happens because it is the destiny of this body-mind organism and the will of God is the final understanding—which can only *happen*.

GABRIEL *It is in fact very universal, because Africans tend to believe God does everything. It is very universal.*

RAMESH That's what I'm saying, Gabriel: that is the universal phenomenal truth, or rather the basis of any religion. And yet there are religious wars because the basic concept in every religion is interpreted in different ways. I read today or yesterday that in Afghanistan your hair must not come onto your forehead because then the devil lives there. So there are barbers waiting to chop your hair off. That is an *interpretation* of Islam. And the basis of Islam—I am told—is universal love.

Every Muslim frequently says, "Insh'Allah," which means "God willing." One man will ask another, "When are you going? Tomorrow?" And often the reply is, "Insh'Allah—God willing." So the basis is nothing happens unless it is the will of God. "Thy will be done" in another religion. In the Hindu religion one says to God, "You are the doer, you are the enjoyer." The basis is the same, and yet it is not accepted.

PHILIPPE *Any sense of oneself is a separating process.*

RAMESH That is correct. Absolutely correct. In fact the

whole problem arises, Philippe, because each individual considers itself a separate entity—separate from the rest of the world...

PHILIPPE *Yes but then whom do you address when you say "your" true nature?*

RAMESH You see, it is only that I am addressing it to that fictitious entity who comes to me and asks the question.

PHILIPPE *Yes, but it is tricky because it seems that you consolidate this illusion when you say "you" have a true nature. Who is that "you"?*

RAMESH This fictitious entity asks me a question, and I can either answer it—give an answer to this fictitious entity— or sit silent. What do you want me to do? You see?

PHILIPPE *It's a matter of language, of course, but in anything that is written or said, the use of the personal pronoun, the impersonal formulation is much easier...*

RAMESH But the point is the impersonal formulation. The Upanishads say it all: "Consciousness is all there is!" An impersonal statement: Consciousness is all there is! If that is accepted, "who" is going to ask "what" question? "Who" can ask "what" question? Consciousness is all there is, which I expand into saying: Consciousness has scripted the movie, Consciousness has produced the movie, Consciousness is playing all the characters, Consciousness is witnessing the movie. What is the basis of all this? Consciousness is all there is! If that is accepted; if that impersonal specification is accepted—Consciousness is all there is—"who" will ask "what" question, Philippe? "Who" is there to ask any question? There can't be any individual to ask any question. You see? That is why the Upanishads say the final word: Consciousness is all there is. If that is accepted, "who" can ask any questions? And I quite agree with you. The moment you get away from the impersonal and start with the personal concept of God, all kinds of problems arise. I agree. Consciousness is all there is. You accept it—end of it!

Many body-mind organisms which are programmed towards knowledge—*jnana*—will accept this. But what happens is that many intellects are not able to accept this impersonal specification. A body-mind organism which is programmed towards devotion— *bhakti*, basically duality—such a body-mind organism will say to me, "I'm sorry I'm finding it very dificult to accept this impersonal Consciousness, or Awareness. You tell me that everything happens according to the will of God. That I can accept." That body-mind organism has been programmed based on duality. So seeking is happening in both body-mind organisms—one is programmed towards knowledge, and the other is programmed towards devotion. A third body-mind organism is so programmed he says, "I don't want your God and I don't want your Consciousness. Tell me I must do this for social good. That I can accept." So that body-mind organism has been programmed for *karma yoga*. You see? So seeking is happening. There is no individual seeker. What kind of seeking happens, happens according to the way the body-mind organism has been programmed.

PHILIPPE *When you say that this process...*

RAMESH Yes...

PHILIPPE *...In* Duet of One *the process which begins in a body-mind organism can go on for several lifetimes?*

RAMESH Yes.

PHILIPPE *Whose lives?*

RAMESH That is the point! Several lives. Lives have been happening for thousands of years, Philippe. Whose lives? There have been lives happening for thousands of years. Body-mind organisms have been created and then they die. A body is created; a body dies. If you must ask whose lives, then in duality I can say God's lives. You see? Lives, yes, but not "whose" lives.

PHILIPPE *So there is no relationship?*

RAMESH No, there is no relationship from one life to another life. That is my concept. Why does this theory of rebirth come in?

PHILIPPE *Social control...*

RAMESH No. One basic reason! The ego says, "I cannot but accept. It's a fact of life that the body will die. But what is going to happen to 'me'?" That is why this rebirth, you see. So with this question the "me" is told by certain religions to do good so that in "your" next life you'll have a nice life.

PHILIPPE *Yeah. That's where the social control steps in.*

RAMESH That is the point. Therefore the basis of this rebirth instruction is socio-economic. It tells you to be a good boy so that in your next life you'll be a better boy! And it goes to such extent as to say that if you do bad things you'll be reborn a frog! You see it goes to any extent. Once you are a human being you cannot become a frog. Why not? *(both Ramesh and Philippe laughing)* You go into conceptualizing.

GABRIEL *Buddhists say that.*

RAMESH That's right. So it's all conceptual. My basic question is only one thing: if Philippe is supposed to do good deeds so that Philippe will have a good next life, then in the next life will there be a Philippe? *(everyone laughing)* Or will there be a "Robert"? And Robert wouldn't care a damn for Philippe just as Philippe now knows nothing about his previous life. So Philippe cannot have a new life. In a new life there will be a new ego.

PRAKASH *That is a concept.*

RAMESH   It is a concept. You must have heard me say it one hundred times: whatever I say is a concept. Whatever any sage has said at any time is a concept. Whatever any scripture of any religion has said is a concept. That God is a concept and that there is no God are concepts. The only thing which is not a concept is that which no one can deny—that he exists—I Am, I Exist. *Impersonally* there is existence. *Personally* there is no existence.

PHILIPPE   *Yeah. That's tricky because that sense of existence as soon as it is captured, is a "me" again.*

RAMESH   Sure. So you see, that I Am is always the Present Moment. The I Am *is* the Present Moment. In the I Am there is no need for any one to say "I Am"—because there is no one who says "I'm not." You see? That is why it is impersonal Awareness. It is impersonal Consciousness.

So when a body-mind organism wakes up in the morning, at that split-second of waking up there is this impersonal existence. Almost immediately Philippe comes on: "I'm Philippe!"—and the day begins, life begins, and the problems begin.

JAY   *There is a question about what Nisargadatta Maharaj meant when he was talking about beyond I Am That. I Am is just the arising of the thought I Am. That's correct?*

RAMESH   What is the source of I Am? I Am is Consciousness aware of Itself.

JAY   *But was he talking about something beyond Consciousness, or is it just a matter of using different words?*

RAMESH   Yes. Consciousness being aware of Itself is I Am. Then what is the Source of I Am? Consciousness *not* aware of Itself. So Consciousness not aware of Itself becomes aware of Itself as I Am.

JAY   *How could Nisargadatta be aware of himself in that state?*

RAMESH "He" can't be, that is correct. Did he say "he" was aware of that state?

JAY *I'm not sure how the book described it, but he was in that state...*

RAMESH Did Nisargadatta write that book?

JAY *No I don't think so.*

RAMESH He didn't know any English. He couldn't have written that book. The book was written by somebody based on translation done by somebody else or five or so others. So how can you say Nisargadatta says this? Therefore whatever you read is just a translation of what he said in his own language. In any case, having understood what Nisargadatta Maharaj says, how does it give or get you anything?

JAY *It gives me confusion if I think there's anything beyond the I Am.*

RAMESH The I Am is the impersonal sense of Presence which is Consciousness aware of Itself.

JAY *Is that before the thought arises of I or any recognition or cognition?*

RAMESH There is no thought in the I Am. "Whose" thought, Jay? When you say a thought, it is somebody's thought, isn't it? Somebody's thinking. So Consciousness not aware of Itself becomes suddenly aware of Itself. That is Its nature. Consciousness unaware of Itself is Potential Energy, and Potential Energy becomes aware of Itself by activizing.

JAY *So in our present functioning here we are aware of...*

RAMESH "Who" is aware of "what"? What are you talking about? You are interested in the Source of I Am. What I am telling you is that Potential Energy—which is Consciousness not aware of Itself—becomes suddenly aware of Itself because Potential Energy activizes Itself. Why does Potential Energy activize Itself into this manifestation? Because that is the nature of the Potential. If the Potential did not activize Itself sometime, Potential would not be Potential. It would be dead matter.

JAY *Would that be Noumenon?*

RAMESH   Potential Energy is the Noumenon—or Consciousness—not aware of Itself. Potential Energy activizes Itself into this manifestation. That is the nature of the Potential—to activize Itself. And when this activization takes its course it goes back into the Potential.

JAY *And that would be all in the field of perfection then, because it's all coming from the potential Perfection.*

RAMESH   Yes that's right. And so all this *knowledge*—how does it help Jay in any way? You understand that there is a Potential Energy which activizes Itself into this manifestation. And Jay—that is to say this body-mind organism—is part of the manifestation.

DANIELLA   *Why is God doing this? Just for fun?*

RAMESH   Yes! *Lila.* The word in the Hindu philosophy is *lila.* It is God's game. This is a sort of movie He has already made. The movie is there.

DANIELLA   *There's no purpose?*

RAMESH   There is no real purpose. It's entertainment. You see if a movie is made with all good characters, who is going to see it? You go and see a movie because it creates interest. There's a hero and there's a villain. So in his movie God has created heroes, and villains, and love stories, and tragedies, and comedies. God or Consciousness has written the script for the movie, produced the movie, has directed the movie, is playing all the characters in the movie—this is the important point—and is suffering and enjoying whatever is happening to each character. Consciousness has made the movie and Consciousness is witnessing the movie. And the characters in the movie are complaining!

ERIC *Hey, I want a better role!*

RAMESH Yes. I want to be a Mother Teresa, I don't want to be a psychopath! That is the whole problem.

HOPE *Shakespeare said all the world's a stage. The players have their entrances and they have their exits.*

RAMESH Yes that's right. That's all that is happening. You see if you really see that, that this is a movie which is already there, already finished...

DANIELLA *For all time?*

RAMESH For all time! There is no way to alter it. That is why I said, "'Who' is complaining?" The character is complaining, but the movie is already done. So my role is already finished.

LAUREL *It is the character's role to complain.*

RAMESH Quite right.

HOPE *Ramesh, don't you think God would let you change roles if you wanted to? I mean, if he wanted to let you change roles.*

RAMESH In this movie a good man can become a bad man; a bad man can become a good man; but it is part of the movie. The movie is already there. An enemy can become a friend; a friend can become an enemy—which is happening in life all the time.

HOPE *But the manifestation does not know.*

RAMESH The character does not know what is going to happen at the end of the movie.

JAY *This is for all characters.*

RAMESH   For all characters. And the only thing is: a character who has realized that he is only a character does not care anymore.

JAY   *And there is no cause and effect, there is no karmic situation which creates the movie for the future?*

RAMESH   Yes. But in the movie how does the plot develop, Jay? Because of causation something leads to something else that leads to something else—which is the whole plot; which is the design.

JAY   *Then there's nothing that can happen haphazardly. It's all cause and effect to keep the movie going on into infinity.*

RAMESH   Yes.

WOLFGANG   *Is there any overview of the objective or goal? The sages say that ultimately all sentient beings will be enlightened. Do you subscribe to that?*

RAMESH   No. It is a hopeful concept.

DANIELLA   *But isn't it boring for God if all is finished already?*

RAMESH   He will make a new movie. You see the Potential Energy has activized Itself, and when this activization comes to an end—with that burst of energy having exhausted itself—it goes back into the Potential. And then It again activizes Itself.

JAY   *A recreation.*

RAMESH   It is the nature of the Potential to activize Itself. So God will make a new movie when this movie is over.

DANIELLA   *What's the meaning of the concept of Ramana Maharshi's words, "from the knot of the Heart"?*

RAMESH   Again, "the Heart" is a concept because there is the concept of the mind. If there is no concept of the mind there is no need for the concept of a heart. Because you say "I understand intellectually," you have created a concept of intellect. Therefore, you create a concept of the heart. That means in the intellect there is a "me." In the heart there is no "me." That is the difference. So when the understanding goes from the intellect to the heart, what happens is in the intellect you say, "I understand," and in the heart there is only understand *ing*. When the "me" is not there, you're in the heart.

HOPE *It would seem to me that a model for how to deal with this phenomenon would be I Am as the ideal parent. This would mean a parent who accepts that the child is the way he or she is would be a good mother or father.*

RAMESH There is nothing to prevent a parent from trying to be a good parent. But he will not be a good parent if he or she does not bear in mind that the child has its own destiny and tries to force his or her own views on that child. "Good parent" means that the parent does his or her duty to tell the child what is accepted behavior in society. Having done that they have to remember that the child has its own destiny. And if the parent is a doctor, what happens if the parent wants the child to be a doctor? Whereas the child may be programmed and destined to be an accountant or a comedian. "My son a comedian?" You see? Being a comedian is not accepted.

HOPE *But can you alter that child's destiny? If a parent wanted him to become a doctor, so he becomes a doctor. That is his destiny.*

RAMESH It is. And then he'll be an unsatisfied doctor. But then that would be his destiny. In other words, it would be the destiny of that child to have an unwise parent.

WOLFGANG *Everything is programmed?*

RAMESH That is my basic point. That is the bottom line. Every human being is merely a programmed instrument or a uniquely programmed computer. There are no two humans alike. Each human being is a uniquely programmed computer through which God brings about an output exactly that he wants. There is only God and the body-mind organism. "You" just don't exist. The relationship as far as the functioning is concerned is merely between God and the body-mind organism. God by his hypnosis has created a "me" which says, "I am the doer." And because of that the movie goes on. Interhuman relationships—love, hate. All that is happening because without it the movie wouldn't have any interest.

LUCA *I see that God is a little bit cruel.*

RAMESH That's what I told you, a character is complaining that the producer has been unfair. He gave me a bad role. That is why when you *truly* understand, three lovely things happen—no guilt or frustration, no pride, no hate. Then you go with the flow and accept whatever happens.

BLAISE *It's tempting to argue with it, but that means I'm still holding on to some sense of doership that resists totally accepting the fact that I don't have it. So that is how it should be.*

RAMESH I wouldn't say "should" be; rather as it's "supposed" to be.

BLAISE *Subtle difference. What's the difference?*

RAMESH Somebody says, "This should be." I say, "Everything is as it is supposed to be."

BLAISE *More objective.*

HOPE *Is it better to say, "Everything is as it is."?*

RAMESH Quite right.

HOPE *And that's the way it is.*

LUCA *What about meditation? Can it be useful?*

RAMESH Oh yes. It can be useful, certainly. It is part of

effort, isn't it? Now supposing you say, "Meditation is a must, I *have* to meditate." Someone will say, "I just can't meditate." He's not programmed to be able to meditate. What does he do, Luca? Therefore my answer is: if you can meditate and you like to meditate—meditate. If you can't meditate, don't worry about it.

WOLFGANG *I was leading meditation for many years. It was also my observation that ninety-nine percent meditate with a sense of doership. And it's very rare that you come across someone who meditates with no purpose. Everyone wants something and is desperately trying to be successful.*

RAMESH You see what happens in meditation is you meditate for half an hour—good. So the "me" says, "I feel good if I meditate for half an hour, I will feel better if I meditate for two hours." So he tries to meditate for two hours. He can't do it. He's frustrated. Or he's able to meditate for two hours and then he says, "I am better than somebody who cannot meditate for two hours." You see?

LUCA *I am not able to meditate for two hours. I'm very lazy about it.*

RAMESH So take heart from the fact that it is not a must. But if it happens, it is good. That meditation is true meditation in which there is no individual meditator. That understanding is true *understanding* in which there is no "me" to say, "'I' understand." That acceptance is true acceptance in which there is no "me" to say, "'I' accept." And there is only true surrender where there is no "me" to say, "'I' surrender." You see—meditation happens, understanding happens, acceptance happens, surrender happens. And when that happens you know it—because there is a feeling of emptiness.

回 回 回

Maajhyaa manaa laago chhanda / nitya Govinda Govinda / /
Tene nirasela bandhana / mukhi vade Narayana / /
Bramharoopa hoee kaayaa / maayaa jaeela vilayaa / /
Hoya sarva sukhadhani / chuke janma marana khaani / /
Mhane Ekaa Janardan / sadaa samaadhana mana / /

May my mind passionately sing:
  "Govinda (Lord Krishna), Govinda" all the time.
Narayana (Lord Krishna), in accepting Your will
  there is freedom from the sense of doership,
  and involvement gets cut off by itself.
The body then has a sacred mission.
Your hypnosis is totally destroyed therein.
Your grace begins to operate
  through the body-mind organism.
Life becomes a festival,
  and there is no thinking mind
  to worry about birth and death.
Eka Janardan says:
  There is eternal peace.
  No more questions, no more doubts.

▣

Maajhaa bhaava tuze charani / tuze roopa maaze nayani / /
Saapadalo ekaamekaa / janmojanmi nohe sutakaa / /
Tvaa todili maazi maayaa / mee to jadalo tujhya paayaa / /
Tvaa maja mokalile videhi / myaa tuja dharile hridayi / /
Naamaa mhane gaa sujaanaa / saanga latike kone konaa / /

All my feelings are concentrated
  at Your feet, my Lord.
Your form is always in my eyes.
After meeting You, I cannot think of myself
  as separate from You.
You liberated me from Divine hypnosis.
I surrender at Your feet
  with deep gratitude.

209

You took me beyond the thinking mind.
I always keep You imprisoned in my heart.
Namadev says:
  Be careful friends.
  Without being authorized by the Master,
  we can only create confusion
  while talking to each other.

Scene 9

"Why" is most necessary in material life and scientific progress, but it is an impediment in the spiritual search.

What conceptualizing and vocalizing the thoughts do is to prevent us from direct, intuitive perception.

It would be more difficult for a human being, however intelligent, to understand the will of God or the Cosmic Law, than it would be for a child in the first grade in school to understand the theory of relativity.

🐢

ARNIE *Ramesh, I see a copy of Suzanne Segal's book on the table. Some others also may have read it, and I would be interested on hearing your view of her story.*

RAMESH Frankly, I read it very cursorily because she sent

me the manuscript and wanted a comment from me, which comment has appeared on the back of the book. The book merely describes the traumatic experience which she had. So what I have said in my comments is that enlightenment to me is the total annihilation of the sense of personal doership. Whether a traumatic experience is necessary for enlightenment to occur is a moot point. I mean it is debatable. I think it is not necessary. Enlightenment or understanding can happen in a perfectly smooth manner. Suzanne describes her traumatic experience in great detail and with great feeling which make it interesting.

BOB *Fourteen years.*

RAMESH Yes. And what is more, I understand that the fear was still there after the book was published. That's what I was told.

BOB *Was that not her mind trying to understand what had happened to her?*

RAMESH Yes it was, indeed. Therefore the mind was still there.

HOPE *The fear was that she'd lost her ego. We're scared to give it up, but she'd already lost it, and she was still scared.*

RAMESH Now wait a minute. "Who" had lost "what," Hope? Who had lost the ego? She *was* the ego.

HOPE *Thinking mind isn't therapy. She was enlightened. Isn't that right? She had had this enlightened experience.*

RAMESH No. She had an experience. Who is to say whether it was enlightenment? Therefore I explain what I mean by enlightenment. Enlightenment means the total annihilation of the sense of personal doership.

HOPE *That's what she describes in her book.*

ARNIE *That's what I thought too. There was no Suzanne anymore.*

RAMESH The therapists, I am told, have a word for it. They call it "dissociation" or something like that. I am not sure.

BOB *There really is a difference between psychological processes and spiritual processes.*

RAMESH Yes.

BOB *And I've felt hers was more psychological than spiritual.*

RAMESH That would seem so. And that psychological process has been identified with some people as spiritual. So what has been happening may not be spiritual at all. Because if the personal sense of doership is lost there is a tremendous sense of openness.

HOPE *In other words, she would not be fearful if she had really lost her sense of doership.*

RAMESH That's my point.

NAN *Maybe this would be a good time to tell my story and that I was not afraid after I lost myself. I was listening to music on the way home on the freeway. I exited the freeway and was sitting while waiting for the lights to change. The music was going, and I was feeling wonderful. All of a sudden I was out of where I was. I was not in the car anymore. It was great. I couldn't see down, but it was different. I felt that oneness. I didn't know where I'd stopped, and everything else was just all one. I felt an absolute peace, and I didn't need to struggle anymore. Everything was taken care of. It was the biggest relief. I just sighed this huge sigh of relief. The other thing I felt was I knew everything there was to know. Don't ask me because I don't feel it now, but I just knew.*

RAMESH What you are describing now, it lasted only for a little while. I mean by "little while" maybe even two years or two days, but it was temporary, was it not?

Nan *Right. And I recognized that it was an enlightenment experience, but I still didn't understand what I was experiencing. It has taken me a long time to get through and...but I do feel that now I am understanding better. I also think it's very important not to try and recreate that state.*

Ramesh Yes. That is the important point. You see, I keep repeating that when an experience happens of the I Am— the experience of just being—it means the absence of the "me." Maybe for a few minutes or a few moments, but those moments occur in the case of almost everybody even during a normally busy day. The feeling arises of oneness. There is no feeling of separation. It arises only for a few moments, but in those few moments one of two things happen if there is a certain amount of understanding. If the body-mind organism has been programmed to seek spirituality, and there is a certain amount of understanding, and because the experience is not total, then the thinking mind which is still there says, "I like that experience. I want more of that experience." Or if there is no understanding and there is no seeking for spirituality at all because the body-mind organism has not been programmed for spirituality, then the thinking mind says, "What are you doing wasting your time? Do something!" Either way the thinking mind comes in and disturbs that experience. So what is to be done when there is an experience like that? Leave the experience alone!

Nan *But I have no control over that.*

Ramesh You have no control over that. So what happened later, Nan?

Nan *For two months I was very euphoric. I still read spiritual things and understood them immediately, but the intensity was not there. Then I moved to a different state and I became depressed, and I still had the old trouble with my shoulder. I had to work through a lot of things, and then I started to get busy with architecture again. What I notice now is that I can easily feel love for people. That's just very easy.*

RAMESH You see, the result of the experience is that there are some after-effects—like you feel more love towards others.

NAN *I feel a oneness. I've been there and so I know it's there some place.*

RAMESH Yes. The feeling of oneness that you had—if you leave it alone—has its effects. As you say, you know that you've been there. In fact the only advantage of a drug is that it tells you that there is such a state. The disadvantage of a drug, of course, is that you may become a drug addict. Therefore if you can get that experience by meditation, it is a much safer way to do it.

NAN *My daughter had some experience with LSD. I really believe that the LSD helped her to enter that place and make her more at peace.*

RAMESH There are people who genuinely wanted to have that experience and took drugs—LSD or whatever. Once the experience happened, they were satisfied knowing that there is such a state which the mystics have been describing and that it is not an illusion. Then they have given it up. I think Aldous Huxley was one of those. He said that the drug has this advantage.

HENRY *I recently came across how Rimpoche wrote in his* Tibetan Book of Living and Dying: *"Do not mistake knowledge or understanding for realization, and do not mistake realization for liberation."*

RAMESH Yes. And do not mistake liberation for something else. *(laughs)* Anyway it's a play on words, you see.

HENRY *It seems to me like Nan's story. It has to do with this liberation business, if you know what I mean.*

215

RAMESH   Now "liberation" is a good word, Henry. Liberation from *what* ? Liberation from the sense of personal doership.

HENRY *Liberation from trying to understand what liberation is.*

RAMESH   Quite right. Because "who" wants to know what liberation is? The wanting to know is the individual sense of doership—"'I' want to know." Therefore Ramana Maharshi repeatedly said, "If the question arises, do not try to answer the question. Find out who wants to know." If you really go into "who wants to know," the "who" will disappear because there is truly no "who."

The arising of the question is not in your control, or whether you take delivery of that question and get yourself horizontally involved. The arising of the question is a vertical happening. Getting *involved* in that question is a horizontal involvement. So the horizontal involvement is avoided with this question: "'Who' wants to know?"

GAIL *So going into who you are, is that a horizontal activity?*

RAMESH   You see the asking the question "Who wants to know?" is the working mind. The arising of the question is vertical, the involvement of the *thinking mind is horizontal*. The working mind is *not* horizontal. The working mind is in the Present Moment. So in the Present Moment the working mind asks the question "Who wants to know?" and if the thinking mind doesn't come in and try to answer the question, then the "who" disappears. That is the theory of it. Ramana Maharshi didn't bring in this "thinking mind" and "working mind." These happen to be concepts which occurred to me, but that is what he meant.

GAIL *Ramesh, maybe I have misunderstood you but did you say that enlightenment can be sudden, or is sudden, but that liberation sometimes lasts longer?*

RAMESH   No. A Zen master said that awakening is always

sudden, deliverance may be gradual.

GAIL *Now what's "deliverance"? What's the difference between deliverance and...*

RAMESH He didn't explain. That is where the joke is. The joke is the thinking mind gets into what is deliverance. But my point is where enlightenment has happened— where the awakening has happened—there will be no one to wonder about deliverance or to care about deliverance.

GAIL *There might be other people around to wonder what it means.*

RAMESH When the sudden awakening is there, there will be no one left.

GAIL *That's wonderful.*

RAMESH I personally think this Zen master was being mischievous when he said that. He wanted the thinking mind to get involved.

MATTHEW *Ramesh, when we talk about awakening or having an awakening experience, whatever, it seems to me that even after that there has to be a kind of process in time for that kind of realization to become permanent.*

RAMESH Say that again and you will find the answer to your question.

MATTHEW *After waking up.*

RAMESH After waking up you are awake!

GAIL *But you can go back to sleep again.*

RAMESH Sure, but then that is not waking up.

MATTHEW *Right. So there does seem to be some kind of process that happens with people unless it is somebody like Ramana Maharshi.*

RAMESH   Now wait a minute. The process happens before the awakening is final. In fact the seeking is a process in phenomenality. Seeking is a process in time, and when the final awakening happens it is vertical and time is cut off.

MATTHEW   *So what you call the "final awakening" isn't a few seconds of having a realization.*

RAMESH   No. On the contrary. You see that is what I call a flip-flop—waking up and falling asleep again. That is "I understand, I don't understand." The understanding has come, then it's gone. That flip-flop is part of the process.

What happens is that the seeking, as a concept, is like a staircase. You don't know how many steps you have to climb. Someone may have three thousand, someone may have three hundred, someone may have only thirty steps. And how many steps there are to climb will depend upon the receptivity in that body-mind organism, which is part of the programming. In the case of Ramana Maharshi the receptivity was total. So when it happened, there was no question of earlier *sadhana*—no seeking even. Normally there is seeking.

Suppose there are a hundred steps to climb. When you are at eighty or eighty-five or ninety you begin to see the light. But the light is still farther away, and beginning to see that light can be a dangerous affair because someone says, "I am already enlightened." So only between the ninety-ninth and one-hundredth step is the awakening sudden. Between ninety and ninety-nine the flip-flops will keep happening. So there is no need to feel disappointed with these flip-flops. The understanding happens and then it leaves. Let it happen and leave. Let the flip-flops be there. Accepting the flip-flop itself is a big step.

LUCA   *When the last step happens, you never come back?*

RAMESH   Then you never come back. That is correct. Why do you not come back, Luca? Because there is *no one* anymore to go up or down! There is no more Luca to go up or down. That is what I mean by the sense of personal doership. It gets totally annihilated.

LUCA *And when this experience happens, is it shocking?*

RAMESH You see, what happens is it may be shocking or it may not be shocking. It depends on the destiny of that particular body-mind organism. When I say you have to climb one hundred steps, I'm not saying that the climbing will be step by step. It may *not* be step by step. If it is gradual it is the destiny of that body-mind organism. So step by step there will not be much of a shock.

GAIL *The second or third day I was here there was this understanding, "Who cares if I get enlightenment or not."*

RAMESH That's a very good feeling to have.

GAIL *But it only lasted for a few hours.*

RAMESH That is indeed the flip-flop I'm talking about.

GAIL *A strong feeling.*

RAMESH You had that feeling—"I really don't care"—then the caring happened again. So there is a flip-flop. Let the flip-flop happen. My point is worry happens because the worry is a vertical arising over which you have no control. Where does the horizontal involvement come in? If you worry about the worry and say, "I don't want to worry. I don't want worrying to happen" then there is horizontal involvement. The answer is don't worry about worry. If the worry happens—let it happen.

If you don't accept compassion as something which *comes*, then the ego gets fattened—the ego says, "I am a compassionate person"—which is the horizontal involvement. Fear arises, anger arises, so too compassion arises, and each may take its own course. Compassion arises and that compassion may turn into giving somebody

219

something which he needs. Or compassion may arise and just disappear. The arising of the fear, anger, or compassion is a vertical arising.

The anger arises. Anger may arise even in the case of a sage. If the anger arises and it takes its course, then where does the horizontal involvement happen? The horizontal involvement happens when there is the supposed individual—the sense of doership—and the thinking mind says, "I was angry. I shouldn't get angry. I must control my temper." All that is horizontal involvement. Andwhen enlightenment has not truly happened the *supposed* sage will get horizontally involved and say, "I must not get angry. If I get angry what will people think? People will think I am not a sage. People will think I am not enlightened." All that is horizontal involvement.

MATTHEW *So as long as the flip-flop does happen, it is okay?*

RAMESH Oh, indeed!

MATTHEW *What about if it is just the flop? I mean if you have one flip and then you flop. Does that happen? Can that happen also?*

RAMESH Anything can happen. I mean there is nothing which cannot happen. Again to use Ramana Maharshi: "Who" wants to pin it down?

MATTHEW *Well, I think just my mind.*

RAMESH It is the thinking mind which is the ego, which is the sense of personal doership that I am talking about.

MATTHEW *Something in me wants to keep the sense of doership: "I am doing this. I am getting enlightened."*

RAMESH Therefore, Matthew, the final stage when enlightenment or awakening is likely to happen is the genuine acceptance that enlightenment may not happen. The final stage is when you say: "I truly don't care whether I get enlightenment. It is not in my hands."

There is a story of Lao Tzu and a disciple of his. The disciple went to Lao Tzu, his face shining with achievement. He says, "Master, I've got it!" Lao Tzu put his hand on his shoulder compassionately and said, "Son, you haven't." So this disciple went away. He came back later. The mind says, "How much later: one weekend, one week, one year?" That is immaterial. *(laughs)* But he came back later and very humbly said to the master, "Master, it has happened." So Lao Tzu knew that this time it was there. Lao Tzu asked him, "What happened in the meantime?" The disciple's answer was, "You told me that enlightenment had not happened, and I accepted it as God's truth. I accepted your word. But I also had come to the final conclusion that I had done everything I could possibly have done. There was nothing more I could do. I was as sure as your word that enlightenment had not happened. So two things were accepted as God's truth. One, I had done everything I could. There was nothing more I could do. And two, it had not happened. Therefore I stopped trying for enlightenment and went about my duties. Then suddenly there was a realization: This is it! No one wanting anything. No one wanting enlightenment—no more questions. This is indeed enlightenment. There is no 'me' wanting even enlightenment. The disciple had ceased seeking enlightenment.

So the final stage when enlightenment is likely to happen is when the seeker no longer seeks enlightenment. When there is no longer a seeker seeking enlightenment— enlightenment is likely to happen.

MATTHEW *So do you find with people who come to see you that in some cases the flip-flop stops, or do you talk about the climbing of steps?*

RAMESH You mean have there been cases? That's what you are asking, isn't it?

MATTHEW *That's what I'm trying to say.*

221

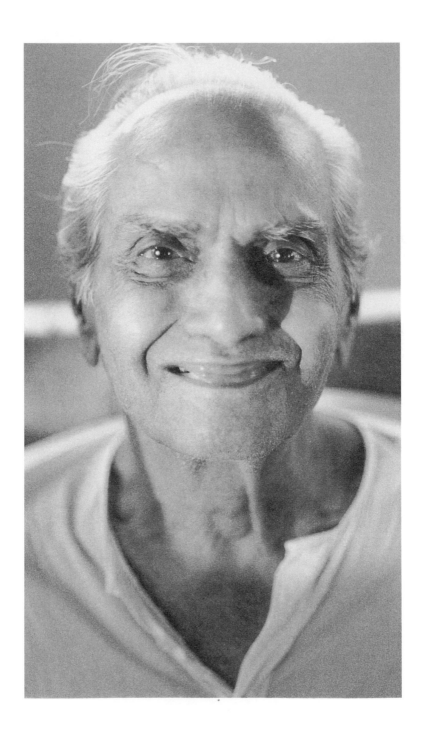

RAMESH   The answer is, "Yes!" There have been cases when this flip-flop has stopped and the awakening has happened. Yes there are cases. So there is no need for total disappointment. *(everyone bursts out laughing)*

Yes. So Mauna, shall we continue our yesterday's conversation?

MAUNA   *Just to start with: thinking mind and working mind— would you please explain?*

RAMESH   Have you read *Consciousness Speaks*?

MAUNA   *Yes.*

RAMESH   It's very simple, Mauna. The thinking mind is the ego, the working mind *is not* the ego. Now Ramana Maharshi says that understanding can only happen— enlightenment can only happen—when the ego is cut off at the root. By doing *sadhana*, by trying to purify your mind, what you are really doing is merely cutting off the branches which will grow back again. So he says that the ego must be cut off at the root. And yet he says, "Even in a sage the ego arises." Even in the sage, even in the wise man, the ego arises. You see? But he says that for the sage the ego is not dangerous; that the sage's ego is like the ash skeleton of a burned rope. The shape is there, but it is useless—you can't tie anybody with it.

So the question can arise: How can the ego arise in a sage when Ramana says that it has been cut off at the root? That question can be answered by the conceptual division of mind into thinking mind and working mind. As Ramana says, "Even in a sage the ego arises." The ego that he speaks of is merely the working mind which is necessary for the body-mind organism to function. You see?

Ramana didn't use the conceptual distinction between working mind and thinking mind. The question which the mind asks as a result of Ramana Maharshi's words is answered by this distinction. So that which is cut off at the root, as Ramana Maharshi would say, is the thinking mind. The working mind, which includes identification with name and form, continues and is the ash skeleton ego that Ramana Maharshi is talking about.

MAUNA *So from the book I understood that the thinking mind is that identification with name and form...*

RAMESH   *And* as a "me"—as the ego's personal identity. Therefore anything that happens the thinking mind says, "How is this going to affect 'me'?" The thinking mind being the ego-doer—"me" and "mine"—says: "Something is happening. 'I' am doing something. How is it going to affect 'me' in the future?" That is what the thinking mind does. You see? The thinking mind is concerned with the future. The working mind is not concerned with the future. The working mind is only concerned with the Present Moment—doing what it is supposed to do. The working mind *merely* does what it is supposed to be doing at that moment, whatever the work. Having done that, the working mind is *not* personally concerned with the future consequences. It is the thinking mind—the ego with the sense of doership and the "me"—which is personally concerned with future consequences. This is the basic difference. *(silence)*

GABRIEL   *Is the thinking mind* manas *and the working mind* buddhi *?*

RAMESH   Look, I'm not concerned with the synonyms! If you are using synonyms, "you" deal with them! *Manas,* good deeds...you are creating problems, Gabriel! You see *that* is the thinking mind! The working mind says, "Yes, I understand the distinction." Finished! The thinking mind says, "Can I call it this? Can I call it that? Can I compare it to this? Can I compare it to that?" What's the point? Any concept is merely used to point at the Truth. So once you have got the concept, once you have understood the purpose of the conceptual distinction between thinking

224

mind and working mind, let it finish. Let that concept go...*(silence)*

MAUNA *I asked this question about thinking mind and working mind because I also have to come back to Suzanne Segal. Can you put it like this: her working mind was functioning and in this she felt also that there was the feeling of fear and emotions?*

RAMESH Not that fear which arises as the spontaneous reaction of the brain, but the anxiety—horizontal anxiety extending in time which she felt—was the thinking mind. Therefore the thinking mind hadn't gone!

MAUNA *Do you mean that for an enlightened person there are no emotions coming up?*

RAMESH Sure the emotions come. But supposing an emotion came into this body-mind organism. What would I do? Merely notice it. Watch it arising. It is witnessed "as if" it is somebody else's, *not "mine"*! You see, the emotion which arises is the reaction of the brain to something which is seen, or smelled, or heard. So someone comes here and keeps asking questions, the brain reacts to that, and a feeling of great compassion arises. It arises, but it is also known that there is nothing I can do to help that person to get rid of those emotions which he is concerned with. The emotion of compassion arises because of the suffering of the other person who is not easily able to accept the teaching. So you see, compassion arises, but along with that compassion is also the understanding that what happens is the destiny of that body-mind organism.

The compassion which arises does not become a burden for me. The fear which arises does not become an anxiety for me because there is no thinking mind thinking it is my responsibility to make him understand. An ordinary teacher would be very much concerned that it is his or her responsibility to make students understand. So there is the thinking mind which is the involvement!

In this teaching there is no involvement because there

226

is no question of any responsibility to make someone understand. The understanding is that whether the understanding happens or not depends on his destiny! If there were a thinking mind in this body-mind organism, then that thinking mind would say, "It is his destiny, and it is my destiny too because if I don't make him understand, then he will go telling people, 'Don't go to Ramesh, it is useless!'" You see? But the thinking mind is not there! So if he goes and tells people not to go to Ramesh—good! Less people here! Then I don't have to go out into the big room. I can stick to this little room.

So Claudia, it makes you laugh? It is funny, isn't it?

CLAUDIA (laughing) *It is funny! It's very funny.*

RAMESH So, Anya, do you think this is funny?

ANYA *Yes. It is funny.*

RAMESH Yes, Mauna? So anything further?

MAUNA *First I have to digest that.*

RAMESH Yes, yes, yes. But is it clear?

MAUNA *The concept, yes.*

RAMESH Intellectually the concept is clear? That is all I'm concerned with, Mauna.

MAUNA *Now I will try to explain it to myself.*

RAMESH Yes! If you were to explain this concept to somebody, how would you do it? If somebody asked you, "What is the difference between the thinking mind and working mind?"

MAUNA *I would say that all actions we do belong to the working mind.*

RAMESH That's right.

MAUNA *And all that which is judgment about something...*

227

RAMESH   So when the thinking mind judges the effect of what the working mind is doing, it is thinking in terms of the consequences.

MAUNA   *I see... And that's when the suffering comes, the involvement comes!*

RAMESH   Yes! For example the working mind is working as an artist. The artist works at something and the working mind is happy with the result. The working mind says, "This is as good as I can do." The working mind does not say, "What will happen if it is not sold?"

MAUNA   *But the working mind might have values. This is also judgment when the working mind says, "This is good or not good."*

RAMESH   Sure, the working mind also dips into the past like the thinking mind. If you are working at something, whatever it is you are working at...what is your...

MAUNA   *I also paint.*

RAMESH   You paint. So suppose you are a mechanic or a surgeon. When you have to do something your working mind says, "Do I do this or do I do that?" Then the working mind remembers that in an earlier job it did this, which went wrong. Therefore the working mind says, "No, this time I'll do it another way which may be successful." The working mind chooses to do this or that— which is judgment!

MAUNA   *Which still belongs to the working mind?*

RAMESH   It still belongs to the working mind! Supposing you are in an executive position: you have two assistants, and you have to promote one. Will you not have to judge who is the better worker? That is the working mind. The working mind says, "Between A and B, A is a better worker." The thinking mind says, "But I like B better."

MAUNA *That's where the judgment comes.*

RAMESH I know. That is why the person becomes unhappy. So if the person's programming happens to have some character—sense of justice—then the working mind will say, "I like B better, I know, but I also know that A is a better worker. Therefore I should promote A." That is the working mind. If you promote B, that is the thinking mind.

So the working mind also makes judgments but in the Present Moment. *The working mind is always in the Present Moment.* What the thinking mind does is to work in the future. The thinking mind would say, "I should promote B. B is well-liked. My boss also likes B, so my boss would like me to promote B. And if I promote B the boss will be happy with me." That is what the thinking mind is involved with— *the personal future consequences* of the action. The working mind says, "A is better. I'll promote A." What happens later, the working mind is not concerned. The working mind also judges—make no mistake! But that judgment is *in the Present Moment* and not concerned with the personal consequences.

LANCE *Supposing in any case, when the working mind is busy with the job at hand, prior to that a mental planning process takes place. That is also the working mind?*

RAMESH *That* is *also* the working mind! I've told you: if a sage has to catch a plane at twelve midnight, the working mind has to plan. "The plane leaves at twelve o'clock. I have to be at the airport at ten o'clock. Therefore I must leave from here at nine o'clock. Thus I have to start packing my things by eight o'clock, and I must have my meal at half-past seven." All that is planning! Isn't it?

MAUNA *But he also considers the consequences.*

RAMESH He considers the consequences in making a judgment— *in making a plan*! The flight may be missed regardless of the working mind's planning. The sage is not concerned with the consequences of missing the flight. That is why the Sufi says, "Trust in God, but tie up your camel!" It is the working mind that ties up the camel and makes sure that the rope is properly tied. After that it is the thinking mind that is concerned with what happens if somebody steals the camel.

You see, during the very first seminar at Kovalam Beach in 1988, I did not have this concept of working mind and thinking mind. It came later. So at the seminar I remember saying that it is *the involvement* which is the problem. When I said this one lady promptly put up her hand and said, "But Ramesh, I'm a teacher and when I teach I'm totally involved! Is that bad?"

The moment I used the word involvement there were different implications. So now I can explain that involvement. The lady's involvement with her teaching is the working mind which is exactly as it should be. The more the involvement of the working mind, the better the job! It is the involvement of the thinking mind—or the ego—concerned with the future which causes misery.

MARKUS   *When enlightenment has happened there is no thinking mind, or are the thoughts that might come up only thoughts of the working mind?*

RAMESH   Any kind of thought may arise, but in the sage there is *only* the working mind. There is no thinking mind.

▣▣▣

Teertha Viththala kshetra Viththala /
  deva Viththala devapoojaa Viththala / /
Maataa Viththala pitaa Viththala /
  bandhu Viththala gotra Viththala / /
Guru Viththala gurudevataa Viththala /
  nidaana Viththala nirantara Viththala / /
Naamaa mhane maja Viththala saapadala /
  mhanoni kalikaalaa paad naahi / /

Reciting Vitthala's (Lord Krishna) name
  is my bath in the sacred rivers.
Remembering Vitthala is
  my pilgrimage to holy places.
Vitthala is God,
  and the worship of God is Vitthala.
Vitthala is my origin.
He is my father and mother.
All my relatives are Vitthala.
My Master is Vitthala,
  and my acceptance of the Master as God
  is itself Vitthala.
Vitthala is my treasure.
Vitthala is eternal.
Namadeva says:
  I have understood
  that Vitthala is all there is.
  Now there is no 'me' to get
  involved with manifestation.
  I merely witness it as a dream.

Scene 10

*When you are about to judge someone's
action, pause a moment and ask yourself:
Whom am I judging—man or God?*

*Meditation means BEING when there is no
meditator.*

*Not being able to understand the theory of
relativity does not make the seeker
miserable. Not being able to understand
God's will makes him miserable.*

*We are constantly being deceived by God —
through Divine hypnosis — so that life as we
know it may go on.*

RAMESH   What is the understanding that you think you
have now? Ramana Maharshi was your inspiration. Did

233

you go anywhere over the years? Did you do anything about it?

HANS *Maybe I can tell you that about twenty years ago, by chance I met Nisargadatta Maharaj.*

RAMESH Oh, did you. I see.

HANS *I had no understanding. I had no...*

RAMESH How did you happen to meet Nisargadatta?

HANS *I was staying somewhere near his house.*

RAMESH Oh, really.

HANS *Yes, and my host said, "There is a man you should see." I didn't know anything. I went and I was sitting in the upstairs.*

RAMESH That's right, in a small room not even the size of this room.

HANS *It was very low and very long, and I was sitting there and I didn't know what was going on. I did not understand anything.*

RAMESH No, but tell me: somebody said, "He's an interesting man." If he were a juggler would you have gone to see him? If somebody had said, "Here is an interesting man, a very good juggler." Would you have gone to see him?

HANS *I came to India in order to find men of truth. That was my main inspiration.*

RAMESH I see, yes. What was your first impression when you met Nisargadatta?

HANS *I can't tell. It was later when I read the book* I Am That *after being trained by a Guru for many years, suddenly it opened up...*

234

RAMESH   You were trained by a Guru for many years? Now, could you tell me about that training over many years? *(Hans laughs)* What was that training? What did you get out of that training, Hans? What did you understand?

HANS   *The training was again and again having the experience...*

RAMESH   Where was this?

HANS   *In winter time Tiruvannamalai, and during the summertime in Switzerland. The same man. He was a devotee of Ramana Maharshi.*

RAMESH   I see. Was he an Indian?

HANS   *A German. And he in the German way just went at it very hard. But he had the capability to transmit this state of no mind. Again and again we were put in this state.*

RAMESH   Now wait a minute, Ramana Maharshi didn't speak of any "no mind," did he?

HANS   *No, the terminology differed. We called it the experience of the "I." And when everything else dropped off it was just this beingness. Again and again this was shown more or less clearly, more or less deeply. Of course, it faded away and the old stuff came up stronger and stronger. The deeper the experience, the more rubbish came up. However, I feel that the experience of "I-ness" is what the central point is in life—to be able to stay more and more in this consciousness.*

RAMESH   I see. So "who" is to stay more and more in this consciousness?

HANS   (laughing) *Nobody.*

RAMESH   So you say this is what you understand: that the more someone does something the more and more someone is in deeper consciousness.

HANS *The more I let go of all ties, the more I give, no, the more this "I"—my ego—dissolves, the more this state is there.*

RAMESH Quite correct. The more the ego dissolves the more prominent is this I Am state. Correct. So how does the ego dissolve itself so that the I Am state will prevail? Have you been given the instructions for the "I"—the ego—to dissolve itself so the I Am state can prevail?

HANS *That's a great mystery.* (laughs)

RAMESH So how has the mystery been solved, Hans? After twenty years, how has the mystery been solved?

HANS *It just comes like a gift—just wells up. I don't know, I really don't know.*

RAMESH I mean, that really is the answer, isn't it? When you say "I" you mean Hans, don't you? When you say, "I don't know," what you mean is Hans does not know.

HANS *Exactly.*

RAMESH Does it not really mean Hans *cannot* know?

HANS *Yes, of course.*

RAMESH Hans cannot know.

HANS *He must disappear.*

RAMESH Then what is Hans looking for?

HANS *For his own disappearance!* (everyone laughing)

RAMESH So can Hans make himself disappear?

HANS *No.*

RAMESH You're quite right. As Hans disappears more and

more, the state I Am prevails more often—more deeply. That is the thesis. I Am is like the sun covered by clouds. As the clouds disappear, the sun—the I Am—shines more brightly. But the problem is that Hans has been trying to get rid of Hans.

HANS *Quite so.*

RAMESH   And has Hans been told how to do it? In these twenty years, has your Guru, who is Ramana Maharshi's devotee, told you how?

HANS *No. He was able to remove the clouds, and so the sun was shining. And when he was not present the clouds came back more or less quickly.*

RAMESH   What is the answer then?

HANS *His answer was...*

RAMESH   So you have to be with this man all the time?

HANS *That's why I'm here.* (laughter)

RAMESH   I mean if you depend on that man or this man to remove your...I mean—what's the point?

HANS *It's pure bondage.*

RAMESH   It's bondage if you depend on someone to remove the "me," Hans.

HANS *So after twenty years I decided, Hans decided, to get it from a different angle.*

RAMESH   So you're looking for that angle here?

HANS *I feel some connection. It is my experience again and again that it is this* darshan *—this direct transmission—which makes the sun appear very clearly. And so Hans can do nothing. All Hans can do is to seek this transmission—this* darshan *or* satsang.

RAMESH So what is your final understanding, Hans? Now Hans is still looking for something, is he not? Hans is still looking for something which will remove Hans. That is the position now, isn't it? So is Hans in a position to remove himself?

HANS *No.*

RAMESH So what is the answer? We have come to the point where Hans agrees that for the I Am state to prevail—Hans has to be removed. And Hans cannot remove himself. So what is the next step, Hans? In other words, we have agreed that there is nothing Hans can do. Therefore what Hans thinks is, "I can do nothing, but this Guru or that Guru may be able to do it."

HANS *My experience is that there is a power within my body-mind. It is a power rising up, coming up, and it seems the more Hans is aware of the occurrence of this, of this life rising up, the more this presence is there. Up to now I felt that the best plan would be to sit, to meditate, to let this happen and also carry on during daily duties, daily life. This step-by-step approach. I also have the experience that it just happens like this. It has happened like this, but every time it somehow faded away.*

RAMESH Yes. So what is Hans doing now? He's still doing something, is he not?

HANS *Listening.*

RAMESH I know, at this moment he's listening. But what I'm saying is before you came here, after these twenty years, what is the *understanding*, Hans? Would I be right in saying that the understanding is still that Hans is able to do something which will make Hans disappear and this state of I Am to prevail? And for that, Hans thinks he should go and be in the presence of so-and-so. In the presence of A, this experience happens and disappears; or perhaps in another presence—B—this will remain forever. Or if B is unsuccessful you'll go to C.

HANS *We call it shopping.*

RAMESH This is called Guru-hopping. *(general amusement)* This is what is happening, isn't it? So what is the basic thing to understand—for Hans to understand Hans?

HANS *The basic thing is that he can do nothing.*

RAMESH That is the point, Hans! There is nothing that Hans can do. And one additional thing—there is nothing anyone else can do for Hans either. You see? So Hans is searching for Truth. Twenty years ago how did that happen? Did you decide at any particular moment you will do the seeking from tomorrow—you will go to Tiruvannamalai?

HANS *It just happened.*

RAMESH It just happened! So this disappearance of Hans can *also* just happen! Just as the seeking happened, the process of the seeking has also been happening. The final end, if it is to happen, can only happen. And the more Hans tries to do something about it, the longer it will take. So what has Hans to understand?—That anything that he's looking for, "he" cannot achieve. It can only happen. Therefore with this understanding that there is nothing Hans can do to achieve anything, what does Hans do? How does Hans live his life? What do you do for a living, Hans?

HANS *Sculpture.*

RAMESH I mean, you can make a living out of sculpture?

HANS *Not anymore. Now it has turned more into a business of doing tombstones.*

RAMESH So that brings in sufficient money for you to live reasonably comfortably?

HANS *Right.*

RAMESH So Hans who creates tombstones now has to answer the question: "Nothing that I am seeking can I achieve. It can only *happen.*" And with this understanding what does Hans do? How does Hans live his life? That is the question really, isn't it?

HANS *Of course, of course.*

RAMESH You come to the *final understanding* that what Hans was seeking to achieve, Hans *cannot* achieve. It is out of Hans's control.

HANS *Exactly.*

RAMESH In whose control it is, is really irrelevant. The relevant point is that it isn't in Hans's control. If the mind still wants to know in whose control, you can say that it is God's will or the impersonal functioning of Consciousness. But it is not in Hans's hands. So if it is not in his hands, how does Hans live his life? With the understanding that Hans can do nothing about it, nor can anyone else do anything about this, what can Hans do? What is the answer, Hans?

HANS *Just accept the fact.*

RAMESH Yes, and having accepted this fact, how does Hans live his life? How does Hans live his life in the future?

HANS *Just in letting go of this wanting to grasp.*

RAMESH Can you let go of yourself? No you can't. That is what is understood. That is what has been accepted—you can't let go of yourself. It can only happen. Having understood this, even intellectually—having accepted the fact that nothing is in "my" control—then whatever is to happen can only happen if it is God's will or the impersonal functioning of Totality. "Letting go," or whatever you call it, is the final acceptance. With that final acceptance, Hans is still there. And Hans's question is: "Having understood this—having understood that nothing is in 'my' control—how do I live my life?" Difficult!

HANS *It's very clear, but it's almost not possible to answer. That's the riddle.*

RAMESH You're saying it is a riddle, and I'm saying it's extremely simple. Do you know why I'm saying it's extremely simple?

HANS *Because it cannot be* done.

RAMESH Oh, it *can* be done, all right. What does Hans do in the future with this understanding and acceptance? What does Hans do? Hans goes on doing tombstones. Hans goes on cutting stones into tombstones, selling them, making money, living his life as it *happens*. With this understanding Hans's life need not change at all! Hans continues to live exactly as before with the *deep understanding* that nothing that happens can ever be in Hans's control. With this understanding what does Hans do? Hans just lives his life. Hans just lives his life with the deepest possible understanding that Hans is not living his life. Life is *being lived* through Hans. So part of the acceptance extends to this understanding that Hans doesn't live his life. Hans is merely the name given to a body-mind organism. The body-mind organism is being lived. Lived by whom?—By Consciousness.

So the final understanding is that this body-mind organism does what it is born and trained to do. That is all the body-mind organism can do. Life lives through this body-mind organism, and this body-mind organism does whatever he has been doing so far with only one understanding—that "he" has not got control over "his" life. *This understanding makes no change at all in your life.* The body-mind organism continues according to the way it is programmed. It has no choice. This body-mind organism has been programmed.

By programming I mean certain natural characteristics which were stamped at the moment of conception: physical, mental, temperament. And this body-mind organism has been conditioned by the environment. You had no choice about your parents, you had no choice about the genes or DNA, you had no choice about the environment; therefore, you had no choice about the conditioning which this body received as a child. And by programming I mean genes plus conditioning.

So what happens to Hans? Hans merely watches the life being lived through this body-mind organism. Hans merely witnesses things as they happen, knowing that they are not Hans's actions. That is why it is not a riddle. The mind makes it a riddle. It is the mind which turns the simple fact of life into a riddle. So there's no problem.

HANS *In '76 or '77 when I met Nisargadatta...*

RAMESH Oh, that was much before my time. I started to go to him in 1978.

HANS *I remember somebody asking him, "How did you do it?" And his answer was, "I just believed my teacher." And that was for us, of course, no answer. But now I get a feeling for it.*

RAMESH What is the feeling, Hans?

HANS *It just happens.*

RAMESH It just happens! You see, *what* just happens, Hans? What did Nisargadatta used to say? What he used to say was, "I went to my Guru reluctantly. I did not want to go to my Guru." Because what he used to do before going to his Guru was to go to a temple and sing *bhajan*s along with several others who sang *bhajan*s. So that body-mind organism was quite happy after the day's work to go to the temple and sing *bhajan*s. In other words, truly there was no seeking. So a friend of his suggested that he should go along with him to his Guru. He wasn't interested. Then this friend forced him to go to the Guru, so he went. And the Guru told him: "You as such don't exist. All there is is a body-mind organism through which Consciousness functions. All there is is Consciousness. It is Consciousness functioning through every human being, but the acts which Consciousness produces through a body-mind organism the fictitious person 'me' thinks 'he' is doing.

"There is truly no 'me.' All there is is Consciousness and a body, Consciousness and a human being, Consciousness and an object. So all the functioning through that object is done by Consciousness. There is no 'me' doing anything. Therefore is it your life? You don't live your life. There is no 'you' to live 'your' life. All there is is a body-mind organism through which Consciousness lives the life—which is the destiny of that body-mind organism." So Maharaj said, "I heard him and I accepted it." The question is why was *he* able to accept it and not most others? It was the destiny of that body-mind organism with a simple mind to accept this. Again, it just happened. This is all I have to say, Hans.

HANS (laughing) *It's enough. It's enough. It's the same feeling. It's the same atmosphere.*

RAMESH Yes. But nobody brings it about. It happens. Repeatedly, repeatedly as the *understanding* goes down into the heart two things will happen again and again. Two thoughts will come up: one, *it happens—everything just happens—*and two, *whatever happens doesn't really matter. I can't control it anyway!*

HANS *All these pictures emerge: what I experienced with Nisargadatta at that time. Now when I look into your eyes, it's just like as if I looked into his eyes.*

RAMESH I see.

HANS *It's puzzling.* (softly laughs)

243

RAMESH But basically it's so simple, isn't it?

HANS *Yes, and we make such a big fuss about all this.*

RAMESH How does the fuss arise, Hans? What is the basic problem?

HANS *It's asserting the ego.*

RAMESH I know, but what is the problem about the ego? What is the problem about the ego?

HANS *Because it is nothing, it has no substance. It wants to be something, and to be something it makes all these big philosophies.*

RAMESH So how does the ego disappear?

HANS *When it realizes that it has no substance—that it is just happening.*

RAMESH The answer is, but the words are slightly different: Not when the ego realizes, but when the *realization happens* that the ego has no substance. And how does the realization happen that the ego has no substance?

HANS *When the time is ripe?*

RAMESH No, no. How? I mean what do you have to do, or what has to happen, or what has to be understood to know that the ego has no substance? The only thing to be understood is: *how does the ego arise?* The ego arises, Hans, *because Hans thinks "he" is the doer!*

HANS *Right.*

RAMESH If Hans didn't have the idea that he is doing things, Hans wouldn't be there. So the only way to understand that Hans doesn't exist is to understand that Hans does *nothing*. Any action that happens through this body-mind organism, Hans thinks it is "his" action, isn't it?

HANS *Yes.*

RAMESH Any action that happens through this body-mind organism, Hans thinks it is "his" action; therefore, Hans is. Why is there Hans's existence? Because Hans thinks he is doing things which happen through this body-mind organism. So Hans is really the identification with this body-mind organism. The only way Hans can disappear is for the understanding to happen that Hans is not the doer! And how can you understand that Hans is not the doer? Only by the understanding that some other power is bringing about actions which happen through the body-mind organism called Hans. Whatever Hans thinks is "his" action—what is it really, Hans? Do you know what it is? It is merely the reaction of the brain to an outside event. A thought comes, the brain reacts, and that reaction of the brain is what you call "your" action! There is only the reaction of the brain to an outside event over which "you" have *no* control: "you" have no control over what thought is going to come, "you" have no control over what "you" are going to see or hear. The brain reacts and that reaction is what "you" call "your" action.

JIM *And with the* jnani *it's the same?*

RAMESH Sorry, what?

JIM *With an enlightened being is it the same? He has no control over the thoughts that come?*

RAMESH Are you saying that even the enlightened being— the body-mind organism in which enlightenment has happened—has no control over what thought will come? You are right! That is precisely what I'm saying.

JIM *Is thought not ego?*

RAMESH *Thought* is not the ego! *Thinking* is the ego!

JIM (laughs to himself)

RAMESH Thought arises, the brain reacts to that thought and it leads to horizontal thinking. A thought arises vertically. Even a sage has no control over what thought will arise.

JIM *But thinking produces further thoughts?*

RAMESH I make a conceptual distinction between *a thought*—the original thought which is *independent* of the body-mind organism—and the *subsequent* horizontal *thinking*. A thought comes or you see something—anger arises. So the reaction of the brain to what is seen or heard is anger. Anger is a natural reaction of the brain. Anger may arise in any body-mind organism, whether a sage or an ordinary person. The sage does not say, "'I' am angry. 'I' should control my temper." There is no "me" there to get involved in thinking! So anger arises and takes its course. The sage merely witnesses the anger, and it takes its course. However, in the ordinary man the ego gets *involved* and it leads to *thinking*, horizontal thinking: "'I' am angry. 'I' shouldn't get angry. 'I' must try to control 'my' temper. How do 'I' control 'my' temper? This is what 'I' must do!"

JIM *Must there not be an "I" to feel anger?*

RAMESH No. Anger arises. And whether or not the person takes delivery of that anger and says, "'I' am angry" is the difference between a sage and an ordinary person. Anger arises and whether or not the delivery of that anger is taken by a "me"—the ego—is the difference between a sage and an ordinary person. The sage does not say, "'I' am angry." The sage *witnesses* the anger arising, taking its course, and then disappearing.

JIM *Arising in whom?*

RAMESH In the body-mind organism. The brain reacts and the reaction is anger. There is no "who." That is my whole point! The brain reacts to an outside event, which can be a thought or an input from the senses, and that reaction by the brain is not "someone's" reaction—not an ego reaction. Only when "someone" *reacts to that reaction of the brain* is there involvement. That is the "me" coming in with horizontal thinking. So in a sage, when the brain reacts to a thought and a feeling arises, there's no "to whom" the feeling or thought arises. The brain's reaction may be anger, it may be compassion, it may be fear...

JIM *But do not the feelings or thoughts change that arise to an enlightened being? They are different?*

RAMESH No. The thought is the same; the feeling is the same—the reaction is different. The *reaction* is different. I told you anger arises. The ordinary man says, "'I' am angry." The sage does not say, "'I' am angry." In the sage anger which arises is witnessed. There is no "me" to become involved.

JIM *So the identification creates more thoughts...*

RAMESH Yes! *Identification gives rise to thinking.*

ALLEN *It gives rise to an appearance that thoughts are other than Consciousness. When the thought arises it is nothing else but Consciousness.*

RAMESH Where does it come from? You can either say God sends the thought or it arises from Consciousness. The brain is inert matter. The brain cannot create a thought. It is only a reactive agent. The brain can only react to a thought which, as Allen says, comes from Consciousness, or God. Whether you say that God sends the thought or whether you say that it comes from Consciousness, to me it makes no difference. What happens subsequently is the difference between a sage and an ordinary person.

JOCK *So even during very strong anger the sage is still present witnessing?*

RAMESH Yes!

JOCK *The I Am is still...*

RAMESH Let me put it this way. Anger arises in another body-mind organism. The sage witnesses it. Anger arises in his own body-mind organism, and this is also witnessed exactly as if it had arisen in somebody else's. So to the sage, his body-mind organism is no different from any other body-mind organism. The brain in each body-mind organism reacts according to the way each is programmed.

JIM *If it is the truth that we cannot do anything, why do the sages say we have to do things?*

RAMESH The sages do not say you have to do anything. In fact, Ramana Maharshi says that effort is bondage. Ramana Maharshi says in as many words that effort is bondage. What does he mean when he says this?

JIM *It means the identification.*

RAMESH That is the point! Therefore if effort happens—it happens! For "whom" is it bondage? Only if you say, "'I' make the effort. 'I' must make the effort. Without effort, 'I' have been told, 'I' will get nothing. 'I' must make the effort." That "I" making the effort is the bondage. Effort is not the bondage! If effort is to happen, it will happen. The ego...

JIM *It's not better to make no effort?*

RAMESH The ego says, "'I' made the effort "

JOCK *...or "'I' didn't."*

RAMESH   ...or "'I' should have made the effort, 'I' didn't make the effort." I'm not saying that some Gurus do not give you a list of *do's* and a list of *don'ts* and an implied promise that if you do this you will become enlightened.

JIM   *What is with that promise? It's wrong?*

RAMESH   Yes, if the promise doesn't happen after thirty or forty years *(Hans laughs)* all that happens is a frustrated *sadhaka*.

JIM   *But out of this I understand that you don't have to make an effort.*

RAMESH   You don't have to make an effort! Effort, if it is a necessity, will happen. I'm not saying effort will not happen. On the other hand, if a body-mind organism has been programmed not to be able to make an effort—it will not happen! You are told to meditate. But some body-mind organisms are programmed to be so restless that they cannot meditate! So if that body-mind organism is not made to meditate what else can result except frustration? Now that restlessness...

JIM   *If you ask yourself "Should I meditate or not?" is this the wrong question?*

RAMESH   No, it is not! The answer can be very...

JIM   *But if you meditate, you will meditate. If you don't meditate, you won't?*

RAMESH   What is the answer? The answer is...

JIM   *You don't have to ask the question?*

RAMESH   No, you ask the question. What is the answer? If you like to meditate—meditate! If you don't like to meditate—don't! That is the answer! You see? If you like to meditate—meditate. So there is no question of right and wrong about meditation—or anything.

ALLEN *What is the ultimate goal? Is this some sort of pastime, this* lila *for God?*

RAMESH Yes. This is a *lila* for God.

ALLEN *And there's no ultimate goal?*

RAMESH There is no ultimate goal for "whom"? There is no "who," therefore there is no ultimate goal for a "who." You see, you take a child to the seashore, give him a bucket and a spade, and he spends a lot of time creating a sand castle. You tell the child it's time to go home, and he will kick it. He will demolish it and go. So if you ask the child, "Why did you create it with so much patience and trouble and then destroy it?" the child will not understand your question. But if you persist he will say, "I created it because I liked it. I destroyed it because I liked it." Where is the aim? Where is the goal? To create a sand castle, where is the goal?

JOCK *All goals are created by the ego.*

RAMESH All goals are created by the ego. And it is the ego which says, "Life must have a goal."

WENDELL *The thinking mind is still seeking something.*

RAMESH And why is it so?

WENDELL *Because it has to be.*

RAMESH But why does it have to be? Because it is its nature. Why is a monkey so restless? That is its nature. You know, there is a story of a sage who found a scorpion struggling to climb up a riverbank out of the water. So he picked it up. It stung him; it bit him. You see? So someone said, "What did you do? You picked him up, you saved his life, and he stung you." So the sage answered, "I acted according to my nature, and he did what was his nature." So every living being does what it is supposed to do. So what is functioning? Nature is functioning. And it was the destiny of that scorpion to be saved; therefore it was saved. If its destiny was not to be saved, someone else would have pushed it back down into the water.

ALLEN *Well, a sage does sometimes feel hate and anger in his body-mind organism?*

RAMESH "Hate" I wouldn't say. Revulsion or anger may arise. In his body-mind organism the brain may react with revulsion or anger, but he does not feel revulsion *towards* anybody.

ALLEN *In other words he doesn't blame people in quite the same way as somebody else might.*

RAMESH He doesn't blame. It is part of What Is. That doesn't prevent him from doing what he can to redress whatever is happening. It doesn't prevent him from helping people to the extent that he can.

ALLEN *And if he were a hangman it wouldn't prevent him from hanging them either!*

RAMESH Quite right. It wouldn't prevent a judge from sentencing a man to be hanged. And the hangman wouldn't feel guilty for hanging him.

JOCK *Would he kill mosquitoes?*

ALLEN *Ramakrishna did.*

RAMESH Yes, why?

JOCK *If he is programmed to kill mosquitoes.*

RAMESH No. The mosquitoes were destined to die by Ramakrishna's hand. The mosquitoes were destined to die by being hit by Ramakrishna. But Ramakrishna didn't think "he" was killing mosquitoes. Ramakrishna didn't think "he" was creating a sin. That is the difference.

CINDY *Ramesh, now there's all this pollution which happens, and the destruction of nature is like the child demolishing the sand castle, isn't it? I always had problems accepting how this could be God's will, but this way it's just God's "sand castle."*

RAMESH The child demolishes the sand castle which he has built with great trouble and patience over a long time.

TOM *What is karma?*

RAMESH Karma simply means action. The theory of karma means causation. In life certain actions happen. They will have their consequences. And those consequences may be long-term. So for long-term actions to happen, God creates new body-mind organisms through which those effects will happen. So it is causation, cause-effect, and the effect becomes a further cause. And that is the whole basis of life.

WENDELL *That's what you call horizontal.*

RAMESH Oh, indeed. Karma is causation in time. But what I'm saying is there is no individual to be connected with the happening of the karma, with the causation.

WENDELL *When you talk about a vertical arising, in what sense is that a causation? Is it a causation at all?*

RAMESH That vertical thought creates horizontal causation.

WENDELL *But there is an arising from Consciousness. Now what is that? The thought appears...*

RAMESH Yes.

WENDELL *...that's not a causation?*

RAMESH That is the cause of the causation. The thought arises...

WENDELL *which is beyond cause itself.*

RAMESH   Yes. That is beyond cause. Although that may be the reason causation is started.

WENDELL   *But we see it as a causation because we think of it in time.*

RAMESH   We see it as a causation, but it is an input which God puts into a body-mind organism, into a conditioned or programmed instrument so that a certain action will happen. So that is an input. A thought is an input which brings about an output which leads to causation.

WENDELL   *The thought itself isn't a cause, really?*

RAMESH   No. It's an input.

GERALD   *The thought happens in the moment and causation is in time?*

RAMESH   That's right.

WENDELL   *The moment is out of time.*

RAMESH   The Present Moment is out of time.

WENDELL   *The horizontal thought happens without any time?*

RAMESH   Horizontal means in time. Vertical means in the Present Moment—which is out of time.

WENDELL   *We look back at the moment as though it had a structure, as though it had a basis and went up. But there's nothing like that in fact in the moment.*

RAMESH   No. But make no mistake. I keep repeating it: All this is a concept. Make no mistake. It is a concept.

WENDELL   *But people seek the truth through that.*

RAMESH   Yes.

CINDY   *So it's not the truth that there is no free will?*

RAMESH   No. I told you: the only Truth is I Am—I Exist. That is the *only* Truth. Everything else is a concept. Rebirth is a concept. Your karma is a concept. "There is no karma which is yours, all that happens is God's will" is a concept. But the concept that only God's will prevails— *that* concept gives rise to a simple life: no guilt, no pride, no hate. The concept "I have free will" leads to frustration and pride and hate.

CRAIG   *Ramesh, though it is a concept, I find that mostly people who believe in free will have not really thought about the whole matter.*

RAMESH   That's correct. That is why I say if you believe that you have free will, find out from your own experience in the past six months or six years to what extent your free will has prevailed. From your own experience you'll find that really there's no free will.

WENDELL   *Ramesh, if we accept the concept that there's no individual entity, that solves a lot of problems, doesn't it?*

RAMESH   It makes life simple, Wendell. How does it make life simple? Because if I am not the *doer* then why should I feel guilty, why should I feel pride, and why should I hate people? So no guilt, no pride, no hate make life simple. I mean other than that, what does one really need in life? Forget about spirituality. Forget about seeking. Forget about enlightenment. What is it that one needs in life? No guilt, no pride, no hate make life simple. It means *peace*.
   You're quite right. If you seek peace in this life, then the only thing to understand is that you are not the doer, that you're truly not responsible for anything that you do. You are not responsible for anything that you do. But that doesn't mean that you have to be irresponsible. Because the answer ultimately is do whatever you like according to any standards of morality and responsibility you have. The standards of morality and responsibility are part of the *programming*, and you cannot act other than your

programming.

MARY *So it's "do what you like and take the consequences."*

RAMESH Indeed.

MARY *Which is what a lot of people would say is responsible, in that sense.*

RAMESH Yes.

MARY *That we accept the consequences of actions.*

RAMESH Therefore do whatever you like with whatever standards of morality and responsibility you have. I am not saying cut your responsibility. I'm not. On the contrary I say, "Do whatever you like by any standards of morality and responsibility you have, and the standards of morality and responsibility will be part of the programming."

MARY *We don't have to change them.*

RAMESH You *can't*! So somebody says, "You can do whatever you like." Can I go and take a machine gun and kill people? The answer is: if you are programmed not to do it, not to lift a hand against somebody, how can that programming allow you to do a kind of action like that? Not possible, you see?

WENDELL *But also some psychopaths will use teachings like this to justify themselves.*

RAMESH Yes.

WENDELL *You'll get people who will do the most horrible thing, and use spiritual reasons to justify it.*

RAMESH The spiritual fact says "you" don't do anything. An act happens through a body-mind organism as part of its destiny. What happens to that body-mind organism because of that act is also the destiny of that body-mind organism. Some act happens, good or bad, through a body-

255

mind organism. That is its destiny. Depending on whether it's good or bad, the consequences will happen, and the consequences will also be the destiny of the same body-mind organism. So who suffers the consequences, good or bad? It is the body-mind organism whose destiny it is. So there is truly no "you" to be concerned.

Yes, Hans. So, at the end of the talk, what is your reaction? What has happened to twenty years of searching?

HANS *When Hans tunes in to Ramesh, Ramesh's life shows it as it is. And everything seems clear, it's just so obvious. But when you turn away, suddenly the clouds come back.*

RAMESH Why, Hans? Why do they come back?

HANS *It's the old conditioning.*

RAMESH That's right. The old thoughts come back because that is God's will. And when will these outside thoughts stop coming, Hans? When will they stop coming? Only when God wills. So they keep coming now—the thoughts or clouds keep coming now because it is God's will. They will stop only when it is God's will.

HANS *You see, when the clouds are there, there is unhappiness.*

RAMESH Of course there is.

HANS *But when awareness is there, it's no problem.*

RAMESH I know. So why do the clouds happen?

HANS *According to this teaching, because it's God's will.*

RAMESH And why is it God's will that this should happen? It is also God's will that there should be suffering. It is God's will that these clouds happen and cause suffering. And when will they disappear? Only when it is God's will. So therefore my question is: in the meantime until God decides to remove those clouds—what does Hans do? He continues to build tombstones! You see?

HANS *You see, this spirituality is like heroin. Once you have had it, you just want it so badly.*

RAMESH Quite right.

HANS *So you can't forget it. There is this continuous drive to be in the light, to be in the sun. If you are not in the sun, it's cold, it's painful.*

RAMESH What does it all boil down to? It boils down to just one fact—the "me" keeps on coming. So the thinking mind keeps on happening to cloud the sun, and the thinking mind will continue until it is God's will for it to cease. In the meantime, what does Hans do?

HANS *Goes on.*

RAMESH Hans goes on with his life, knowing that he is not in control. What else can Hans do? Nothing, except go on with his life.

HANS *And this is grace acting?*

RAMESH Yes. For this misery to happen, by seeking as you say, is it not God's grace?

HANS *Yes, it's a gift.*

RAMESH It is. That you are a seeker is itself God's grace. You didn't choose to do it, Hans. That you are seeking what you are seeking is God's grace. Therefore the speed with which the process happens is God's grace. When it ends—if it ends—is also God's grace. But the important thing is that you are a seeker, which has happened because of God's grace. And for that Ramana Maharshi gave encouragement to the individual wanting enlightenment impatiently: Your head is already in the tiger's mouth.

HANS *I would have, in fact, drawn it back long ago if it would have been possible.*

RAMESH   Yes, quite right. You'd have pulled your head out, but you can't. Ramana adds one thing—There is no escape. Your head is already in the tiger's mouth. There is no escape.

◙ ◙ ◙

Pandharichaa vaasa Chandrabhaage snaana /
  aanik darshana Vithobaache / /
Hechi ghado maja janmajanmantari /
  maagane Shri Hari naahi duje / /
Mukhi naama sadaa santaanche darshana /
  jani Janardana aisaa bhaava / /
Naamaa mhane tuze nitya mahaadwaari /
  keertana gajaree sapremaache / /

Vitthala (Lord Krishna), all I ask of You
  is a residence in Pandharpur,
  a bath in the river Chandrabhaga,
  and a glimpse of Your image.
May I always have Your sweet name on my lips.
Keep me among those people
  who have surrendered at Your feet.
Bless me with the feeling
  that You have become the manifestation.
Namadeva says:
  I will stand outside Your temple
  and sing songs portraying
  the love between You and Your devotees.

SCENE 11

*The final truth: "I Am That I Am" or "The
tao that can be named is not the Tao."*

*The fact of the matter is that the human
being cannot ever know Reality, because we
are not apart from Reality—we are It.*

What can be more real than nothing?!

*Whatever you think you know is ignorance;
whatever you cannot know is knowledge.*

*The bottom line? We really and truly can
know nothing!*

[*Scene opens with no new visitors and the tiger hungry.*]

RAMESH   So Ananda, would you like to say something

today? There is no fresh meat. *(laughter)* For years you have studied, written about and lectured on the Upanishads. Everybody knows that. *(explaining to everyone)* Ananda Wood is an Indian physicist living and working in Pune who has written two beautiful books on the Upanishads. One is *From the Upanishads* and the other is *Interpreting the Upanishads*. Both are excellent books. And I don't know how he has managed to keep the price so low. He says because there is no publisher. He's published them himself. So the Upanishads and what I say here—is there, I mean there can't be a contradiction really?

ANANDA *No, there is not.*

RAMESH How do they blend?

ANANDA *How do they blend?*

RAMESH You see, the Upanishads have nothing to do with day-to-day life. Isn't it? They say the truth. They don't refer to life as we know it. Do they?

ANANDA *No, basically not.*

RAMESH Basically they say, "This is the truth. Take it or leave it!"

ANANDA *Yes.*

RAMESH Very concise.

ANANDA *Yes, that's right. Very, very condensed. No explanation.*

RAMESH So they're not really meant for the ordinary person, are they?

ANANDA *Um, no.*

RAMESH They're really meant for someone who has

reached a certain level of understanding. Would that be right?

ANANDA   *Yes, but I think particularly they're meant for a teacher to use.*

RAMESH   That's right.

ANANDA   *They need to be heard from a teacher. They're extremely simple. The language is very simple, and the content is very simple. There are no complicated arguments.*

RAMESH   Yes, but they are so compact that they need explanation. So they're really meant for the teacher, as you say.

ANANDA   *They were meant for a teacher to sort of..."use." He'd give a disciple a short statement from the Upanishads and get him to repeat it. So actually, they had two aspects. One is the "mantra" aspect which is the "yogic" aspect.*

RAMESH   Can you explain that?

ANANDA   *Yes. You see, the shape of the sound—for example take something like aham brahma. Now the shape of the sound, as such, is like music. If you keep on repeating it, the shape of the sound will eventually create a certain mood.*

RAMESH   Like Om?

ANANDA   *Like Om. Of course, Om is the classic.*

RAMESH   Om is the classic one, isn't it, where sound is concerned.

ANANDA   *Yes, where sound is concerned. And that leads to a kind of state, a detached state of experience...a mystical state that is supposed to help. This is a preparation only, a help to lead to the right kind of mood. Now unfortunately, this is what most people see about the Upanishads...the mystical aspect which can lead to special states of experience by chanting. But the heart of the Upanishads is not any mystical state at all. The essence is what the Upanishadic statement* says. *And that is something which only a Guru can tell you.*

RAMESH   Yes.

ANANDA   *The statement is meant to be repeated by a disciple, and it's meant to raise questions as one goes on repeating...as one goes on thinking more and more deeply about it...*

RAMESH   Yes.

ANANDA   *...so that one comes to an understanding aided by explanations from the teacher. That's why the Upanishads have these short statements—one of which is* Prajnana brahma, *Consciousness is all there is.*

RAMESH   Yes. Consciousness is all there is. I didn't know that when I first used this statement it was in the Upanishads, as I hadn't read them. So I didn't realize I was stealing it from the Upanishads. *(laughing)*

ANANDA   *But the thing is, at the beginning of the* Isha Upanishad, *there is something that is, in a way, a summary of your teaching—your approach.*

RAMESH   What, Consciousness is all there is?

ANANDA   *No, not that. A summary of the approach about there being no free will and about surrender.*

RAMESH   Oh, really? Can you tell us something...

ANANDA   *Yes. But I must admit that when I first studied it I didn't notice that aspect of it.*

RAMESH   I see.

ANANDA   *It was about "God" and so I didn't pay much attention to that. But after hearing you, a different meaning of it struck me. What it says is* Ishavasyam idam sarvam, yat kinchid jagatyam jagat. Ishavasyam *means "the place where God lives."*

RAMESH   Yes.

ANANDA   *So what it says is: "The universe is the dwelling place of God." Meaning it belongs to God.*

RAMESH   Yes. The universe is the abode—is God's abode.

ANANDA   *Is "God's place." It says that everything which moves and changes in this moving and changing world is God's place. That means everything in the universe.*

RAMESH   I see.

ANANDA   *Then it says: "With this renunciation."*

RAMESH   With this "renunciation"?

ANANDA   *Yes, it calls this* understanding *a "renunciation"— giving up. In effect it means giving up all things to God.*

RAMESH   Yes.

ANANDA   *With this "giving up" you can enjoy your life more fully than ever before. Completely...you can enjoy your life completely, with nothing held back. That's what the verse goes on to say next.*

RAMESH   Yes. In other words nothing belongs to anyone other than God.

ANANDA   *That's right.*

RAMESH   Isn't it? That's what it says. All there is—all that can be manifested and seen or heard—belongs to God.

ANANDA   Yat kinchid jagatyam jagat: *Everything that moves in this changing world, this moving world, belongs to God.*

RAMESH   I see.

ANANDA   *God is What Is or I Am—neither changing nor changeless. Anyway that's the point which for me represents your particular approach.*

RAMESH   Yes. That is why when I say "you" surrender to God, usually the surrender to God takes the form of: "I pray to you. Therefore you are obliged to give me what I want." *(laughing)* You see? So the only thing that any individual can give—and this is not in "his" control—is his fictitious belief that "he" has free will. *(laughing)* What have "you" got to surrender to God?

ANANDA   *I forgot to mention the end of the verse.*

RAMESH   Yes, please.

ANANDA   *The ending is a question: "Whatever property there may be, to whom does it belong?"*

RAMESH   *(laughs)* Yes. You see? So if I surrender something to God, then what can I surrender? I can only surrender what belongs to "me," but the *Isha Upanishad* says that *everything* in the universe is God's. It is God's place. So there's nothing that belongs to "me." Everything—including "me"—in the universe is God's. So *what* can I surrender and to *whom* do I surrender? There is no "me" to surrender "mine" to "whom." (laughing)

ANANDA   *That's basically what the Upanishads ask: To whom does anything belong? Where does it come from?*

RAMESH   Yes. I see.

ROSE   *But it also says* tera tujh ko arpan. *That is: "What is yours has now been given back to you."*

ANANDA   *I don't know...That is Hindi and there are no capital letters to distinguish the exact meaning:* tera *can mean either "Thine" or "thine,"* tujh ko *can mean either "to Thee" or "to thee"—just as in old-fashioned English. The Hindi word* arpan *means either surrendering or offering. So the possible meanings are: God surrendering to God; God surrendering to a person; a person surrendering to God; or a person surrendering to a person.*

264

ROSE   Tera tujh ko arpan.

RAMESH   I know. But in *tera tujh ko arpan*, "who" is the "one" surrendering, and to "whom"?

ROSE   *You are also* tera tujh ko arpan . *The whole concept is yours. It goes back to you.*

ANANDA   *In the particular verse I was quoting from the Upanishads, what's said is that it wasn't yours in the first place. It says that everything in the universe belongs to God and all you have to do is to realize it. It's not a question of giving...*

RAMESH   Understanding is everything.

ANANDA   *Understanding is everything. But what it calls a "renunciation," it means understanding.*

RAMESH   Understanding is all there is.

ANANDA   *And it says that once you have this renunciation, then you enjoy everything completely. In that sense, I suppose, it's "given back to you."*

RAMESH   Yes.

ANANDA   *The way to enjoy everything is to renounce it...to understand that it isn't yours in the first place. (To Rose) But the saying you quoted is in Hindi. Is there a Upanishad from which it comes?*

RAMESH   Do you know the original?

ANANDA   *It sounds like a* bhakti *saying. So if the original is from an Upanishad, it must be one of the later, devotional Upanishads—not one of the classical ones. Because the classical Upanishads don't normally talk about God or religious worship at all. You see at the time the classical Upanishads were composed, there were both the Vedas and the Upanishads. Today the Vedas are regarded by Hindus as the fountainhead*

265

of all knowledge. But from the standpoint of the Upanishads, the Vedas are worldly.

RAMESH   Yes.

ANANDA   *Worldly documents. They are about getting ahead in the world.*

RAMESH   Yes.

ANANDA   *They're about making various assumptions concerning the gods and so on, and using these gods to achieve various objectives that you want. Whereas the Upanishads are not about getting along at all, but about getting to the bottom of things.*

RAMESH   What Is.

ANANDA   *Yes, getting to What Is. So they're basically questioning what God is.*

RAMESH   Yes, and thinking of that, didn't the Vedas ultimately come to the conclusion: "Not this, not that"— *"Neti, neti"*?

ANANDA   *I don't think* Neti, neti *is in the Vedas.*

RAMESH   The Vedas say *shruti.*

ANANDA   *Yes, it is in the Vedas in a more general sense as denoted by the word "shruti," when it is considered that the Upanishads are the culminating part of the Vedas.*

RAMESH   Oh, I see. So my interpretation of it is the Vedas trying to understand.

ANANDA   *Ahhhh!*

RAMESH   The Vedas tried to understand the original Source and then came to the conclusion, or the basis, that *knowing* something means there's a subject-object relationship. And if *all there is is That*, then "who" is to say "this" is That?

Therefore the two-part question is: "Is *this* God?" and the answer is—"No." "Is *that* God?" "No." So the ancient answer is *neti, neti*—not this, not that. That means, in other words: What is being said is the *tao* that can be described is *not* the *Tao*.

ANANDA *Of course.*

RAMESH You see? It cannot be described. You can't. "Who" is to describe "what"? That is all. And the same thing is— I think Moses is supposed to have asked God what he should say when asked what God's name is. And God said, "I Am That I Am." And what is I Am? I Am That I Am. Beyond I Am there is nothing you can say. I read that Ramana Maharshi said this, and also that the name Jehovah means I Am.

ANANDA *Doesn't that have something to do with the burning bush?*

RAMESH Moses asked God, "What are you?" And God said, "I Am That I Am." And God further said that the answer to I Am That I Am is *I Am*. That's all. I Am—the *impersonal* awareness of existence—is all there is.

ANANDA *Even in the Vedas proper—I mean the original four Vedas which do not include the Upanishads and other "Vedic" texts—there are hymns which suddenly change the whole tone and start enquiring. The* Nasadiya *is the famous one.*

RAMESH Which one?

ANANDA *The* Nasadiya— *"In the beginning there was neither being nor non-being."*

RAMESH I see. Do you know that?

ANANDA *I've forgotten most of it, but the end is the relevant part. It says the gods were born* after *this world's creation.*

RAMESH Yes!

ANANDA *They themselves belong to the world. They belong to creation.*

RAMESH Meaning they are concepts.

ANANDA *Yes.*

RAMESH Isn't it? *(laughing)* If they were born after the creation...they are merely concepts.

ANANDA *And then it finally ends by saying: "He who sees this, who witnesses this..."*

RAMESH Yes?

ANANDA *"from the highest heaven, perhaps he knows and perhaps he does not."* (Ramesh laughs) *It asks: "Who knows this?"*

RAMESH Yes. Again to the same thing. Knowing is relative knowledge. Knowing is subject knowing an object.

ANANDA *I mean, that's what is asked in the end. What sort of knowledge is it that...*

RAMESH You see, that can only be relative knowledge. Relative knowledge meaning a subject knowing an object. And that is the reason I say, "How can the human mind-intellect know its own Source? It can't." So that is why in Tukaram's beautiful *abhanga* he says: *Dev pahaayas gelo, Dev houniya aalo*—"I went to see and know God, and returned being God." So all your efforts to see God and know God—that intensity of longing turns into being God. And this is exactly what Lord Krishna says in the *Bhagavad Gita*: *Tesham satatayuktanam, bhajatam pritipurvakam / dadami buddhiyogam tam, yena mam upayanti te* —"When the intensity of a devotee reaches a certain degree, I give him the lamp of knowledge, the receptivity to understand." So the *bhakti* must ultimately end in knowledge.

ANANDA *In the non-dual.*

RAMESH That's right. Non-dual. So Tukaram started as a *bhakta* saying to God, "For those who want to see you as formless, for them you'll be formless; but for me always, please, be in your form which I can worship and adore." And this same Tukaram, you see, when he gets this knowledge, when the *bhakta* becomes a *jnani...*

ANANDA *But did he return to* bhakti *later on?*

RAMESH Yes. But you see, his verses have not come down to us in chronological order.

ANANDA *So we don't really know.*

RAMESH So we don't know. But at some stage Tukaram says, "You fools! Why do you go to the temples? Why don't you worship the God within?" *(laughs)* Same Tukaram!

ANANDA *Probably after that he still went back to devotional worship. The same thing happened to Ramakrishna. When he was doing Advaita sadhana his Guru, Totapuri, pressed a sharp piece of glass against his forehead. Then he had a vision of Kali in which he used his discrimination as a sword and "cut her into two." This resulted in a nirvikalpa samadhi which lasted for three days, and he came to an understanding of Advaita. But afterwards he went back to worshipping Kali.*

RAMESH Yes! Because once you know that both are the same, you see, you'll go back to what...So Totapuri, on the other hand, had no inkling of *bhakti*. He was an *Advaita jnani* pure and simple—knowledge only. No *bhakti*. So they say Totapuri was Ramakrishna's Guru, but it was destiny that Ramakrishna also became Totapuri's Guru. As the story goes, one night Totapuri flew into a rage and was about to beat a man for something. Ramakrishna laughed because Totapuri had been explaining Brahman and the illusoriness of the world when suddenly Totapuri was involved in a fit of passion. Supposedly Totapuri

269

became embarrassed. Shortly after this, Totapuri developed a severe attack of colic pain. It kept him from being able to concentrate on Brahman. He was a yogi, but with all of his yogic powers he couldn't bear the pain. He didn't care about the body so he tried to commit suicide. He walked into the Ganga all the way over to the other side, and the river is deep. He was stunned as he looked back across the water. Suddenly he saw the presence of the Divine Mother everywhere in everything. Consciousness-in-action is the Mother. Consciousness is all there is. There is no free will. Totapuri couldn't end his life because it was not his destiny. It dawned on him—the grace of God's grace. The happening of that Knowledge is itself God's grace. *(laughing)*

◻ ◻ ◻

Aataa kothe dhaave mana / tuze charana dekhiliyaa / /
Bhaaga gelaa sheena gelaa / avaghaa zaalaa aananda / /
Premarase baisali mithi / aavadi laathi mukhaasi / /
Tukaa mhane aamhaa joge / Viththala ghoge khare maapa / /

I have been blessed with a vision
  of Your holy feet, my Lord.
Where can my thinking mind run now?
The feeling of being separate from You
  has totally disappeared, and so has the idea
  that I have free will.
There is peace.
A great joy is felt in embracing Your feet.
The tongue enjoys the continuous reciting
  of Your name.
Tukaram says:
  We who have found peace
  at the feet of the Lord
  are not infatuated by earthly pleasures.

270

SCENE 12

If we accept what the physicist says—that there is really no such thing as past, present, and future—can there really be any such thing as birth or death?

□

At one time, a physicist declared that "no man can split the atom"; at another time another physicist declared that "heavier-than-air flying machines are impossible." So is there really any difference between knowledge and ignorance?

□

The only constant thing in phenomenality is change.

□

In spite of all the theories, equations, and symbols of the scientist, the unknowable remains unknown.

RAMESH   So what do we talk about? You know, when I went to Maharaj I was the new one, I was the new man. There were many who had come earlier. I used to be of help to Maharaj: giving him generous donations, finding out what he needed in the house, providing for him, taking him for a car ride in the cool of the noon *(laughter)* after the talk was over. Maharaj liked me for one reason alone—not because of these things, but because the first thing he said to me was, "You've come at last, have you? Come and sit down."

There was a certain amount of heart-burning among the others. Maharaj said, "You have been coming here for twenty years. Here is this man just come, and he takes over as if Maharaj belongs to him." That was the sort of feeling. At that moment a thought flashed to my mind that the only way to look at what Maharaj does is not to think in terms of Maharaj doing anything, but something happening.

You see, there is a story about Buddha. He had a favorite disciple called Ananda, and the others didn't like it because they thought it was favoritism. But they didn't talk about it didn't dare talk about it when Ananda was present. So once what happened—they were all about to cross a stream when Buddha told Ananda to fetch something. Buddha and the other disciples crossed over and Ananda remained to do what he had been asked. Upon reaching the other side the other disciples thought it was a good opportunity to complain to Buddha about his discrimination of favoring Ananda. So what Buddha did was to shout in extreme urgency, "Ananda!" Ananda heard it and came with such earnestness that he walked over the water. You see? *(laughter)* The master wanted something urgently, so Ananda just walked across the water. There were no more complaints. *(laughter)*

And this happens all the time. For Ramakrishna, Vivekananda was a great favorite. In fact he used to be quite upset if Vivekananda was not in the vicinity. And there was quite some talk about it including bad thoughts:

"Why did he need Vivekananda? What kind of relationship was there between Vivekananda and him?" That kind of thing.

So I would say that the easiest way of living in peace is very simple—not to think, "Why is she doing that to me? Why is he doing this to me?" I mean, it is bound to come up in life. And every time it comes up, if there is some understanding, then that understanding will automatically bring about the sudden thought, "He is not doing anything; it is just happening through him. No one can do anything. Everything just happens." So if that is understood, life can become simple.

(To a visitor) So you have come after some time? How has the teaching been treating you, Brigitta?

BRIGITTA   *Very deep. Very good.*

RAMESH   Good. Would you like to say something about it?

BRIGITTA   *Yes. It's always in my mind. It is always in my life. It is very sweet.*

RAMESH   I see. How does it work in life? That's what I'm always interested in. How does the teaching function in life?

BRIGITTA   *It's a deep need in me always to think about it, and always to...*

RAMESH   Yes, but now, thinking about this teaching, doesn't it interrupt what you are doing?

BRIGITTA   *I have had many fears, and I think the deepest part is that I've lost some fears. When there is a fear—like I'm very afraid of flying—it helps very much, this teaching in this situation.*

RAMESH   Can you tell me how it helps, Brigitta?

BRIGITTA   *It's a feeling that I don't carry anymore all these things. They're not on my shoulders. All that happens—the*

273

fear also—is God. And that is very helpful for me.

RAMESH I see. Even this arising of fear is not in your hands? You can't control it? Is the fear only of flying?

BRIGITTA *Oh no, I have many fears. They are there but they are not so big, not so prominent.*

RAMESH I see. I understand. They arise, but they don't bother you so much?

BRIGITTA *Not so much.*

RAMESH What have you done earlier?

BRIGITTA *Astrology.*

RAMESH So you were an astrologer?

BRIGITTA *Yes. Was. Now it has changed.*

RAMESH Yes, I understand, but you were an astrologer? Astrologer doing what? Merely analyzing the character of the person, or predicting the future, or both?

BRIGITTA *No. Through astrology I was able to realize that the pattern of life was already there, and there was no need in judging it or valuing it.*

RAMESH I see. What you are saying is astrology says that if you can predict something, then that something in time, in the future, is already there. Isn't it? And the whole basis of astrology is to what extent you can see the future, depending on the gift you have.

I had a very good friend who was an astrologer. So I asked him, "How many of your predictions are right? What percentage of your predictions turn out to be correct?" I thought he would say seventy-five, eighty, or something. Do you know what he said? "Fifty percent." He said fifty percent. When he saw I was surprised, his reaction was, "You ask an honest doctor how many of his diagnoses are correct, and an honest doctor will have to say fifty percent." *(laughter)*

And yet there are predictions. Have you heard of the nadi, the predictions written on dried palm leaves? I had an experience with this, long ago in 1950. Somebody told me that there was a reader of these things in the area. I'd heard of them, so when I was told, I went. There was no privacy—I mean everybody sat there and took turns. In some cases he would say, "I don't have your leaf." The person would be disappointed and would go. In one case I remember there was a Jewish man in poor health who asked for a reading about his condition. The nadi reader had a leaf for each section of one's life: money, marriage, love-life, profession, spirituality, health, like that. So the reader got the leaf pertaining to this man's health, and reading in the Tamil language in which the leaves are written, told him about a specific diet and a special prayer. I remember the precise instructions on the palm leaf: "You should use this prayer morning and evening"—and the reader repeated the prayer. The Jewish man became absolutely angry and puzzled at the same time. He said, "No one but a rabbi is supposed to know that prayer." On that ancient leaf was reproduced a prayer which only a rabbi was supposed to know. *(laughter)*

The remarkable thing, Brigitta, is that in a *nadi* reading there is no interpreting; it is just read as written long ago. Before this *nadi* reading experience happened, some people had asked me if I believed in astrology. I replied, "I believe in astrology, but I do not believe in astrologers." *(laughter)* You see? Because often the Indian astrologer, wanting to make more money, will read or predict while watching your face to make sure you are pleased. He'll change his prediction to what the customer wants to hear. But with *nadi* readings there is no interpreting; the leaf is read exactly as it was written down long before. The man who read my leaf told me that he knew very little about astrology.

At the beginning of the reading which I had, he gave me at least fifteen family names to verify that he was reading the correct leaves. He mentioned my name, my wife's name, my father's and mother's names, my brothers' names, and so on. The actual names were mentioned. You see, when I mention this to people, they are usually interested in having a reading, and readings are still available in the south: Bangalore, Madras, Chidambaram, various places. But I caution them, "You will be cheated if you are not careful, and the only way to be certain is to make the *nadi* reader give you the names of your family members. The names have to be there. Then whether the prediction turns out to be right or wrong is another matter, but at least you know it was your reading."

So in the reading I asked for my spiritual chart. He brought it out and read, "This subject is born a Hindu brahmin, but he is not interested in Hinduism, he is interested..." He went on to generally describe *Advaita*, you see. And he continued, "He has been quietly seeking for a Guru all his life. He'll meet one five or six years from now, and that association will last about twenty years. However, nothing much will come of it. He'll meet his real Guru one year after retirement, and then the result will be quick." As I told you, this was in 1950. After the reading I just put it aside. Looking back, these events happened when and as foretold.

But what I'm getting at is people persist in saying, "No, no, I am the master of my destiny. I can do what I like. I have free will." And yet, if somebody says to them, "You see that man over there? He is a very good palmist," they promptly jump up and show him their hands. Now, if they are masters of their destinies, then why are they interested in their futures? Why? Because deep down they know that what is going to happen to them is already there. Deep down they know it. And why do they know deep within? Because of their past experiences. From these experiences they know that whatever things have happened to them, they themselves had very little to do with it. Every person must know that things have been happening over which he or she has had very little control.

So, Brigitta, you were here last year. Can you repeat what you think is the basis of the teaching? Do you remember what the basis of the teaching is?

BRIGITTA *That there is no doer—life happens, feelings happen. Sometimes there is a feeling of doership, but deeply I am feeling that...*

RAMESH Yes, I understand. Deep down you know, but the feeling of doership arises every now and then. So why does the feeling of doership exist in everybody, Brigitta? Why does this feeling of personal doership exist? Has everybody created that feeling of personal doership?

BRIGITTA *Nobody has created it.*

RAMESH Nobody has created this sense of doership, and everybody knows it because this sense of doership is unhappiness. The spiritual seeking is really everybody trying to get rid of this feeling of personal doership, isn't it? So has it not struck you to wonder: "Why has this feeling of doership arisen?"

BRIGITTA *Sometimes I wonder, but...*

RAMESH There is no answer?

BRIGITTA *I think my mind could never get an answer to it. My mind is always churning, but I never get an answer...*

RAMESH But you see, if you stick to the basics you will get the answer. And what is the basic point? Everything just happens; "you" don't do it. What do I mean everything happens? What I mean is that everything happens according to God's will, or Consciousness. What Consciousness wills, happens. So whatever happens, happens because it is the will of God. God or Consciousness is the Source of everything. So the question is: "Who created this sense of personal doership?" Isn't it? I mean if you accept that the Source of everything is God, then the Source of this sense of personal doership must also be God's work. You can say God has been very mischievous in creating this sense of personal doership which causes so much unhappiness. Can't you? So why has God created this sense of personal doership in everybody?

BRIGITTA *So life can go on.*

RAMESH That is the point. Because without this sense of personal doership which everybody has, this sense of love and hate wouldn't arise. Human relationships wouldn't be there. Happiness and unhappiness wouldn't be there. Life as we know it cannot happen without this sense of personal doership. You see? So for this impersonal functioning of Consciousness, or God, through manifestation or life as we know it to happen, then the basis of life is the sense of personal doership.

BRIGITTA *And to fight against it is like fighting against the air or...*

RAMESH Yes, quite right. How did this sense of personal doership arise? What I say is God has hypnotized everybody into feeling that he or she is a personal doer. It's Divine hypnosis. You see, if a reasonably good human hypnotist comes and makes 2,000 people believe something is there when it isn't, or believe that something is not there when it is, then why is it so difficult for God to hypnotize every being into thinking that he is the doer? What the human being is trying to do is get rid of this hypnosis. You see? You can't get rid of something which God has done. So who can get rid of something which God has done? Only God can do it. And that is why the seeking began when you were fourteen years old. You read something, it stuck in the mind, and your mind began thinking about it. So the seeking began at that time. But later on, Brigitta, the seeker comes into the picture and says, "I am seeking this, and I want this." That's when the trouble begins. You see?

One of the basic things I mention is that there is never really any seeker. There is never any doer. But even intellectually how do you come to the conclusion that there is no doer? You come to the conclusion intellectually that there is no doer when you truly understand that it is all God's will. You didn't decide, "From tomorrow I shall seek." You didn't decide. Seeking happened.

My point, Brigitta, is that ever since a baby is born and seeks its mother's breast intuitively, life is nothing but seeking. *Life is* nothing but *seeking*. And the seeking is strictly according to the natural characteristics, the destiny and programming, of the body-mind organism through which the seeking is happening.

SALILA *But you always have a choice.*

RAMESH No! *You don't have a choice!* You *think* you have a choice. And why do you think you have a choice?

SALILA *Maybe that's what rises in this program, that I am continually aware that I have a choice.*

RAMESH That is correct.

SALILA *So for this program, that is my destiny.*

RAMESH That is correct.

SALILA *And if I don't have a choice, then that won't be my destiny. But what you give us is concepts.*

RAMESH Yes. But what I'm saying is that if you think you are able to make your choice, then do what you like.

SALILA *Right, if it's coming from the doership...*

RAMESH That is exactly what God wants you to think. And that is why he has programmed you to think so. So if you think you can decide, that is what God wants you to think. So decide. You see?

SALILA *Yes.*

XAVIER *I read last year, since there is no choice, the only choice you have is to identify with the Self. It is this being the witness.*

RAMESH   Say that again, Xavier.

XAVIER *You don't have any choice, everything is predestined. The only choice you have is to not identify with all this and identify with the Self. You try to be the witness...*

RAMESH   Do you *have* that choice, Xavier? Do you have that choice? You see, what you are saying is, "I have the choice to seek my True Nature or God or whatever." That's what you are saying, isn't it? What are you saying?

XAVIER *To step out of the way.*

RAMESH   So the only choice is to step out of the way and become a spectator of what is happening.

XAVIER *Do I have that choice?*

RAMESH   I don't think so. If you had, Xavier, why didn't you do that years ago? *(everyone laughing)* Why didn't you do that years ago—be a spectator, and not be concerned with the suffering of the world?

XAVIER *It seems that you say that it is also predestined if you can be a witness. It's also a destiny.*

RAMESH   No. What I'm saying is this: if you are seeking God or whatever you call It, that is not material, then you are seeking God because you did not choose to seek God but because God has programmed this body-mind organism in such a way that that kind of seeking will happen. If this body-mind organism had been programmed to seek only money and fame, then that is what would have been sought through this body-mind organism.

XAVIER *Yes, this has become very clear here.*

RAMESH   Even that is not your choice. I know that Ramana

Maharshi said that it is your choice to seek the Self. But that he said out of his compassion. But I say you don't even have *that* choice.

XAVIER *Yes, that is what I'm asking.*

RAMESH I'm saying you don't have even *that* choice. What you are seeking is God's will and for that reason he has programmed this body-mind organism in that particular fashion. So if you are seeking God that is because God wanted you to seek God. And therefore, God created this body-mind organism with such programming that seeking God is happening. Seeking is part of doing, isn't it? So if you consider yourself the seeker that means you are the doer. Seeking means part of doing, and no doing is your doing. So even the seeking is not "your" seeking. In other words, what I am saying is that you are not the seeker. The seeking is happening.

ROHIT *Ego also has some function?*

RAMESH Sure! To me *ego is the maximum function. Ego has the basic function.* Ego has the basic function to make you think you are a separate individual with power to do what you want. *Ego is the basis for life as it happens to happen* . Each individual being has to think he is an individual doer. Without that, life as we know it would not happen. Therefore, who created the ego? The Source created the ego so that life as we know it could happen. You see? So that Source—or God—has created the ego, and who can remove the ego? As Ramana Maharshi said, "The ego cannot remove itself." So only that Power which created the ego can demolish it. Therefore he said: Your head is already in the tiger's mouth. Be grateful for it and let God continue. You didn't start the seeking. So let that Power which started the seeking continue with the seeking. Why bother?

DURGANAN *Is there a place for* sadhana *? For realizing?*

RAMESH Sure.

DURGANAN *Can you yourself do that?*

RAMESH No. Basically there is the understanding without which no *sadhana* can get you anything. The purpose of any *sadhana* is to bring you to the basic conclusion that "I" can do nothing. "I" am merely a programmed instrument through which the Universal Energy functions. Who is this "me" who wants to achieve enlightenment? If the *sadhana* is happening, whichever *sadhana* you're doing, it will ultimately lead you to this conclusion.

So is *sadhana* necessary? My answer is very simple. If *sadhana* is necessary and if it is the destiny of the body-mind organism, which is the same as God's will, then *sadhana* will happen. You see what I'm getting at? A body-mind organism may want to do *sadhana*, but if it is not programmed to do the *sadhana* then it would say, "I would like to meditate, but I cannot meditate. How do I meditate?" You see? That body-mind organism has not been programmed to meditate, so it will not be able to do so. On the other hand, that body-mind organism may be programmed to do social service. So social service will come naturally to that body-mind organism, whereas it may not come to the one which is doing the meditation. Whatever the kind of *sadhana*, it will happen if it is supposed to happen according to the destiny of each body-mind organism. That is what I say about *sadhana*.

DURGANAN *There is not any particular* sadhana?

RAMESH Sure. There is a particular *sadhana* according to the programming of each body-mind organism. You see? So there is no universal *sadhana*. There is no road which *every* body-mind organism is supposed to follow. This is very often the problem with religion for certain body-mind organisms. What I'm suggesting, Durganan, is there is no need for you to worry about *sadhana*. If *sadhana* is to happen, it will happen. Why worry about it?

DURGANAN *I just continue to do what I feel?*

RAMESH   Yes. Again correct. Do whatever you feel like doing. You have been meditating. You like to meditate. By all means continue to meditate. The only thing I'm saying is do not at any moment think—and even that is not in your control—"'I' have been meditating for twenty years, 'I' should be entitled to something, at least some visions, and nothing is happening. It's not fair!" That is the problem about "someone" meditating—a "meditator" meditating with a certain objective. If the objective does not happen, then there is frustration. So if you like to meditate, you meditate without any expectation! If you like to play tennis, play tennis. But don't expect that tennis to get you enlightened! Only that *sadhana* is pure and effective which is not done with a sense of personal doership. I repeat: *only* that *sadhana* is pure and effective which happens without a sense of personal doership. What more is there to say?

PETER   *What do you mean when you use the words "conceptualizing" and "understanding"?*

RAMESH   Thinking. Conceptualizing is thinking.

PETER *And understanding?*

RAMESH   Understanding is something which *arises*. The understanding, as I understand, is an impersonal understanding.

PETER *Outside the mind.*

RAMESH   Outside the mind. That is correct. Pure Understanding transcends the mind. Pure Understanding transcends the mind so that there is no individual *comprehender* that says, "'I' understand." You see? When there is a feeling of "'I' understand," it's a subject understanding an object.

PETER *May I ask another question?*

283

RAMESH Sure.

PETER *Many Gurus stress love, and you also do it in your books. During the last two days I never heard the word "love" here. Can you talk about the role of love? Then, what is "love"?*

RAMESH That is what I want you to tell me. You are asking about love, so what do you mean by love?

PETER *I read the word "love" in your book, what do you mean? And what do you think others mean? What does Osho mean?*

RAMESH I have no idea what Osho means by love. But what I mean by Love is the absence of separation. The absence of separation. If there is no separation, there is Love. But there is no need to *talk* about Love. The moment you *talk* about Love, Love becomes a concept. So I talk more about the disappearing of the ego, which is what covers the Love, which is I Am.

PETER *Would you use "self-love" in some context, or is this not a word for you?*

RAMESH I don't bother with words. Why bother with words? Because that's part of conceptualizing, you see. The mind, the ego, loves labels, loves formulas. That's what the mind wants, a label on which to hang itself. If there is meditation, there is freedom. If there is meditation, there is freedom from what?

MATT *The ego.*

RAMESH Freedom from the ego. Freedom from conceptualizing. You see? Meditation is freedom from the ego, from conceptualization. What I'm saying is that whether meditation happens or not depends on the way the body-mind organism has been programmed!

MATT *And you're not really talking about sitting cross-legged and just witnessing?*

RAMESH   That is correct. I mean, I don't think that meditating really means cross-legged all the time, with the mind saying, "Is my back straight enough? I'm supposed to keep my back straight." So meditation "sitting straight" is not meditation. Meditation can happen in any pose. Meditation can happen when you're walking. Meditation means the absence of conceptualizing. Meditation means the absence of thinking.

PETER   *You said the "I" in I Am is not the ego. But what is it? I did not get it when you said the I-I.*

RAMESH   You see, Consciousness not aware of Itself, Potential Energy, is a concept. Make no mistake! I-I, I Am, I am Peter—the whole thing is a concept in order to understand your true nature. So I-I is Potential Energy before the manifestation.

PETER   *The manifestation of me.*

RAMESH   No. The totality of manifestation.

PETER   *So this is totally nonindividual, this I?*

RAMESH   Right. Well, actually, whether it is I-I, I Am, they are not two. I-I becomes I Am in manifestation. I-I becomes aware of Itself as I Am. But it is the same one Consciousness.

PETER   *Is it a name for Consciousness? Is it a label for Consciousness?*

RAMESH   That is right. A concept. That is why I keep saying that I Am becomes a concept when you *talk* about it. This pure Awareness of Existence is the Truth, but the moment I *talk* about It, It becomes a concept.

PETER   *What is the relation between Consciousness and the word "I"?*

RAMESH   It is just a name given to Consciousness.

PETER   *Oh! Yes. It is just what you call a label.*

285

RAMESH Yes, it is. You see, even "Consciousness" is a label. "God" is a label.

PETER *Yes. Confusing using the "I" that we use for our individuality in this context.*

RAMESH Therefore I say I-I, I Am, and I am Peter.

PETER *These are three different I's.*

RAMESH Or it is the same Consciousness, but the relevance is to a different point.

PETER *Yes. The last one for the ego.*

RAMESH The last one for the ego.

PETER *The middle one, I Am...*

RAMESH Impersonal Consciousness.

PETER *And the I-I...*

RAMESH Is the impersonal Consciousness before...

PETER *Potentialization, manifestation.*

RAMESH Yes. Quite right. Again they are words to explain something. You see?

PETER *Yes. Yes.*

DURGANAN *This Consciousness, or God, has no characteristics...*

RAMESH It has no characteristics. Characteristics refer to an object, and *This* is pure Subjectivity. The Source of everything.

DURGANAN *Intellectual potentials, bliss, and things like that.*

RAMESH Those are concepts created by the mind. And "bliss" is a very misleading word. "Bliss" is the word which makes the ego seek enlightenment because the ego says, "I have enjoyed everything in the world, but "this" bliss must be something tremendous. So I want to enjoy that bliss." But as a word, I prefer—again, a word is a concept—"calm" or "peace."

DURGANAN *The concept of calm can be considered as bliss, as similar to bliss?*

RAMESH No. If the ego hears that this is only calm or peace, it says, "No, I don't want it. I want excitement." Calm or peace is the absence of excitement or bliss or misery. Calm or peace is a concept used to transcend opposites.

▣ ▣ ▣

Pandharinivaasaa sakhyaa Pandurangaa /
  kari angasangaa bhaktaachiyaa / /
Bhaktakaivaariyaa hosi Naaraayana /
  bolataa vachana kaaya laaja / /
Maage bahutaanche fediyale rina /
  aamhasaathi kona aali dhaada /
Vaaramvaara tuja laaja naahi devaa /
  bola re Keshavaa mhane Naamaa / /

Panduranga (Lord Krishna), my dear friend from Pandhari,
  You remove the misery of devotees
  by giving them the knowledge of Oneness.
Narayana (Lord Krishna), You always rush to the rescue
  of the devotee who has surrendered to Your will.
I don't feel shy in chanting Your name, my Lord.
You have been generous to so many devotees in the past.
Why this injustice and delay in my case?
I am not ashamed of reciting Your name
  again and again and again.
Namadev says:
  Dear friends, go on reciting the name of the Lord with great feeling
  and understand that it is His will which prevails.

SCENE 13

You may never be able to see God—or know God—but you can always tickle his creatures and make them laugh.

Instilling fear and hope are the only refuge of the shallow spiritual teachers.

The human animal makes every effort to love his neighbor, but is always ready to cut his throat if his theology is not what it should be.

Cynicism is to delude people and degrade them; wisdom is to know that they are already deluded and degraded.

You are told to be like a child. What does it mean? It means that a child reacts naturally to an event—it does not judge either itself or others.

[*This scene opens with Consciousness manifesting as Director*]

RAMESH   Little louder, little slower.

INES   (taking a few breaths and looking at the English she has carefully written from her native German)

RAMESH   Little louder, little slower.

INES   (reading again) *Beloved Ramesh, you said that there are two possibilities that thinking mind is quiet. First is the working mind is busy, and the second is simply witnessing. I know a third possibility—when there is love in the heart of a* bhakta *the thinking mind is also quiet. And thank God that he gave me the heart of a* bhakta. *Thanks God.*

RAMESH   So talk about it. What do you mean, Ines? You are quite right. You are absolutely right. You're 100% right.

INES   *So what can I say? If there is love in the heart, there is no thinking mind.*

RAMESH   What you mean is *when* there is love in the heart there is no thinking mind. Isn't it? Quite right. When there is love in the heart is what the majority of these *abhangas* that are being sung at the end of *satsang* are mostly about. Why? Because the *abhangas* are written by *bhakta*s. Although there is one which Kalindi usually concludes with that is written by a *bhakta* but is pure *Advaita*.

Wolfgang, would you like to say something more on this point? Did she tell you about this note?

WOLFGANG   *Oh yes.*

RAMESH   Now, what was your reaction to it? I mean what do you have to say about it, about this or anything, Wolfgang? All I'm saying is talk for a while. You have a good understanding so please talk for a while.

WOLFGANG   *The question is what is meant by love?*

RAMESH   Yes. Quite right. Good point.

WOLFGANG *We usually write with capital letters to indicate the difference from what we usually understand as love. Normally we mean there is someone loving somebody else or something else.*

RAMESH Quite correct.

WOLFGANG *So there's still a duality of the lover and the beloved object, and what we understand as Love—capital letter—is that the duality is no longer present. There is just oneness or non-duality. Then the understanding that what the other is, is the same as what I am—not only the understanding but also the experiencing of It—That would be called Love.*

RAMESH Yes. And how does it arise, Wolfgang?

WOLFGANG *It happens.*

RAMESH You see, even in duality the *bhakta* sings "all I know is you." In one of the *abhangas* he says, "I don't know anything about knowledge. I don't have any experience of pilgrimages. I don't have any knowledge of *shastras*. I don't have any knowledge of scriptures. All I know is I love you." So what I am saying is there remains that duality, the duality between the *bhakta* and God.

WOLFGANG *Yes. And usually there is a longing to merge with the beloved object—with the Guru or with God. This longing remains as long as there is still the experiencing of a duality.*

RAMESH Yes. Sure.

WOLFGANG *But when the duality is merged, then the longing disappears and is purely the experience of oneness.*

RAMESH Yes. So what I'm saying is that the love of the *bhakta* for God is still in duality, you see? The *bhakta* longs for his God, and in one case, in one of the *abhangas* the *bhakta* sings, "I went to see God, and I came away being God." You see, in one of the *abhangas* that is a line, "I went to see God and returned being God."

WOLFGANG *With the understanding that there is only God, nothing else.*

RAMESH Yes. That is why Kavita said she wanted silence. But "she" cannot have silence. When Kavita is not, silence is there. When Kavita is not there, deep sleep is there. So Kavita cannot know deep sleep, she can only be in deep sleep. Addressing exactly this is a verse in the *Bhagavad Gita* in which Lord Krishna says: When the intensity of a *bhakta* reaches a certain degree, when the intensity of a *bhakta* reaches a certain degree of being unbearable, then I give him the receptivity to get knowledge.

WOLFGANG *And it seems for the jnani it's the opposite way. It may start with the intellectual understanding, but as the understanding deepens and it reaches the heart, then there is also Love.*

RAMESH Quite right. Knowledge blossoms into Love. You see? And Love blossoms into Knowledge. This is why almost every *jnani* says there is no difference between *bhakti* and *jnana*. There is truly no difference between *bhakti* and *jnana*.

The Adi Shankara—you know, he was the epitome of *Advaita*—wrote some very moving poems about Shakti, about Devi, the female energy. There are some people who are only *Advaita*, who are knowledge and nothing else, and they can't understand how a basic *Advaitin* like Adi Shankara could have written poems like this. They don't understand that when there is *true* Knowledge, the *true* Knowledge blossoms into *bhakti*, you see. The true Knowledge blossoms into Love and *Bhakti*.

PIERRE *When I first read Ramana Maharshi, he made a comment that the path of* jnana *is so narrow that it can only be done single file. What do you think about that?*

RAMESH I don't know, I haven't come across it. What exactly did he say?

PIERRE *It means essentially that there is no room for another.*

RAMESH So true *jnana* means Oneness, isn't it? Doesn't it mean that? *Jnana* ultimately means Oneness. That is to say, so long as there is a duality, true *jnana* cannot happen. Therefore, so long as there is the difference between a *bhakta* and his God, then his or her love remains in duality and there is no room for *jnana*. And so, in the *Bhagavad Gita* Lord Krishna says: When the love of the *bhakta* for his God reaches a certain intensity, I give him the receptivity to receive Knowledge.

PIERRE *So where is the room for another in it?*

RAMESH There *is* no room. That is why he said single file. I mean I haven't come across that particular sentence, but this is the way I would interpret it.

PIERRE *I agree. It's just the ramifications of this. In the West there is a very, very intense focus on relationships. So how does that work into this knowledge?*

RAMESH It means so long as there is a duality of relationship, the relationship between man and woman or man and man. Isn't it?

PIERRE *Yes, whatever.*

RAMESH That's a relationship, and a relationship is in phenomenality, isn't it? So how can they go together? The relationship may continue. I mean it's not that when Knowledge happens all relationships disappear, but rather the relationships have no attachment. The relationships have no attachment.

PIERRE *I guess I've never seen one like that. I mean to have absolute freedom in relationships seems somewhat contradictory. I've never seen people not experience jealousy or hurt or...*

RAMESH In which case there is no Knowledge. Knowledge hasn't happened. Transformation has not happened.

PIERRE *So the other person is absolutely free to do whatever he or she wants?*

RAMESH Yes, certainly. The other person is absolutely free to do what he or she wants. Certainly. Vasan, you came some time ago, you said? So now, you know the teaching? Will you tell us what the teaching is? If somebody asks you, "What is the teaching that you are going to? What does Ramesh have to say?"

VASAN *I would say that the whole thing is Consciousness.*

RAMESH Yes, that is one thing. So he will want to know more about it. What is meant by the words "everything is Consciousness"?

VASAN *Human beings are designed, then given hypnosis, thus what we see is not the real thing. It's all unreal. There is something else which has to be experienced.*

RAMESH I see; then the next question would be, "How do you experience it? How do you experience this oneness that you are talking about? Does the teaching say anything about this?"

VASAN *First of all that knowledge has to be there; that this is not real, we are under Divine hypnosis,* maya. *So first that understanding should come; next the contemplation should start, and then you have to start exploring it. I have to remind myself that I am not the body, I am not the mind. That's what I think.*

RAMESH I see. Do you have to remind yourself? I mean, how will you be able to remind yourself? You are busy. You are busy all the time. So only "you" will remind yourself when "you" are not busy. Isn't it?

VASAN *Initially I will start reminding myself when I'm free, but when it starts, I can put brakes on the thoughts.*

RAMESH Can you really do that?

VASAN *I've been doing it. I have been successful.*

RAMESH   I see. What have you been successful at?

VASAN *Suddenly I am not doing it. I'm not an individual.*

RAMESH   So what you are saying is "suddenly," isn't it?

VASAN *Suddenly. Suddenly I can apply the brakes.*

RAMESH   So, suddenly the brakes are applied, or do "you" apply the brakes? If "you" are applying the brakes, why suddenly? *(Vasan laughs)* Why not all the time?

VASAN *Because you are caught in a thought. You are flowing in a thought.*

RAMESH   I know. You are flowing in the thinking and suddenly "you" apply the brakes, or do the brakes get applied? My point is, is it in "your" hands to apply the brakes, or do the brakes get applied?

VASAN *No. It is happening.*

RAMESH   It is happening. That is the point. So if it is happening, and it is happening more and more frequently, then what happens is the involvement becomes less and less, doesn't it?

VASAN *Usually what happens is—because I don't practice it, it doesn't happen. I should be conscious and be a little aware.*

RAMESH   Have you tried it, really?

VASAN *Yes, I've been trying it.*

RAMESH   So, that is why it doesn't happen more often— because you have been trying it. If you let it happen, then it will happen more frequently. Otherwise it becomes an obstruction the more you think "you" are applying the brakes, because "you" *are* the obstruction. This understanding itself will produce the sudden realization that "you" are involved. It is this understanding which will produce the...

VASAN *Obstacle.*

RAMESH   No. "You" are the obstacle. "You" wanting to apply the brakes is the obstacle. You see? So if you keep on doing whatever you are doing without trying to do anything, then this sudden realization of the involvement will happen more frequently.

VASAN *I'm trying that also.* (both laugh) *Like I say, it is happening.*

INES *You say if I have an idea of Ines, for example, this is a thought, but it's not only a thought. In my experience there can be no thought without there also being a feeling of Ines.*

RAMESH   Yes.

INES *Also there is a feeling of Ramesh, for example, but this is not a thought, it's a coloring. It's like if you say you are red and I am yellow. If there is also love, then these two colors together are a new thing, it is like orange.*

RAMESH   I see.

INES *It's as if a new quality is there. It feels like one. And if the attention is on this new color, it fades out more and more. It becomes more transparent. Do you understand what I'm saying? So this which we are, we can't experience because it's...,*

RAMESH   It is there.

INES *Yes, it is there, and the last thing I can experience is this color...*

RAMESH   This I Amness, this Beingness, isn't it?

INES *Yes. And the attention is on that point.*

RAMESH   I see. Now, what you said about color is interesting.

Can you say more about this color which you have described?

INES *To say that this is a color is only a word, because this is a feeling of...*

RAMESH So the colors mean only differentiation. Is that what you mean?

INES *For example, it's the feeling that I have when I have the feeling of Ramesh, but your color is nearly transparent, it's not so easy to get a feeling.*

RAMESH I see. So normally, when you talk of a person, you think of that person with some color?

INES *No, it's not a color, color is only a word. It's not the yellow or orange which is important. It's only to find a descriptive word for the feeling I have of a person.*

RAMESH Of a separateness?

INES *No, it's a special temperament. Temperament is also something, it has nothing to do with the way one speaks or with the way one talks. It's a feeling of someone.*

RAMESH Yes, I see.

INES *It's very, very subtle. It's a feeling of someone. There is a difference between the feeling I have from you or I have from myself. This is nearly nothing, but it's a difference.*

RAMESH I see. So what happens? What happens to this difference?

INES *So the attention is on this feeling I have from someone. It's not a thought.*

RAMESH Yes, I understand. It's a feeling. I mean, human relationships are basically feelings, aren't they? Human relationships are based not on thoughts but on feelings. So you have a feeling about someone. That's what you are saying? What happens to that feeling, Ines?

INES *If the attention is on this feeling, the feeling of Ines and the feeling of someone else, for example, then the only thing that is there is a feeling of both together. This is not two things. It's not a merging because there are not two. It's one feeling, and this feeling, yes, is only what is experienced.*

RAMESH I see.

INES *This is one experience of something, it is not two. And if the attention is on that, then it is one happening. It is not separate from what the experience is. It's one...it's not so easy to find words for it because it's very subtle.*

RAMESH I see. So what you mean is there is truly no difference?

INES *There is no difference. The coloring of Ines and the coloring of Ramesh is the same.*

RAMESH I see.

INES *It's not so easy because it's nothing you can touch or you can describe.*

RAMESH That I can understand, yes.

WOLFGANG *Ramesh, it seems to me sometimes that if one applies your concept of enlightenment, the disappearance of doership, to mystics or masters who are known or have passed away, then it seems many of them don't fit into that concept. Let's say like when I read Aurobindo, now I find it doesn't correlate with your concept.*

RAMESH And that is why I say this is *my* concept of enlightenment. The concept of someone else may be different. You see? Someone else can say, "There is no enlightenment unless there are *siddhis*. There is no enlightenment unless there is the arousing of *kundalini*." So there may be various concepts. But Ramana Maharshi made it clear that the happening of enlightenment or transformation has nothing to do with the arising of *kundalini*. In other words, the arousing of the *kundalini may* give rise to enlightenment, but enlightenment is not presupposed by the existence of the *kundalini* arising. You see? So there are various concepts. My concept is there is no enlightenment—I repeat, it is *my* concept that there can be no enlightenment unless the sense of personal doership is totally gone. This is the same as Ramana Maharshi's.

WOLFGANG *And this concept seems to me also very true. It feels like the truth. I can only say that some years before, I had a different concept. When I was with Osho, for example, I considered him the greatest enlightened being in the whole history of man, but it was only according to a certain concept I had at that time.*

RAMESH So what was that concept which you had, Wolfgang, about Osho?

WOLFGANG *I had the idea that enlightenment is connected with some radiation of energy, a strong energy field. When one comes near this enlightened being, one feels this strong vibration of energy, and the ashrams in Pune and in Oregon seemed to be based on this energy phenomenon. He was creating big meditations, mass meditations, something like* darshans *where the energy was getting increased more and more. Probably the idea of all the* sannyasins *with Osho at that time was that when the energy got to a certain point, then the mind got blown away somehow. That was considered as enlightenment. It was also my idea at the time.*

RAMESH I see. But it happens and then the mind comes back again, doesn't it?

WOLFGANG *Yes, yes, yes. Energy phenomena were happening. People were falling unconscious because of energy.*

RAMESH Oh, sure!

WOLFGANG   *But the habit of the mind came back, of course, after a while. The feeling of doership was still there.*

RAMESH   It was back again, yes.

WOLFGANG   *Then one had to meditate to gain back that high state of energy, to gain this no-mind state. But the idea that there is someone who is meditating...*

RAMESH   That is the point.

WOLFGANG   *...who has to gain this no-mind state was still there. That was the hindrance.*

RAMESH   Yes. Yes. That was *indeed* the hindrance. You are quite right.

WOLFGANG   *I was doing many kinds of meditations there, including leading meditations for many years in the Osho meditation center. So I had my meditation experiences, and I could see that after thirteen years I was basically the same as in the beginning.*

RAMESH   Yes.

WOLFGANG   *Maybe some psychological changes were there, but basically I was the same.*

RAMESH   Yes. Now, when you say "basically I was the same," what do you mean, Wolfgang?

WOLFGANG   *I mean I still had the feeling that I was someone...*

RAMESH   Doing something! Doing the meditation or doing whatever.

WOLFGANG   *Wanting to reach something.*

RAMESH   Yes.

WOLFGANG   *And in the end I was just so frustrated that it made me ready for your teaching.* (the room bursts into laughter)

RAMESH   In this case Lord Krishna says: When the intensity of the devotion of a *bhakta* reaches a certain stage, I give him the receptivity. So Lord Krishna says: When the intensity of Wolfgang's frustration reaches a certain stage, *(sparkling laughter while speaking)* I give him the receptivity to have knowledge!

What is your experience, Kavita?

KAVITA   *When you said yesterday that the liberation is* from *the notion of a personal doer that has to be liberated, it just...*

RAMESH   It made sense?

KAVITA   *Yeah, totally. When that notion is not there then liberation is there.*

RAMESH   It *is* there. So, precisely speaking, when the sense of personal doership disappears   *it* does not lead to transformation. Transformation   *is* the annihilation of the sense of personal doership. One doesn't   *lead* to the other. One *is* the other. You see?

KAVITA   (pause) *I think before, I still had a concept that liberation was from the production of thoughts, images, any identification with those things. But when you said yesterday, "Okay, let the mind be...these things may still be produced..."*

RAMESH   Sure.

KAVITA   *But I, as a separate entity, am not producing them.*

RAMESH   That is correct. So what produces the images, Kavita? What produces the images? The Energy produces the images in a body-mind organism according to the way it is designed and programmed. Here I am using the word "design" for genes. You see? So design plus conditioning is programming, and according to the programming the Energy produces images.

KAVITA   *So it doesn't matter.*

RAMESH   It doesn't matter that the images come and go.

Let them come and go. You see? But if you say "I" have these wrong images,"I" would like to have the correct images...

KAVITA *I had this idea that I could stop them, and until I could do that...*

RAMESH Yes. So now it feels better? (laughing knowingly)

KAVITA *Yes. Wonderful.*

RAMESH That's why God sent you here; and who knows, maybe God will send you somewhere else.

So Bianca, you are leaving? Now is your chance to speak. All these days you have been only painting.

BIANCA *It's also a way to speak, no? It's a silent way to speak.*

RAMESH Yes, but from what has been said, doesn't it provoke something for you to say?

BIANCA *Provoke?*

RAMESH Yes. I mean doesn't it make you say something about what Ines said, what Wolfgang said, what Kavita said?

BIANCA *That's all words, no?—Words and concepts.*

RAMESH Quite correct, they're still all concepts.

BIANCA *And the truth is beyond. So it's better to forget all the concepts and all what I have heard here and...*

RAMESH Quite correct.

BIANCA *... and then be free, or be.*

RAMESH So really, freedom is freedom from concepts. Freedom is freedom from concepts and the worst concept is the "me."

BIANCA *Yes, and when this is understood...*

RAMESH   When this is understood, nothing more is to be understood. Isn't it?

BIANCA   *Mmm, yes.*

DUNWOOD   *I keep getting into these moods, and I want to stabilize. When I come here it is very soothing, and it lessens that crabbiness.*

RAMESH   I see. So what brings it about, Dunwood?

DUNWOOD   *The circumstances are very constricting at the moment. I feel I'm very, very suffocated. I feel I'm not able to express myself.*

RAMESH   So what is it about this teaching that gives you a sense of...you do have a sense of peace?

DUNWOOD   *Yes.*

RAMESH   Now, what do you understand by peace, Dunwood? What do you really understand by peace? You said there *is* a certain amount of peace. Now, how does that peace come about?

DUNWOOD   *I don't know, really. Just sitting here and just sort of listening in a resigned state...just taking it in. It just creates a kind of feeling afterwards.*

RAMESH   So are you telling me that the moment you stop coming here this peace will disappear?

DUNWOOD   *No.*

RAMESH   Because you say that this peace arises as a result of your being here.

DUNWOOD   *It's not so bad.* (both laugh)

RAMESH   Therefore, my questions are: by being here what is it that brings about peace, and what do you really understand by peace?

DUNWOOD *Well, I've always been very angry.*

RAMESH I see. Are you talking of anger or frustration?

DUNWOOD *Both.*

RAMESH I see. Because they are closely aligned aren't they?

DUNWOOD *Yes, but all the negative things. Yet, when you say that there is nobody to blame because everyone is just performing their role...*

RAMESH Quite right. In other words, what I'm saying is there's no personal doership. Nobody *does* anything. Anything that anybody thinks he or she does is merely the reaction of the brain to an outside impulse over which he or she has no control, according to the programming in the body-mind organism over which a person also has had no control. So, it is this understanding that there is truly no individual doer, either in your own case or in the case of others, which produces the peace. Isn't it?

What produces this peace?—The understanding that nobody is truly doing what he or she thinks he is doing. That is what produces the peace, isn't it? As a result, there is no sense of personal doership when there is this understanding that whatever happens happens because it is supposed to happen, according to the way people have been programmed. The understanding is that there is truly no personal doership which produces this peace, is it not? So if *this* understanding of nondoership is there, then with *this* understanding you know that "you" had nothing to do with "your" being here. You see what I am getting at?

DUNWOOD *But I heard it here.*

RAMESH Oh yes, sure.

DUNWOOD *I didn't know it before.*

RAMESH So, you can say you are grateful to me. All right, be grateful. But what brings about the peace? That is my point. It is *this understanding* which brings about the peace, and not just *because* you are here. You see? If this were the case, then the peace would disappear when you left. But if this understanding goes with you, then that peace will be with you always, so long as the understanding is there. Right, Bianca?

BIANCA   *Yes. It's true.*

RAMESH   So what produces the peace is not your being here, but the understanding that you got from being here. You see?

WOLFGANG   *I find it very helpful that you always hammer on these same basic points again and again.*

RAMESH   For that reason, the talks over the recent years have become extremely focussed. They *have* become—there was no design. You see, earlier there was a fair amount of rambling, but in the last few years there has been an extremely deep focussing, and therefore, it is possible to repeat it again and again.

VASAN   *Ramesh, you have been telling us that things just happen, and in my case, which we were speaking about before, "putting on the brakes" just happens?*

RAMESH   That is what you have to understand.

VASAN   *The understanding has to come?*

RAMESH   The understanding has to *be, not* to come. The understanding has to be that "putting on the brakes" happens, and "you" are not the doer. This is the very *basic* principle to understand. Otherwise, how can the sense of personal doership disappear? It could never disappear. If whatever happens you continue to think in terms of "you" doing it, how can the sense of personal doership disappear? It cannot even become less.

You see, the only way it can become less is for the

understanding to be firmly there, and even that is not in your hands—it just happens. You can say, if you like, it happens because it is God's will. It happens because it is the destiny of this body-mind organism. If it is not the destiny of this body-mind organism, then that understanding will not happen. But the point is that this understanding, or lack of it, brings about such changes as are destined in your life. The happening of this understanding is itself not in your control, and what it produces is also not in your control. That is the firm understanding that has to be there—whatever is happening, "you" are not doing it. But more importantly, whatever is happening through someone else is also not "their" doing. You see? When you truly understand this, then when someone else may think he or she is doing something, you know that he or she is *not* doing it. It is just happening.

VASAN *Even when the seeking starts, it's not that "I" am seeking—it happens.*

RAMESH *That* is the whole point!! *(hits the arm of his chair)*

VASAN *The seeking happens.*

RAMESH If the seeking has happened, then who is this seeker who wants enlightenment? Seeking *happens* and is continuing along its own course. How quickly or how slowly it happens is not in "your" hands. Therefore, what can you do? Just watch whatever way this seeking is taking place.

KAVITA *Ramesh, I was reading in* Consciousness Speaks *where you say that the pattern of the universe or the way the universe functions is so vast and so intricate that the mind can't see it, the mind can't know it. But* can *it be known? Is it known?*

RAMESH What I'm saying is, in fact, "who" wants to know

it, Kavita? One individual mind wants to know the functioning of the entire universe. Isn't it? One individual mind wants to know the functioning of the entire universe. So my question to that is, if there is an enormous machine with billions of screws and nuts and bolts, how is it possible for one screw to know the purpose and functioning of the entire machine?

KAVITA *I know that the one screw can never know it, that's obvious. But can it ever be known? Is there an evolution?*

RAMESH I mean, can it ever be known by "whom"?

KAVITA *That's the question. It seems so strange that there's this intricate pattern, a seeming intelligence, yet nobody...*

RAMESH You know, there was a German master named Meister Eckhart. Do you know what Meister Eckhart has said? He said many things, and one I remember is: The human mind can only marvel and wonder at the universe. The human mind cannot *understand* it. It is futile for the human mind to try to understand the universe, God's universe. All you can do is marvel and wonder.

So one little screw can only marvel at the enormity of a machine where there are billions of screws and nuts and bolts. It cannot understand it. There is *frustration* if you try to understand it. Same thing if you try to understand what deep sleep is—you can't.

KAVITA *I can see that the mind can't understand it. Somehow I had the feeling that part of enlightenment was that there's another...*

RAMESH You see, now, that is a concept of enlightenment. The concept of enlightenment which you are thinking of is that when enlightenment has happened, then everything that is going on is known. That is your concept, isn't it, that a *jnani* must know everything which is going on?

KAVITA *It seems, somehow, when one is fully identified with Consciousness or the Source of all appearance...*

307

RAMESH Yes, quite right. *Then* there is no *one* to be interested in what is happening *anywhere*! *(laughing)* You see the point?

PETER *And then whatever information needs to come, it comes.*

RAMESH It comes. You see? That is the point. There is no *one* interested in knowing anything which happens anywhere. It happens. Let it happen.
  Yes, Hella? *(Hella laughing)* Got it?

ALEXANDER *Intellectually.*

RAMESH Of course. I mean, make no mistake, Alexander, whatever you understand has to be only intellectual. But don't dismiss that as being *only* intellectual. It is the intellectual understanding which ultimately has to percolate from the mind down to the heart. "You" can do nothing about it. All "you" can do is *try* to understand it intellectually. You see? So even the intellectual understanding happening is God's will and your destiny. It's important not to discount intellectual understanding. In almost every case there has to be the intellectual understanding in the first place, then the intellectual understanding becomes more and more firm, you see, until the conviction is 100%.

HELLA *Ramesh, it's possible that I know now my design—programming—in the world. I am...I feel that I am the fool in the world. You know what I mean?*

RAMESH You are a...?

HELLA *The fool.*

RAMESH Yes, I see.

HELLA *... designed—programmed—to be the fool in the world because...to bring fun or joke in the world... you know what I mean?*

RAMESH Say it in German. Wolfgang can translate.

W. FOR HELLA *She has understood what this design is for her, means for her. She feels like a fool always in a state of confusion.*

RAMESH Yes.

W. FOR HELLA *Her concept is to break through certain patterns.*

ALEXANDER (HELLA's husband translating) *Hella has a thinking pattern to be the fool in the world, not to be what others think she should be.*

RAMESH Yes, so what is the problem?

HELLA *To believe what I feel.* (laughing)

RAMESH No. You see, the problem is that there is no "that" Hella to play the role of "fool" in this life. *If* that is accepted, *play* the role of a fool! Where's the problem? *(A. trans.)* Problem arises if you *don't* want to play the role of the fool, isn't it? If the role of the fool is what you are supposed to do, *play* the fool! And there is nobody more popular than a humorist or a clown. *(A. trans.)*

HELLA *No, that's not true!*

RAMESH *(laughs)* People think less of you?

HELLA *I'm not serious. I heard it every time: "You are not serious. You have no structure." If I live my life, you know what I mean?*

RAMESH Yes! Then you know what your answer should be?! *(A. trans.)* Your answer should be, "You don't know how lucky I am!" *(laughter in the room)*

HELLA *It's true!*

RAMESH It is. I know it is true, Hella. *(laughter)*

HELLA *But the others say to me that I'm...you know what I mean?*

RAMESH Yes.

HELLA *That's my problem. Now I know it.*

RAMESH So *now* you tell them, "You don't realize how lucky I am." *(A. trans.)* And quite frankly, these people who denigrate you are jealous of you. I'm not joking. *(A. trans.)* I'm *not* joking.

HELLA *It's true.*

RAMESH Deep down they are jealous of you. They would like to be like you. They can't! Because they are designed in a different way. It's true, Hella. So accept that you are lucky. (A. trans.)

HELLA (through tears) *I am lucky.*

RAMESH *They* would like to be what you are! They can't because they are designed in a different way. They are designed to talk among themselves, to gossip, and be heard, and therefore they try to hurt you. *(A. trans.)* What they are doing is they try to hurt you because they are jealous of you. Understand that and then you will be at peace. *(A. trans.)*

HELLA *I haven't seen, I haven't seen...* (in German to W. who trans.) *She can't perceive that the others are jealous.*

RAMESH Yes, but they are! Take it from...and you know it too, deep down. Deep down you know. *(A. trans.)* Otherwise they wouldn't bother telling you. They wouldn't bother trying to make you like them. *(A. trans.)* They are keen to change you so that you should become someone like them. And then they'll be happy. They want you to change and be like them—unhappy!

HELLA *Ja.*

YVES *A few days ago I was struck by something like a rapid punch on my head. We were talking about concepts, and I had the feeling that we were peeling off, little by little. You said, "God is a concept. Intellect is a concept." There are many*

*concepts like this, you pointed them out. And one I remember
telling you, "So, I Am is a concept too?" You said, "Yes." And
suddenly I felt that all these constructions which are in the
mind, which sustain the mind...*

RAMESH "In the mind" and "sustain the mind" are right.

YVES *Yes, are completely without any substance.*

RAMESH Useless. Without any substance. Quite right.

YVES *Then I felt...*

RAMESH You felt relieved.

YVES *No.*

RAMESH You felt helpless.

YVES *No.*

RAMESH *(laughing)* What did you feel, Yves?

YVES *Emptiness.*

RAMESH Empty, of course.

YVES *But a terrible emptiness.*

RAMESH Yes, but "who" feels this terrible emptiness?
Emptiness is there. "Who" says it is terrible, Yves?

YVES *The one who used to be Yves.*

RAMESH Exactly. And it is Yves who says, "This emptiness
is terrible."

YVES *Yes, because I have nothing to to hold on to.*

RAMESH Quite right. Consequently, Yves, the ego, the
thinking mind, feels helpless. Therefore, I keep repeating
that when you truly understand that "you" don't exist,
that the ego doesn't exist—then Yves truly doesn't exist.
When this is understood, one of two things happens: either
a terrible feeling of helplessness or a wonderful feeling of

freedom. One of these two things. The helplessness is what the ego feels. The ego feels terrible helplessness. And the freedom is from this ego. So when you truly understand that there is absolutely nothing which "you" can do, and more importantly, there is truly nothing for which "you" are responsible...

YVES *That has been taken away, this responsibility.*

RAMESH   If that has been taken away, then "who" feels this emptiness to be terrible? If that has been taken away, Yves...

YVES *You're putting your finger on the terrible thing here, emptiness.*

RAMESH   Emptiness, yes. You're quite right. Whether you call it emptiness, or freedom, or transformation makes no difference. But the word "terrible"—"who" feels this freedom to be terrible? It is Yves, isn't it?

YVES *It is the old fool.*

RAMESH   *(laughing)* All right, as you say, "It is the old fool," but the "old fool" keeps coming back. Ramana Maharshi used to say, "The thief keeps coming back." You see, he had a close associate who was dying. So Ramana Maharshi sat there, out of compassion, trying to help him. He put his hands on the man's chest, and the man then calmed down. You see, he calmed down. After Ramana Maharshi left, the man gathered some strength, and just before he died he said to his family, "Oh, you are all here, I am so happy." When this was mentioned to Ramana Maharshi, Ramana said, "Oh, so the old thief came back." The old thief, the ego—"I," "me," "mine"—returned because it was still concerned with its family. The thief came back. *(pause)* So the thief comes back again and again, you see?

PETER   *Until there is nothing left to steal?*

RAMESH   Until...you are quite right, until there is nothing

312

left to steal—unless there *is nothing* left to steal. That is exactly the point. And what is left to steal is that attachment—attachment to something. So long as that attachment is there the thief comes back to take that attachment, to identify himself with the attachment.

(long pause) So Hella, make no mistake, if you *are* a fool, then remember you are a happy fool which the other "wise" people don't want you to be. You see, all these other "wise" people who are unhappy don't want you to be a happy fool. *Remember* that, Hella. That is a fact! They are jealous of you!

HELLA *For my work it is good, you know, but for normal life it is terrible.*

RAMESH Yes. But I mean, when you understand this, there is no need to feel terrible.

HELLA *Now it feels good. I feel a peace, a freedom.*

RAMESH Peace, yes. Contentment.

HELLA *I feel peace.*

RAMESH Good.

HELLA *It's a good it's a good program.* (laughing)

RAMESH Yes. You see, as Yves said, you can't find peace if you listen to others; only if you listen to your own heart and understand that what you *are* is what you are designed to *be.*

HELLA *Is understanding...really, I am a fool!*

RAMESH *(both laughing)* Now, whether you say—if you must say—you are a fool, at least say you are a happy, contented fool. *(everyone laughs)*

HELLA *Yes, I am.*

RAMESH Good. You are a happy, contented, *peaceful* fool.

(everyone laughing joyously)

YVES *This process of enlightenment becomes something which is really attracting, like a magnet. You know?*

RAMESH   Sure.

YVES *"I want to be enlightened," but nobody knows what it is really, but everybody wants to be there because it seems like a fairy tale.*

RAMESH   No. Basically, what is a seeker seeking enlightenment for, Yves? What is he seeking for?

YVES *He has been programmed, conditioned?*

RAMESH   No. That is *why* he is seeking. But *what* is it that he is seeking? What is it that a seeker is seeking and calls it enlightenment? He seeks it as an object which will give him more pleasure than anything in the world has so far given him. You see what I'm getting at?

YVES *Yes.*

RAMESH   The seeker—so long as there is a seeker seeking enlightenment—is seeking enlightenment as an object which will give him more pleasure than any other object in the world has so far given him, beyond his imagination. Whatever any object in the world has given him, and he thinks *can* give him, *this* object will be a thousand times greater. That's why he's seeking that object.

YVES *So the individual, the ego, everything is still there?*

RAMESH   Very much. Isn't that right, Wolfgang?

WOLFGANG   *Yes, something like eternal cosmic orgasm.*

RAMESH   Something like that, yes.

WOLFGANG   *Bliss twenty-four hours.*

RAMESH   Those are Rajneesh's words?

314

WOLFGANG   *Yes.*

RAMESH   *(laughing)* Cosmic orgasm.

WOLFGANG   *Yes. Like when you take drugs and have good experiences, then you want it more.*

RAMESH   That is, in fact, these drugs which produce this image of an object. You see? *(to Hella)* Alexander said on the phone that you have come for six days? Just the right enough amount of time.

HELLA   *Yes?*

RAMESH   Oh yes.

HELLA   *One week is enough time?*

RAMESH   Yes. What I'm saying is that for one week you listen. You see, what happens is this: the mind says, "I have six weeks, I have plenty of time," but the mind says, "I have only one week, I must concentrate." You see? So a week is a good time. Once or twice is not enough, but five or six times is good.

YVES   *But what about this idea that to be in the presence of the Guru, of the master, to swim in his energy so it takes more than five days.*

RAMESH   Well, if you say it that way, any amount of time. I had the good fortune to be with Maharaj for three years, every morning when I was in Bombay. Every morning I was there for almost three years because I was translating, you see.

YVES   *But is it true that really the Guru has such energy, radiating such energy? It's the grace of the Guru, or whatever? There is such a vocabulary?*

RAMESH   That is what the Indian tradition says, and what I say is it is a concept *(everyone laughs)*.

315

YVES *Yah, because I don't believe it!*

RAMESH *(laughs)* It is a concept, make no mistake. It is a concept.

PETER *But in the moment it may be happening.*

RAMESH Certainly, it could happen, of course. It could happen.

VOLTA *But when you say, "Consciousness is speaking through me," I think, for me, you can feel it.*

RAMESH You see, Volta, what do I mean by that? What I'm saying is nothing that is said is pre-planned. Nothing is planned, it just comes out spontaneously. You see?

VOLTA *I can feel it here.*

RAMESH Yes. Sure.

ALEXANDER *For me it's difficult because I am a fighter and a jnani, and at the moment I have nothing to fight.*

RAMESH *(laughing)* Yes.

ALEXANDER (laughing with him) *Stupid to fight, huh? Something missing.*

RAMESH I know. That is what the ego says...

DINESH *The battle is lost.*

RAMESH *(laughing more)* There is no battle. The ego says, "I like a fight, but there is no one to fight."

HELLA *His wife in the hotel.* (everyone laughs)

RAMESH You have been married a long time?

HELLA *Twenty-seven years. It's a long time, huh?*

RAMESH Long time? Do you know how long my wife and I have been married? Fifty-six years.

ALEXANDER *Tell us about it.*

RAMESH *(laughing)* Well, we *still* don't fight.

ALEXANDER *You're missing something.* (the room explodes in laughter)

HELLA *You're not a fighter?*

RAMESH No, I have never been a fighter. This body-mind organism has been designed to be timid.

HELLA *Timid?* (visitors translate into German for her) *Ah, Tender.*

RAMESH Yes. Ah, you could say tender, yes.

HELLA *A tender fighter.* (laughter filling the room)

回 回 回

Aamha na kale jnaan na kale puraan / /
Vedaanche vachan na kale aamhaa / /
Aagamaachi aati nigamaache bhed / /
Shaastraanche vachan na kale aamhaa / /
Yoga yaaga nem ashtaanga sadhana / /
Na kale daan vrata tapa aamhaa / /
Choka manhe maaza bhola bhaav devaa / /
Gaaeen Keshavaa naam tuze / /

I don't understand words of jnana,
  or what is written in the Puranas.
I don't have the intellectual capacity
  to understand the Vedas.
I don't know why I was born
  nor do I care about what will happen
  after the death of the body.
I cannot really understand all the things

317

that the Shastras prescribe.
I do not understand Yoga
   or the different rituals to please You.
The eight forms of sadhana or sacrifice,
   meditation or going on pilgrimage,
   don't appeal to my heart, my Lord.
Choka says:
   I can only love You, my Lord.
   I will only sing Your sweet name, my Lord.

□

Deva maazaa mee devaachaa | Heecha maazi satya vaachaa | |
Deha devaache deoola | Aata baaheri nirmala | |
Deva pahaayaasi gelo | Deva hovoniyaa aalo | |
Tukaa mhaane dhanya zaalo | Aaja Viththalaa bhetalo | |

God is my true nature.
That is the only truth I know.
The body is a temple where God resides,
   pure light of Consciousness shines within and without.
I went to see and know God,
   but on the way the ego got annihilated and
   I came back being God.
Being God happened
   when wanting to see God disappeared.
Tukaram says:
   Enlightenment has happened.
   Vitthala is all there is.

SCENE 14

The age of wisdom is also the age of
stupidity. The age of beauty is also the age
of ugliness. The age of progress is also the
age of regress. All there is—and ever has
been—is the "Here and Now."

回

What is this anti-matter that scientists are
talking about? What has it got against
matter? And, finally, does it really matter?!

回

Once we believed in a Creator with a white
beard up in the clouds. Soon, perhaps, we
shall believe in—and pray to—the scientist's
singularity principle: "In the beginning we
were all one particle." What is the truth?—
Today's science is by no means the last
word!

回

The human being has intelligence enough to
send a man to the moon. If he also had free
will, why has he reduced the world to the
condition it is in?

回

True knowledge is that physical objects are

as unreal as mental objects.

RAMESH   "The choosing by Consciousness among the QM [quantum mechanics] possibilities is an unconscious process. A personal awareness of that choice comes about one-half second later than a 'readiness potential' that appears in the brain-wave," says brain surgeon Benjamin Libet. "Thus, there can be no free will, that most precious 'possession' in the West. The Indian sage, Ramana Maharshi, said the same thing."

So as I understand it, quantum mechanics says that nobody can know what is going to happen in the next minute, in the next hour. The flight of a particle you don't know where it is going to end. You cannot predict it. That's what Neils Bohr says according to the theory of uncertainty. When this theory was explained to Albert Einstein, he said that he could find no fault with the theory of uncertainty, which says that you never know what is going to happen at any given time. Albert Einstein said that although he could find no fault with the theory, his conditioning and upbringing would not let him accept the theory of uncertainty. He said, "I find no fault with this theory, but I cannot accept that God is playing dice with the universe." Then Neils Bohr replied to him, "God is not playing dice with the universe. You think God is playing dice with the universe because you don't have all the information that God has."

You see, God has the full information, he knows what is happening. He sees the whole picture. It's already there. But we don't possess God's knowledge so nothing is certain. From the wave of probability something happens at any moment to anyone. So when the wave collapses something happens. A thought arises, a desire arises, and it takes a split-second for the brain to react to it and for the mind-ego to immediately take possession and say that it is "my" thought, "my" desire. So the desire arises when the quantum wave collapses. The ego accepts it as "its" desire. Now, you tell me if the desire is of the ego or that of Consciousness.

JOHN *But the path of surrender is the path of no desire.*

RAMESH No, no. That is a mistake. You see, somebody is asked—someone, some ego—to leave desire, is it not?

JOHN *And then the someone surrenders.*

RAMESH Someone surrenders? My point is no "one" can surrender. What will "you" surrender, John? Surrender to whom? God, isn't it?

JOHN *Yes.*

RAMESH You are talking of surrender to God. John says, "I surrender to God." What have you got to surrender, John? Do you have any capital, anything which you can say, "All right, God, I surrender this to you."? Do you own anything of your own which you can surrender to God? What have you got? Nothing! So what will you surrender to God?

JOHN *What about my desires?*

RAMESH I told you, the desire arises, and the ego says, "It is my desire." But the desire arises—it is a Divine desire. Desire arises because you are supposed to have that desire. So if you are supposed to have that desire, how can you give it up?

JOHN *It means that when someone surrenders, he knows that desires will come?*

RAMESH Can you give up the desire, John? The desire arises. Is it possible for you to give up that desire?

JOHN *I can give it up.*

RAMESH How can you give up the desire? If you give up

the desire you are suppressing it.

JOHN *I don't know.*

RAMESH You see, my point is, if you say, "I surrender desire," then the desire gets suppressed. The next moment it comes back with twice the force. It explodes. The only way the desire can be surrendered is if you accept that it is not your desire. The only way to give up the desire is in the very beginning to think that "It is not my desire. The desire just arose. It is not my desire."

JOHN *It means we give less food to the ego?*

RAMESH Yes! Quite correct. And the more you think in these terms, "It is not my desire, it is not my frustration, it is not my anything," then the ego gets less and less food and becomes weaker and weaker.

JOHN *If we give importance to the desire we make the ego stronger?*

RAMESH That is absolutely correct. You see, John, if you think it is "your" desire that is what happens. All these people who are supposed to be gurus, who don't really understand, tell John,: "John give up your desires. Desirelessness is the goal." Can they themselves give up *their* desires? The desire dissolves! And he does not understand it. He thinks, "'I' have given up the desire." So the ego is very much there.

   The question is "who" gives up "whose" desire? So the only way, John, the only way surrender or acceptance can happen—I am not saying the only way you can surrender—the only way acceptance or surrender can happen is when there is no "you" who says, "'I' accept. 'I' surrender." Then the accepting happens. And in that true accepting there is no "me" who says, "'I' accept."

   "Who" surrenders to whom, John? A desire arises. As the quantum mechanics theory says, desire arises. The brain a split-second later reacts and immediately the mind-ego takes possession and says, "It is 'my' desire." A thought arises. The brain a split-second later reacts and immediately the mind-ego says, "'I' had a brilliant idea." That idea, where did it come from? The brain cannot create the idea. The idea arose, the brain got it, and the mind-ego immediately says, "It is 'my' idea."

So whether a desire arises, or anger arises, or an emotion arises—same thing. It arises. And if that is truly understood then John doesn't say, "'I' am angry. 'I' am afraid. 'I' am happy." The fear that arises is witnessed. The anger that arises is witnessed. The feeling of happiness is witnessed. None of these are witnessed as "my" fear, or "my" anger, or "my" happiness.

JOHN *It means you accept?*

RAMESH Correct. You are quite right. The basic ultimate word is *acceptance* or surrender, whichever you like. But the immediate word is "acceptance." Whatever arises is accepted. Happiness arises, it is accepted. Fear arises, it is accepted. Anger arises, it is accepted.

MURTHY *Acceptance means not "taking delivery."*

RAMESH That's right. It means there is no "me" who says, "'I' am angry." Anger has arisen.

LANCE *You are not even accepting acceptance.*

RAMESH That's correct. You are not even accepting the acceptance. The acceptance happens. Truly, there is no "one" who says, "'I' accept." The acceptance happens. When it happens you say, "Who am 'I' to accept anything? Who am 'I' to surrender anything?"

What have you got, John, that you can surrender to God? You have nothing. You came with nothing; you will go with nothing. Because "you" just never did exist. When the body was conceived and created there was no "you."

There was simply the body of an infant, a baby functioning according to its intuition. The baby doesn't say, "'I' am feeding myself on 'my' mother's breast."

JOHN *The baby merely accepts everything.*

RAMESH Yes, because its ego has not developed enough to say, "I accept." Acceptance happens. *(laughter)*

LANCE *So, to say giving up "my" desires is desire itself?*

RAMESH Quite correct. You are absolutely correct. It is a desire to give up desire, isn't it?

JOHN *About these Gurus—they talk about silence.*

RAMESH Silence? All right. What do you understand by silence, John? Silence means, step by step, no questions. No questions means there is no "me" to put up any questions.

JOHN *I am putting up a question and you put up an answer. So where does this answer come from?*

RAMESH This answer comes from Consciousness. You think John is talking, Ramesh is listening, Ramesh is talking, John is listening. The way it is understood here is that a conversation is taking place between two body-mind organisms, both of which are merely programmed instruments of Consciousness or God. So who is creating this conversation, John?

JOHN *I would say that John is questioning.*

RAMESH That is what you are saying. What I am saying is Consciousness is asking these questions through this body-mind organism.

JOHN *So the question comes from the Silence, the Consciousness.*

RAMESH Quite correct.

JOHN *But the Gurus and masters have different answers to the*

324

same question. So is it not God answering all these questions?

RAMESH   Yes it is.

JOHN   *Then why do these Gurus...why do they...*

RAMESH   Because, it is God's wish that the total understanding does not happen in the body-mind organisms of these gurus. A guru may be sincere—I am not saying he is not sincere—but he may not really have understood. Let us say a half-baked guru *(laughter)* let us say there is a half-baked guru. Who created the half-baked guru, John? Is it not Consciousness or God who created the half-baked guru?

JOHN   *Yes.*

RAMESH   So why did God create the half-baked guru? As part of Divine hypnosis.

JOHN   *And why do some people follow these half-baked gurus?*

RAMESH   Because that is their destiny to go to the half-baked guru.

LANCE   *Ramesh, I feel that there is a very good acceptance of this teaching.*

RAMESH   I know there is.

LANCE   *The only thing I just can't get is the concept of destiny. Where did it come from? Is it rational, logical, or...*

RAMESH   You see, everything that happens, just happens. Everything that happens is an act of Consciousness or God. *No thought or act is yours*. Yet the human being judges the acts of Consciousness or God as good or bad. A Mother Teresa or a psychopath has been created by the same Power. So whom do you blame? When you *truly understand*, and this is intuited Understanding and not the "me" understanding intellectually— *the judging stops*.

325

When the judging stops the "me" disappears and there is acceptance of What Is in the Present Moment.

LANCE *I understand this, but I don't understand that if everything is God's act and everything is destiny...the confusion is it's a paradox that things just happen.*

RAMESH Things just happen.

LANCE *So if things just happen, destiny is the answer to the why, why things happen.*

RAMESH That is correct. Destiny is just a concept.

LANCE *Okay.*

RAMESH And a concept is necessary only to understand something.

LANCE *So God can create a new reality every minute.*

RAMESH Yes. Again, that is correct. Every minute, every split-second.

LANCE *So from the point of view of Consciousness, the movie keeps changing?*

RAMESH No, the movie is already there. But what you see is from frame to frame to frame, from moment to moment. But the movie is already there.

LANCE *So it's a fixed destiny.*

RAMESH It's a fixed picture. The movie is already there. Consciousness or God has written the script. Consciousness or God has produced the movie. Consciousness or God has directed the movie. Consciousness or God is playing every character in the movie. And who sees the movie? Consciousness sees the movie.

LANCE *That's what I don't understand. How does one come to understand that it is a movie?*

RAMESH It's a concept—a concept to understand that there is no free will. And the free will itself is a concept. You know what Ramana Maharshi said about concepts? He said a concept is to be used like a thorn which you use to remove another thorn embedded in your foot. And having removed the embedded thorn, you don't keep the thorn which removed it. You throw it away also. So a concept is to be used only for the limited human intellect to understand a certain point. The point being that you have no free will. Today the scientist is telling you that you have no free will. The mystic has been saying it for years.

LANCE *So if a change was meant to happen, it will happen because it was part of the movie for the change to happen.*

RAMESH Quite correct. God sees exactly where the ball is going to land. You don't. That's what Neils Bohr said: "You don't have the full information that God has."

CLAUDE *In scientific language it is fifty-fifty.*

RAMESH Yes. Fifty percent is the scientist's way of saying that he doesn't know. And he cannot know. If a champion is going to play with a beginner, you can say there is a ninety-nine percent chance that the champion will win. But you still don't know. *(laughter)*
    An astrologer may have the gift of seeing into the future, but even a Nostradamus may see a part of the picture, not everything. So we can accept these predictions to be true, but they may not be. How much Nostradamus was supposed to see, you don't know.

LANCE *He could have told a lie.*

RAMESH Now, telling a lie is a matter of intention, isn't it? But what happens is that the telling of a lie is also God's will.

LANCE *So there has never been a lie.*

RAMESH Really, there has never been a lie.

327

CLAUDE *The only thing is Here and Now.*

RAMESH   That is correct.

CLAUDE *So God is everywhere and every time. There is only the present.*

RAMESH   When you say the present, the past and the future come in. So you can only say the Present Moment. That is all you can be in—the Present Moment, What Is.

CLAUDE *And you are God, and I am God.*

RAMESH   Instead of saying you are God, I would say, "There is God."

CLAUDE *And God is everywhere?*

RAMESH   That is correct. So all talk about concern for the future is by the thinking mind, the intellect. It is only the ego which is concerned with the future. God is not concerned with the future. God is the Present Moment. As far as the mind-intellect is concerned, God is in that Present Moment when the mind-intellect is not there. The mind-intellect is not there in the Present Moment because the mind-intellect is only concerned with time: past, present, or future.

CLAUDE *This is connected with surrender and acceptance, being in the Present Moment?*

RAMESH   Being in the Present Moment *is* Acceptance, *is* Surrender; because, being in the Present Moment there is no ego, no thinking mind. Therefore It is Acceptance or Surrender—but not by a "me."

CLAUDE *This also means trust?*

RAMESH   Yes! Of course! You can use the word "trust," you can use the word "love," or whatever. So what is present in the Present Moment is Love and Trust. And the

Love and the Trust are in the Present Moment because the thinking mind is not there. The thinking mind, the ego, *hides* the Present Moment.

CLAUDE *Then why use the mind at all...?*

RAMESH The mind-intellect is still the instrument through which the understanding happens. The mind-intellect is still the instrument through which the understanding begins.

JOHN *Being in the Present Moment I can't understand. I can understand being in the Here and Now.*

RAMESH Then when "you" were understanding something, you were in time and not in the Present Moment. In the Present Moment the Understanding happens! So also the Surrender, Acceptance, Trust, whatever "you" call It, happen in the Present Moment. And in the Present Moment it is not John who says "I" understand, "I" accept, "I" trust. The *Present Moment is impersonal*—*no* personal "I," *or* "me," *or* "mine." The Present Moment is intemporal—no past *or* present *or* future.

LANCE *After the Understanding whatever you do is just happening?*

RAMESH In any case, it's *been* happening. The only thing is that "you" thought "you" were doing it. But whatever was happening was always happening anyway.

LANCE *But the ego thinks it is doing it. And when the ego dissolves to realize that no "one" is doing, it must be funny.*

RAMESH It *is* terribly amusing—that everything has been happening all these years and, like a damn fool, "I" thought "I" was doing it. It is such a joke. Then you laugh, you see?

LANCE *This morning I got angry because someone next to me was smoking. And immediately the thought came, "I am programmed to get angry, so I am angry, but this anger is not really mine."*

RAMESH So the involvement with the anger got cut off and the anger must have dissolved.

LANCE *No, the anger continued.*

RAMESH If you truly accept that it is not "you" who is getting angry but that the anger arises—then the anger collapses.

LANCE *How long the anger lasts is the involvement?*

RAMESH That's right. The arising of the anger is in the Present Moment. The length of the time you are angry is horizontal involvement. The sudden realization which cuts off the involvement is vertical. You might ask, "Who produces this sudden understanding of the involvement?" "You" don't, the ego doesn't, because the ego itself *is* the involvement. So God or Consciousness or the understanding produces the sudden realization. As the understanding goes deeper this sudden realization of the anger and the dissolving of it will be quicker and quicker.

LANCE *So it's an organic process?*

RAMESH That's right. It's an organic process. How long it will take, nobody knows.

LANCE *There is no need to find out why the anger arises, the psychological reasons according to Freud, etc.?*

RAMESH That is absolutely irrelevant and time-consuming, because the moment you do that you are in time, aren't you? You are in the past.

LANCE *You just know that it is not your anger.*

RAMESH Just know that it is not "your" anger. This is what the quantum physics theory says. Anger arises. The brain spontaneously reacts a split-second later, and *then* the thinking mind, the ego, gets involved with it as "my" anger.

DEVESH *If I am going by taxi and the taxi driver takes me on a longer route, then with this understanding I have two options: I can understand that it is his programming to take me for a longer ride than necessary and so I ignore it; or I can reprimand him and take him to the police.*

RAMESH Yes, and whatever happens will be part of the functioning of Totality. And whatever happens will be your destiny and the driver's destiny. Where's the problem? You say that one of two things will happen. If you take him to the police, it was your destiny and his destiny to get involved with the police. If you let him have the money then it is your destiny to lose the money and his destiny to get the money. Where's the problem? Where's the confusion? One of two things will happen. So just wait and see what happens. Whatever happens is not "your" doing. What happens is not in your hands. What happens is the destiny of the body-mind organism named Devesh, and it is supposed to happen. Whatever happens is supposed to happen.

DEVESH *But sometimes things go against astrological predictions. So it means that things can happen against destiny?*

RAMESH Now, astrological predictions are what? They are deductions by an astrologer. So the astrologer can be wrong. An interpretation was wrong. Where is the question of destiny not taking place or going against the destiny? Nobody knows destiny completely. Even Nostradamus—who knows how many of his predictions turned out true?

DEVESH *I had read somewhere that if you can be aware, aware of thoughts, you can change the course of events.*

RAMESH "Who" can change the course of events? "Who" is Devesh? Tell me first "who" is Devesh, and then we can talk about changing the course of events. All I can see is a body-mind organism programmed in a particular way, genes, and conditioning. This body-mind organism is a puppet on which God pulls the strings and makes Devesh do what he is doing. Other than that, where is Devesh? "Who" is Devesh who thinks "he" can change something?

DEVESH *But I have a feeling about myself.*

RAMESH That feeling is merely a personality based on your programming. Genes and conditioning create a personality which Devesh says is Devesh. It is just a picture created by genes and conditioning. It is an impression. Other than that impression, where is Devesh?

LANCE *I am having problems with the I-I and the I Am.*

RAMESH There is no problem because they are not two. They are *not* two. Consciousness-at-rest is I-I. When It is in movement It is I Am. So I-I is a concept with which you are not really concerned. It is just a concept. What you are really concerned with is I Am.

LANCE *I Am is the totality of manifestation.*

RAMESH That is correct.

LANCE *So if you are in the sleeping state, what is it then?*

RAMESH I Am, because there is a body there and because it is in phenomenality.

LANCE *So when there is no manifestation there is just I-I?*

RAMESH Correct.

LANCE *In a book about Ramana Maharshi it says that when*

you take the enquiry Who am I? backwards there is nothingness.

RAMESH   You see, Ramana Maharshi, therefore, does not really distinguish between I-I and I Am because it is useless. I-I is merely a concept about which he said why bother. You are only concerned with I Am and I am Lance. And when Lance is not there, I Am is there.

LANCE   *What is the dream state, then?*

RAMESH   The dream state is identified Consciousness-in-action. What is the living dream, then? The living dream is the dream of the I Am. Lance has a personal dream and I Am has the living dream. So what happens really is that you wake up from your personal dream into the living dream.

LANCE   *In deep sleep there is I-I?*

RAMESH   I Am! You are really not concerned with I-I.

LANCE   *But right now there is a need to know.*

RAMESH   Then where did I Am come from? That is a conceptual question. And for that conceptual question the conceptual answer is I Am is the activized, impersonal Energy in manifestation, and I-I is the Potential Energy. The personal "I" which Lance thinks "he" is, is the impersonal Energy identifying as an ego which thinks it is a doer and needs to know. When there truly are no more questions, then there is no doer. When there is no doer, then there is no ego. And when there is no ego, then the I Am shines forth from a body-mind organism without personal identification. When the body-mind organism dies, then the I Am continues as I Am. And when the totality of manifestation ends, then I Am is I-I, Consciousness-at-rest. And all of this is a concept.

LANCE   *Okay. So from the conceptual point of view, the air around this room is I-I but Ramesh is I Am?*

RAMESH   Well, the air and Ramesh are both in manifestation, are they not?

LANCE *A molecule is I Am?*

RAMESH Yes! *Everything is I Am.*

LANCE *I think that's all I need to know.*

RAMESH   Have you heard of Tao? A Zen master has said that Tao is everything. Then someone mischievously said, "Is shit also Tao?" And he said, "Yes! Tao is shit and Tao is God. Tao is the tree and Tao is the human being. Tao is everything because all there is is Tao."

All there is is Consciousness. Other than Consciousness nothing exists. Other than God nothing exists. Therefore, Consciousness, or God, has to be immanent in everything.

DEVESH *Do you do any puja?*

RAMESH   I have a routine. It includes a puja to Maharaj and Ramana Maharshi. And years ago, about seventy-five years ago, I promised my mother to recite what is known as the Ramaraksha Stotra. It takes about ten minutes. I promised her and I have been doing it for the last seventy-five years. Or, the doing of it has been happening for the last seventy-five years.

▣ ▣ ▣

Hechi daana degaa devaa / tuzaa visara na vhaavaa / /
Guna gaayeen aavadi / hechi maazi sarva jodi / /
Na lage mukti dhana sampadaa / santa sanga dei sadaa / /
Tukaa mhane garbhavaasi / sukhe ghaalaave aamhasi / /

Give me only one boon, my Lord:
May I never forget that Your will alone prevails.
I will joyfully sing of Your glorious deeds.
Give me the association of people
  who have total trust in You.

Scene 15

You are earnest and sincere in your spiritual search, and you exhort others to be earnest and sincere. Where did you buy your earnestness and sincerity? Where does the tiger buy its black stripes and its markings of gold? Why is the scorpion venomous and the elephant benign?

One word says it all: "Awareness."
Two words say it all: "Who cares?"
Three words say it all: "So be it."
Four words say it all: "What does it matter?"

Jens *Last night I had a dream. I met you somewhere in a place, a working place. What happened was that I found my head inside your mouth! It was totally like this, you know* (demonstrating) *And the feeling was awkward somehow. When I woke up my head was wet.*

Horst *And I told Jens about how you frequently refer to*

Ramana Maharshi's image of "your head in the tiger's mouth."

JENS *There is a parallel.*

YOGESH *Ramana Maharshi!*

RAMESH But, Jens, did you know about this?

HORST *No! We talked about it this morning—about the parallel.*

RAMESH Yes, there *is* a parallel! *(laughing)*

BRIGITTE (to Jens) *You never read this story before? You never read and never heard? Never?*

JENS *No. I just woke up I saw Horst, and I told him that I had just dreamt something totally crazy.* (laughing)

CARMEN *Ramesh, I don't understand how you can say "Who cares?" It's bothering me. There is so much suffering and people not caring what happens to each other. Sometimes it comes to the point that I can't take it anymore, and then you say, "Who cares?"*

RAMESH Now wait a minute! You don't understand the *context* in which "Who cares?" is said. The context is meant for the apparent seeker who thinks "he" or "she" is doing the seeking—the seeking of God, or enlightenment, or whatever. "Who cares?" is *not* about life in phenomenality. "Who cares?" means: Who cares whether God is taking me along the path quickly or slowly— *who cares*? That's his business. This attitude has nothing to do with practical life.

Up to what extent does the meaning of the words "Who cares?" have to life in general? An example is that you have two people: one cares a lot and the other cares very little. The one who cares a lot will not stop caring even if he's told to stop caring for others. And the one who is not able to care for others, even if you tell him to do so, will not be able to. Why? Because each body-mind organism has a certain nature—a nature not which "he" has acquired, but which comes with the body-mind organism. One body-mind organism has been created with a deep sensitivity where the caring is part of its nature. If another body-mind organism has been created by the same Source, by the same God, with much less sensitivity, then much less caring will be its nature—over which he or she has had no control. The way one is programmed, one's natural characteristics—sensitive or insensitive—is not in the control of anybody. I'm not suggesting that the attitude in living life be "Who cares?" Rather, these two words refer to the seeker's attitude towards spiritual progress.

From what you heard yesterday, Nirav, any questions?

NIRAV *Yes.*

RAMESH *(laughing)* That was quick.

NIRAV *The* rishi*s are saying that...*

RAMESH How many *rishi*s have you met in your life?

NIRAV *In all my past lives?*

RAMESH Oh, you remember your past lives?

NIRAV *Sometimes.*

RAMESH That is wonderful. I don't. Anyway, what was your question?

NIRAV *What they are saying is that it is impossible to see truth via the senses and that you have to look directly. What exactly do they mean by seeing directly?*

RAMESH I don't know, you should ask them.

NIRAV *I ask you.*

RAMESH No, I mean what somebody else says, I can't explain to you. But my question to the *rishi*s would be "who" is to look directly through to "what?" The *rishi*s tell you, you said, that you should look straight through. They are asking "someone" to look at "something," which means it is "other than." You see? So, what you say is they ask you to see something without the senses. Is that what you are saying?

NIRAV *Yes, that is what they are saying. But this is confusing me.*

RAMESH Yes, naturally. Because as I told you, "whom" are they asking to see "what" without the senses? Without the senses what would you see, Nirav? All that Nirav can *observe* is *only* through the senses. You see? The Source of that which you can see through the senses is the Source, but you can't see the Source. And what they are asking you to do is to see the Totality, or the Source. Isn't it? How can you, Nirav, see It? You are part of the manifestation which is a *reflection* of that Totality within Itself. You see? So how can Nirav, as part of the reflection of that Source, see the Source?

NIRAV *It's impossible.*

RAMESH That's what I would have told the *rishi*s. That is the whole point. There is no Nirav to see anything because all there is is the Source. You can call it Consciousness, you can call it Primal Energy, or God, or whatever you like. But the fact is all there is is the Source. Other than the Source, nothing is. So who can see the Source? It's as simple as that. The *rishi*s ask this "you," this Nirav, to see some "thing." That is exactly the problem. And wanting to see the Source is a problem created for Nirav. The only thing to be understood is that there is nothing other than the Totality. There is nothing other than the Source. So how can Nirav see the Source or know the Source?

NIRAV *Source is now trying to look at Source?*

RAMESH Sure! That is the only understanding, Nirav. That

is the *only* understanding! *All there is is Consciousness*, or Source, and any effort made by Nirav to see It or know It is an obstruction, because there is *no individual doer*. Ultimately, there is no separate Nirav—as part of the *apparent* manifestation which is only a *reflection* of the Source—who can know the Source.

ROHIT *If Nirav is a part of the Source...*

RAMESH No! Nirav is *not part* of the Source. *He is not part of the Source.* Nirav is part of the *apparent* manifestation which is a *reflection* of the Source within Itself. I repeat, Nirav is the name given to the *apparent* object, a body-mind organism, which object is part of the totality of manifestation, which totality of manifestation is a *reflection* of the Source within Itself.

VICTOR *In this body-mind organism, is it one's consciousness which is the reflection of that Source?*

RAMESH No. The Source uses Its aspect of energy to function through this body-mind organism, just like electricity operates or functions through any of the electrical gadgets.

VICTOR *Yes, but what is the nature of that Source in this body-mind organism? Is it one's consciousness?*

RAMESH You can call it consciousness if you like. I prefer to call it energy. The *aspect* of the Source, or Consciousness, which is the *functioning* is energy. You see, according to the Hindu philosophy it is Shiva-Shakti. Shiva is the Potential. Shiva is the Source. So Shiva in Its manifestation is Shakti or energy. Shiva does nothing. Shiva functions through Its mate, Shakti. Shiva, the Source, is undivided. When It manifests It becomes two—Shiva-Shakti—and the entire manifestation is based on duality. So without Shiva, Shakti cannot exist. And without Shakti, Shiva is Potential unmanifested.

VICTOR *Without Shakti can Shiva exist?*

RAMESH Sure, if you mean Shiva as the Source, or Potential, or Totality, whatever you wish to call It.

GABRIEL *So without Shakti, Shiva can exist?*

RAMESH Shiva when manifested, when functioning, has Its aspect of Shakti—so, Shiva-Shakti. Duality is Shiva-Shakti, Consciousness-in-action. Unicity is Shiva, Consciousness-at-rest, Potential.

GABRIEL *Who says Shiva is Potential?*

RAMESH I say it. That is why it is a concept. I told you, right from the beginning.

GABRIEL *And without Shakti, Shiva is just...*

RAMESH It is Shiva-Shakti in manifestation, duality; and Shiva without Shakti, energy, is powerless. The male without the female is useless.

GABRIEL *Indeed.*

RAMESH He cannot create anything.

GABRIEL *Duality?*

RAMESH Yes, but without duality this manifestation cannot happen. So all you have to accept is that manifestation cannot happen without duality. Everything in the manifestation is based on duality...

VICTOR *Suffering, pain and pleasure...*

RAMESH Wait a minute, wait a minute. Hear me out completely, otherwise you'll have problems. *(laughter)* The manifestation is based on duality. Duality means opposites. So duality in the manifestation, in the functioning of the manifestation, is based on interconnected opposites. You

340

cannot find beauty without ugliness in the manifestation. You cannot find goodness without evil. They are interrelated. You cannot find anything beautiful unless you have already decided something is ugly. You cannot find something good unless you have already decided something is evil. They go together. The final understanding is that the manifestation is based on duality, interconnected opposites.

The problem arises because the individual ego wants one and not the other. The individual ego does not accept both. If both are accepted as part of What Is, that manifestation cannot function unless there is duality, then no problem. If you accept both the good and the bad, the beauty and the ugliness, then you don't even have to call something beautiful or ugly. You accept both. But the problem arises because the individual ego says, "I want only beauty, I don't want ugliness. I want only good, I don't want anything bad or evil."

VICTOR *Why has the ego become such a problem if it is part of manifestation?*

RAMESH You see, what happens is that without the ego, life as we know it cannot function. You didn't create the ego. What has created the ego? God or Source or Consciousness has created the ego so that the ego can say, "I like this. I don't like that. I like you. I don't like her."

VICTOR *"I" did this and "I" did that.*

RAMESH "'I' did this and 'I'..." You see? So the sense of personal doership—the ego is the sense of personal doership. Personal doership includes wanting and choosing because without this wanting and choosing, without this separation, life as we know it cannot happen. So God has created the ego as part of the mechanism for the manifestation to function.

IVAN *Ramesh, if the ego creates my problems...*

RAMESH No, the ego does not create "your" problems. The ego creates problems. *(laughter fills the room)*

IVAN *So if I decide to commit suicide...*

RAMESH Then you decide to commit suicide, but whether suicide happens or not is not in your control. I'll tell you an actual story. There was a policeman in Los Angeles who was not programmed to be a policeman, he was too sensitive. As a consequence he had a nervous breakdown. It was severe and he managed to convince the court that his being a policeman had been responsible. As a result he began to receive a pension. The pension solved his monetary difficulties, but the underlying problems, the ego's problems, continued. They became so overwhelming that he decided to commit suicide. As he was walking to go get the gun which he still had from the police force, he suddenly and clearly heard a voice say, "Don't do it." And he didn't commit suicide. So if you are not destined to commit suicide, you won't.

The scriptures say the worst thing a man can do is to commit suicide, that he will burn in hell forever. *(laughter)* You see? But my point is it's the destiny, which is the will of God, of a body-mind organism that determines whether or not death will be by way of suicide. Death has to happen through a body-mind organism, and which way it is going to happen is stamped at the moment of conception. It is God's will. It may be the destiny of a conception not to be born at all, in which case the mother will abort it, naturally or purposefully. If the destiny of a conception is to be born and live for a hundred years, then what happens during those hundred years is also, according to my concept, stamped at the moment of conception. I repeat, it is my concept.

ELAINE *The awareness of I Am, does that exist in deep sleep?*

RAMESH I Am does exist in deep sleep, because if it didn't, then when you wake up how can you say you slept well or you did not sleep well? Unless there was some awareness...

ELAINE *But I don't have a memory of it.*

RAMESH   No, wait a minute. Awareness was there but Elaine was not aware of it. And what Elaine really seeks now, or what everybody seeks now, is that peace which existed in that awareness in deep sleep but which does not exist in the waking state.

So what is the search for? The spiritual search is for that peace which exists in deep sleep and having it even in the waking state. What is the basis of that peace in deep sleep? It is the non-existence of Elaine as the doer. So how can that peace happen in the waking state? Only when Elaine disappears as a doer, as an individual doer who believes "'I' am in control of 'my' life. 'I' do things. Everything that happens through this body-mind organism are 'my' actions."

ELAINE *In deep sleep there's no personal awareness.*

RAMESH   The personal awareness is the sense of doership. You see? So the question really is: "How can Elaine enjoy that peace which exists in deep sleep in the waking state?" And the answer is only when there is the total acceptance that what functions is the body-mind organism, and there is no Elaine doing anything. When this happens the sense of personal doership is annihilated.

When the understanding is that whatever happens through any body-mind organism is merely witnessed as the impersonal functioning of Consciousness, or the impersonal functioning of Totality, then the sense of a personal Elaine is not there, and the same peace exists in the waking state which exists in deep sleep. But this happens only when there is total, unconditional *acceptance* that there is no individual doer. And the happening of that acceptance is not in your control.

HILDA *Doesn't it affect motivation? I mean, one's motivation in work and in everyday life becomes less because there is no ego pushing you into doing anything?*

RAMESH You mean all action will stop in this body-mind organism?

HILDA *No, not necessarily.*

RAMESH The energy inside this body-mind organism will continue to produce actions, physical or mental. And in what way will the energy produce these actions? It will produce them according to the programming and destiny in this body-mind organism.

HILDA *Yes, what I mean to say is what about this motivation— the pushing motivation in a competitive world. That is what I am talking about.*

RAMESH I know. I know you are. You see, you are assuming that "you" are in control.

HILDA *No. To be able to perform, to be able to exist. I mean I won't be able to...*

RAMESH That is totally wrong! You don't have to have any "motivation." That Energy, the pure Energy functioning through this body-mind organism and which functions through all body-mind organisms will continue to produce actions, physical or mental, according to the programming in this body-mind organism, and according to the destiny of this body-mind organism.

Motivation is merely a fiction created by the individual sense of doership: the individual sense of doership that "I" am in control of "my" life; "I" am doing things and in order to do things "I" have to be motivated. What I say is—assuming that there is no motivation, will the Energy not continue to function?

HILDA *Yes.*

RAMESH   And how will the Energy continue to function? It will continue to function according to the destiny of this body-mind organism. That is really the only thing to be understood— *there is no individual doer.* Everything just happens through this body-mind organism purely as a mechanical action or reaction.

What you call "your" action—analyze it from personal experience. I repeat, from your experience in the past or the present, analyze any action, simple or difficult, that you call "your" action, and you will invariably find that it is merely a reaction of the brain to an outside event over which you have no control—the outside event being that a thought comes to you, or you see something, or hear something.

You have no control over what thought will come in your head. You have no control over what you are going to see or hear. The brain reacts to that event according to the programming over which you have had no control, and that reaction of the brain, that mechanical reaction of the brain, is what you mistakenly call "your" action.

And why do you call it your action? Because as one writer has put it, there is a mechanism in this body-mind organism which prevents this organism from seeing its mechanistic nature. You see? There is a mechanism, which is the ego, in this body-mind organism, or body-mind mechanism, which prevents this body-mind mechanism from realizing its mechanistic nature. And this I call Divine hypnosis, so that life as we know it can go on.

Life as we know it can go on only if each individual thinks of himself as a separate being, as a doer in charge of his life, wanting to do what he wants. Without that ego, without that sense of doership, personal doership, life as we know it cannot happen.

DIANNA   *Is attachment also part of doing?*

RAMESH   That attachment is part of the ego.

MAX   *She had a question whether you can perform well with detachment.*

RAMESH   See, the question is whether "you" can perform with detachment. You see? Action just happens. When that is accepted, and *only* when that is accepted, then action happens without a sense of doership.

Attachment is when you say, "'I' do it. 'I' am entitled to the rewards." You see? That is the problem. But the true understanding is that "I" really do nothing, everything is produced by the Energy, impersonal Energy, or Consciousness, functioning through a body-mind organism according to an outside event over which "I" have no control, and according to the programming over which "I" have had no control.

DIANNA   *So much energy is wasted in seeking. It seems a bit pointless.*

RAMESH   So "who" wastes energy? "Energy is wasted," as you say, because it is supposed to be wasted. *(laughter)*

I'll tell you a story—no, not a story, an incident—which I read about Swami Nityananda, the Guru of the more famous Muktananda. I mean famous or infamous, whichever you call it. *(laughter)* This Nityananda used to receive fruit as gifts from people. At the end of the day he would tell his attendant to give it to so-and-so or send it to such-and-such a temple. Once some fruit remained and by the next day it had spoiled. The attendant told Nityananda that he hadn't sent it to anybody so it had been wasted. And do you know what Nityananda said? "No, it has gone exactly where it was supposed to have gone—to the worms." *(laughter)*

ROHIT   *This identification is the ego through the hypnosis.*

RAMESH   Identification is the ego which is brought about by God's hypnosis, the Divine hypnosis, God's *lila*. And That, which has created the ego, wants in some cases to get rid of it. This is the whole problem for the apparent seeker—*only* that Power which has created the hypnosis can get rid of it.

ROHIT *And apart from this identification there is no other identification, there is no entity as such?*

RAMESH The identification *is* the entity. So the final understanding is that there never has been an entity. There never has been a seeker. There never has been a doer.

ROHIT *So then this identification creates objects?*

RAMESH Yes, sure.

ROHIT *Sir, you said "manifestation." Is it only manifestation in the sense of appearance?*

RAMESH Yes.

ROHIT *It is only apparent?*

RAMESH Yes.

ROHIT *It is not real?*

RAMESH Now look, if you go into the sun there will be a shadow. Is the shadow real or is the shadow unreal? The shadow is real because you can see it. The shadow is unreal because it has no existence of its own. For its existence it depends on your body and the sun. So the shadow is real because it can be seen. It is unreal because it has no independent existence. The manifestation is real because it can be observed. It is unreal because it has no independent existence of its own. It is merely a reflection of the Source within Itself.

ROHIT *Therefore the reflection is part of the Source?*

RAMESH When you go and stand before a mirror and there is a reflection, is that reflection *part* of you? How much? One-tenth? One-twentieth? One-fiftieth? How *much* is the reflection a part of you? It is a reflection, Rohit. Where is the question of a reflection being a *part* of anything?

JULIA   *I don't agree.*

RAMESH   You don't agree? Quite right!

JULIA   *I am entitled to my opinion.*

RAMESH   Yes you are.

JULIA   *A friend told me there's a place I could sit quietly, so I came here.*

RAMESH   So the best place to sit quietly is in your hotel room. (*laughter*)

JULIA   *I just don't agree. What can I do?*

RAMESH   *That* is the proper understanding—what can "I" do? It's absolutely correct!

Do you have any questions left?—No?
Is everything clear and transparent?—Yes?
Do you have any expectations at all?—No?
Whatever happens, does it matter?—No?
Then "you" have been annihilated—
The tiger has clamped its jaws!

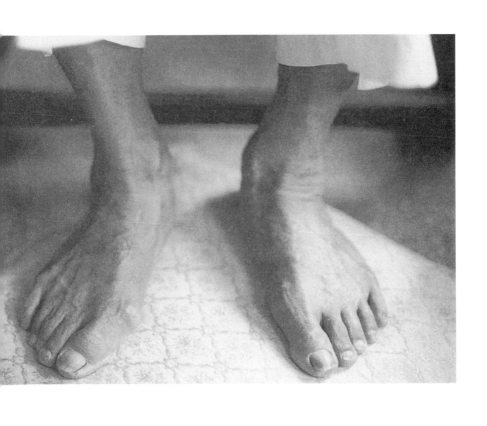

LETTERS

July 20, 1997

Dear Ramesh,

On this Guru Purnima I give to You this set of tapes from my recent series of talks in Sedona. I do this without the slightest expectation that You'll ever listen to them...I haven't listened to them either.

I present them to You as a symbol of how the Teaching is moving onward, of how the Grace of the Guru is transmitted in seemingly the most unlikely of ways by some of the most unlikely of characters, and of what chaos You have wrought by unleashing me on this unsuspecting world.

You tell me You are unsurprised by all of this and I do believe You. To me it remains an ongoing source of amazement...though since that fateful day in the L.A. airport when Your words unveiled my future as Your publisher, I have suspected that You can see far more about me than can I.

You have embraced me as a son, brought me into Your home and given me the gift that "surpasseth all understanding," and there is not enough gold or enough words to express my gratitude. I must remain content with the knowledge that You too know the bhaktic ecstasy of being consumed by the Guru and thus realize that these words, though inescapable, are inadequate and ultimately superfluous.

> The Guru and Disciple are One
> It has always been so
> It forever will be so.
>
> This, according to my
> Dear Ramesh
> Is the Final Truth.

With all my love,

Wayne

◻ ◻ ◻

Y.W.C.A.
Bombay

21-2-98

Dear Ramesh,

I wrote to you last October, from Scotland, asking if I could visit you, as I was very confused. I had read books, been to seminars, and I thought I understood Advaita. But, I still wasn't enlightened!

I have been here now for three weeks. I came with the question "What must I do?" On the very first day, the realization came that there was no me to do anything—no doer at all. I was being lived by Consciousness and the "me" had never existed! It was so clear and so simple. All "my" problems just resolved themselves. I cannot help but do exactly and only what God wills, and I am filled with joy. Life is very easy now.

Since that day, I have returned to your home nearly every day, although there is no need to do so. There is such a feeling of gratitude, and no desire to go anywhere else, while I am in India. If you wish, I will stay away from now on, but I felt I must express the gratitude I feel in my heart, for what has occurred in your presence. Thank you.

Love,

Patti

回 回 回

Mumbai 21 April 1997

Dear Ramesh,

I have written you letters before, but never gave you one, not to spoil your time, and usually and miraculously you answered all my questions the next day, until no more questions are left now.

It is my intellectual understanding and my heart-feeling that you gave me the final Teaching. After listening to your words the search is finished. Maybe it will go on for a while, as long as God wills, because of its own momentum, but I feel I need no more concepts, no more understanding than you gave me.

It may sound funny, but I do not feel great joy or overflowing love or any strong feeling of deep gratitude. I feel like a boxer after a long fight when somebody tells him he was fighting his own shadow. I always saw myself as "a seeker". Seeking enlightenment was the main motivation in this body-mind organism, and it was seen as the purpose of "my" life. It seems quite useless now!

Now you tell me that "I" cannot do anything and have never done anything, it all just happened, and I cannot do anything else than accept it because it is my own experience if "I" like it or not!

In the meantime the experience of spontaneous witnessing and the feeling of "beingness" (which are basically the same) come more often and somehow "deeper".

I want to thank you for your endless patience and your compassion to explain the same concept day after day. Although you will say it is "just happening" I feel deeply moved by this. When you asked me if I felt if I was your disciple I heard myself say yes, and it surprised me. I feel no inclination to touch your feet, or show outward signs of surrender, although I would not mind to do so.

I am not sure if I behave in an appropriate way as "your disciple," but please be sure of my deepest respect and reverence.

Your

Edgar

卍 卍 卍

19th November 97

Dearest Ramesh,

I enclose the photographs as promised. I think there are a lot of good ones. I hope you will have enough for the book.

At present I feel completely inhabited by the teaching; every day is suffused by its effects on the body-mind pulling me deeper into itself. Its sword is drawn, and it cuts again and again freeing grief and leaving only relief. Often it leaves me bereft of anything at all, looking out wordless on a landscape of joy. And then there is action and after that, silence again.

You are often in my mind, your words echoing down its empty corridors, your face filling my mind's eye, my being free of notions of volition and non-volition—for neither can inhabit this silence. How meagre are words in the face of this mystery. In this silence all is played out, and all returns again and again leaving only the enigma of its smile on blessed lips.

And yet all is outwardly as before; life and its functions carry on, business is done, the family life, the work, but ease exists within it all. It seems at the moment judgement is gone and spontaneous acceptance precludes all expectation. How can I name that, that which you rarely refer to, and yet is the bedrock from which you teach. Your words are perfect pointers to that which can only be lived. I am that gratitude and I Love you.

Writing this is in its own way a surprise—the paper was blank and now it is full. It is like consciousness at rest and consciousness in action. What is written must be written, in Beethoven's words "it must be so." How and why do not matter.

In truth I don't know what is happening and don't wish to. Let life take its course! To be at your feet in spirit is a gift above giving, a knowing above knowledge—it is grace, I thank you from the bottom of my heart.

All Love
Justin

Bombay, 12th Jan '98

Beloved Ramesh,

Gratitude, Love, Acceptance

It's GOD, who loves GOD. It's GOD, who is involved. It's only GOD, who creates expectations and disappointments. The pain is GOD's pain and the little calamities in life are GOD's entertainment. Everything is GOD. In relationships only GOD relates to Himself. Who am I to want something different from What Is.

Thank you for your presence and for your teaching. Without your teaching I would sometimes condemn myself for the way I am. But who am I to condemn a puppet of GOD?!

Ramesh, touching your feet—my Guru.

Thank you, thank you, thank you for all.

Love

Ines

P.S. The taxi just passed by Gamadia Road, and it was so clear to me that there is no "you" and "me", just THIS.

ロ ロ ロ

October 10, 1997

Dearest Ramesh,

I, a total stranger, am writing to you, because my heart is overflowing with gratitude. I've known you for a long time, but only through your books, and lately through your tapes.

I read all translated books about Ramana Maharshi in the 60's. And then I found *I Am That* by chance, if there is such a thing, because the title spoke to me. And then read whatever else I could find about Nisargadatta. And then your *Pointers* and then, I believe, your *Experience of Immortality*, and since then everything else that I could find. I've read some of your books many times, and they are all underlined and highlighted, and worn!

As I look back at a long life, I realize that I might have met you with just a bit of luck. In 1954 my husband and I were transferred to Bombay, but because of our 1 day old baby and my husband being sick, the transfer was canceled. A big part of me has always been disappointed that circumstances prevented us from experiencing India.

And then I was in Marin County, in the Bay Area, when you were, but had no idea that you were there. Obviously I'm not in charge and I have known that since 1970. In fact I have known that I'm not, since then. This body-mind will probably never meet you, because I'm too old to travel to India to thank you in person. I've tried to phone you a dozen times or more, but it's been difficult to get through. So be it. I might try again.

It's hard to put into words what you and your sense of humor, and your wisdom, and your clarity, and your loving kindness have given me and continue to give me. Your working mind and so many other gems continue to weave magic in my life. Today I was listening to a tape of yours for the first time and you mentioned Goswami's *The Self-Aware Universe* and I've just finished half of the book. It's difficult reading because Quantum theory is beyond me, but the conclusions are simple and it is such a delight to have a scientist like Goswami write like a mystic.

Why am I writing to you? Mainly because I'm grateful, and I continue to delight in your awareness. I read a page in *Net of Jewels* and am delighted all day long. I was thinking ("working mind?") that there is probably an immense amount of people like me, people who have and are benefiting from your kindness and

357

thoughtful-ness. And it occurred to me that perhaps you might like to know about people like me, who are closet mystics, not by choice but by temperament, or rather by design of Consciousness. And who love you in absentia. I see that same agape in friends, to whom I've suggested your books—I saw it in Ram Tzu who I heard speak the other day here in Santa Fe and I feel it in abundance every day. This body-mind wanted to share this joy with you.

My very best wishes for all good things for you, your wife, and your family,

With loving respect,

Cordially,

Gie

🔲 🔲 🔲

Guru Poornima 97

Dear Shri Ramesh,

You Know me
I Know you—
but there is truly no
me or you
no guru no disciple
no Ramesh no Bianca.
All there is is this *Oneness*
filled with deep love, peace, and gratitude.
So all "I" can offer "you"
is peace and the promise,
so long this bodymind organism
called Bianca is alive
I will be there for you and your lovely family.

Forever yours

🔲 🔲 🔲

Dear Ramesh,

How delighted to hear that Sharda is doing better—Please convey our love to her.

It has been years since my last letter to you—not because I don't want to 'connect' with you—but simply there is nothing to say.

As you have said so many times—"It's all so simple" and indeed it is. So free to not plan, or remember, or convince. So free, just to *be* and not concern oneself with the mind stuff of *"doings"*. So free to dwell in the silence where all thought comes from. So free to be able to act as if all *this* mattered. So free to be unafraid of the fear that the mind and limiting beliefs produce. So free to *allow* it all to arise and disappear.

So free not to have one foot in the past and one foot in the future—thereby splitting myself apart. So free to allow words to transport their own intent and meaning to others without concern for the vehicle of those words. So free to be the direct experience of it all— to come home to the true self that is always present.

So free to be revealed as life wishes me to be revealed. And my dearest Ramesh so free to love you not in form or content but in essence. For you are my true self and I am your true self. Nothing, yet everything—Here now, forever.

Love

Ray

APPENDIX I

Mumbai
20.7.97

Dear Ramesh,

Even before the writing begins, the feeling is that
there are no words worthy enough to express the deep
felt feelings which are often present through the
teaching. At a turning point in life, to be presented with
the teaching is the greatest gift, this (body mind
organism) could have received.

That this body mind is an instrument of God, and
that God uses it for what ever purpose He wants to,
touches something deep within. The thought that to be
an instrument of God and not an individual entity
touches and creates a form of ecstasy which is difficult
to describe. As said earlier words are not worthy
enough for same. With much gratitude and much love.

Indrani

▣ ▣ ▣

20 July 97

Dearest Guruji,

It is with great joy and love that I come to you on this
full moon day in July. More and more the message
becomes clear why the Guru appears in one's life.

There seems to be a tremendous but subtle change
taking place in me. The blossoming relationship to
Danielle, which is so filled with love and the presence of
the teaching together, and also an ever increasing
quietude in the mind. It is having less and less impact on
the thinking mind. Ideas and thoughts slowly losing
their momentum to create any involvement.

I feel it all connected to you. In deep gratitude and
appreciation, I say thank you.

With all my love, Tom

◨ ◨ ◨

June 2nd, 97

Ramesh, you may or may not remember me. I am the young man called Michael from Sydney, Australia. We met in February of this year in Bombay.

There was a very powerful need to write to you and inform you that our very brief meeting has had an enormous effect. How extraordinary it all is that even before I met you or encountered your teaching there occurred that fundamental cosmic insight that you told me is the I-I. I wasn't familiar with the term but I got the idea—no "me" in between. What I felt was so unusual was that on first encountering the teaching I found the most precise and essential expression of what I knew to be true.

However, before actually meeting you and subsequently being drawn joyfully ever more deeply into the teaching I was still confused. Because the intensity of the insight was not always so apparent I felt maybe it had been lost. Also, there was still a sense that it was up to me to respond to it in some way—and to be careful not to contradict it in any way. The drama of volition and the futility of trying to control my behavior gave me no peace.

However, despite the apparent chaos the conviction in the Truth of what was spontaneously revealed remained like an anchor of knowledge. It was my touchstone for what was ultimately true. Then arriving in India it wasn't long before I noticed that what had been awakened was impersonally true and had a life beyond whatever I thought of myself as an apparent individual. Beyond pride and guilt this that had begun to consume the life was choicelessly so.

The conviction is there, the passion for the truth is

there, the Love is there. Michael is not doing it, it is simply there and allowed to be there. There is no effort to control my experience, no more strategizing, volition has been seen through. Everything is indeed choiceless. Nothing could be lost. Nothing could be gained. Life is as it is—and what a joy it is.

The morning I was reading *Experiencing the Teaching*, I think the chapter was "Who, Where and When," there was something in the dialogue about the seeker being willing to accept the whole world as illusion; but when it came down to the "total annihilation of their previous selves" it was a different story. Well, a sense of the utter hilarity of the situation brought about this uncontrollable laughter. It was a real belly laugh, so mad and impersonal. The whole event was so tremendously unburdening and yet nothing was strained or forced. Afterwards there was just a great calm, a sense of weightlessness and a simple joy in Being.

I have also noticed that many apparently positive life changes have occurred and continue to occur. In fact, there is a great harmony in the life that completely amazes me and fills me with awe and gratitude. The truth of the teaching is self-evident. It is like living in a constant flow of grace. All is grace and grace is all. How miraculous it all is. Indeed, it is way beyond anything Michael could have imagined or desired.

One last thing. Recently I attended a *satsang* by a woman called Pratima who is associated with the Lucknow "Papaji." After the *satsang* we got talking and I mentioned that much of what she was saying sounded very much like what you would say. Anyway, she knew who you were and although she hadn't met you she had heard about you through friends of hers that had met you recently in Bombay. We were the last to leave that night so she offered me a lift home. On the way she said, "Would you like to listen to Ramesh?" (She had a tape of the dialogue that took place in Bombay.) It was so wonderful to hear your voice on the tape. I recognized it immediately and there was a delightful sense of being at one with the being of Ramesh.

In Loving Gratitude

Michael

◙ ◙ ◙

Dear Guruji,

I want to tell you a huge meaningful "Thank you." Perhaps you see it in the eyes and there is no need for it to be told.

I knew nothing about you before July 1996, when God brought me to you. That meeting changed a lot in my life. A feeling of freedom started to arise more and more often, even though I was working very hard all this year. Less and less involvement and the feeling of acceptance or trust was becoming stronger.

Having the feeling to express my gratefulness and as you had accepted me as your disciple last year, I thought to come to you here in Bombay, on Guru Purnima day.

So I made an effort to collect the money that was needed to come here and stay with you these 17 days.

Finally, the Truth is very simple. Live my life and do whatever I like to do, or seems right, according to the conditions I live in.

Thank you Ramesh

John

Dearest Ramesh,

My family life doesn't allow me to be with you physically during the day of Guru Purnima. So, with this letter I would like to tell you how deeply I appreciated my last visit in Bombay.

I feel so extremely lucky that God has made it possible to meet you and be at your feet. Change is happening without any doing or controlling of a "me." Life seems more and more like a game in which my role gets played easier and also (I'm surprised) with more pleasure and freedom. I realize that some chain of thoughts have disappeared, and even if some of the old well known patterns arise, they don't seem to bother me so much.

Change seems to happen by itself, just by your grace. Life just happens and I begin to perceive that the mind has nothing to do with it, it just creates artificial concepts and builds up borders where none are needed.

All this has nothing to do with "me" it is all due to the teacher—the reality coming to shake the dreamer. My gratitude is immense—it is all so unexpected and totally different from what can be imagined.

In my daily life I feel your presence, and the teaching shows itself the more the letting go of the "me" happens. Nothing to preoccupy, nothing to worry, no responsibility—just more freedom.

My wife Eveline and myself hope to be able to see you again.

All my love and gratitude

Andre

भ भ भ

20/7/97

To Dear Ramesh

I am so grateful to you for these past three weeks. It means after almost six months in India I don't leave disappointed. It seems now the individual searching has come to an end.

This poem sprang forth after our talk on the 2nd July. Once again I thank you from the deepest depth of the heart.

With much love and affection,

Phillipe

So, there is nothing to do,
No thing to achieve,
No one to do it,
Nothing to perceive.
There is or never was, Phillipe
as a being
Just Consciousness,
Who stamped at conception a
program of seeds.
It happens,
I,I
So, do what I want,
for I is God's will.
Nothing so simple as truth.
The master has spoken,
but more I assure you.
His piercing look of love has
melted the heart.

Bombay, April 8, 1997

Dearest Ramesh,

I had been seeking for a long time. Seeking God, seeking freedom. God was easy because It was just there spontaneously. Freedom was harder because first I believed that freedom from the exterior was not possible and I should try to find freedom within myself. It did help to realise all I had to do is accept the things that came to me and let myself flow with life. It was more or less working because I managed to attain quite a peaceful state and then...

Here I come and meet Ramesh and he tells me that there is no me (smile). So search to free myself from me is no longer possible because there is no one to get free from! So effective! So great! Quite so! Only Consciousness constantly expressing Itself. Now freedom is beginning to pour into this body-mind organism.

It is very, very special the way you pronounce the names of the people who come to you. It seems you get to the core of each one, awakening real understanding and watering the seeds of peace and love.

Through you Ramesh the ego may be annihilated. I alone would not have dared to do it. Thank you for your grace, kindness and love.

BIA (BEA)

▣ ▣ ▣

March 20, 1997

Dear Ramesh,

I want to express my deep gratitude for the divine gift you have given to me. While visiting with you the third week in February, I expressed to you how meeting you was a coming home for me. Well, it truly has been a remarkable coming home in so many profound ways. For the first time in my life I was hearing words for the way I have learned to live life; which is I don't live life, life unfolds through me in mysterious and wonderful ways. Although the path has been filled with hills and valleys and many sharp curves along the way, it is through this journey that I was lead to you through your loving disciple Henry Swift. Curiously enough I have never been a guru seeker or a seeker of enlightenment and soon discovered how odd I was in not knowing the names and places of sages and sacred spiritual vortexes. I became aware of this sitting in your living room and then talking with others every morning as we waited to ascend the steps to your home.

I learned about your teachings from Henry, who showered me with books, which I never read, only skimmed as my hands leafed through the books. Even while traveling in India, it was not known to me that I would actually be seeing you until the week before. It was Singapore Airlines that made sure I came home by way of Bombay and Ramesh. And home I did find sitting in your presence. I am overjoyed in discovering my place in life—which is really no place at all. For me, the mystery of life now has a song. And you, Ramesh, sing this song with every word you speak during the hours you so graciously give of yourself. I am eternally grateful for your gift.

One day, while in Bombay, I found myself sad and crying that I may never see you again. You're old and I am thousands of miles away so the chances of our paths not crossing again are great. These thoughts made me grieve as I looked at you and turned to leave your home. Then, I realized it truly does not matter if I do or do not see you again. I have seen—I have listened—I have heard your message wholeheartedly. It's not your physical beingness, but your spiritual essence that was your gift to me. Your physical beingness is the vehicle that pointed me home. Yet, impersonal Consciousness is homeless in the big scheme of things. So I have had to be homeless to find home only to discover that home really doesn't exist. It is all a projection of my mind. I find my finding home with your teachings and then letting that concept go is so symbolic with my physical life as I write this. I am physically without a home and have discovered a freedom like no other.

It was freedom I found through the songs you sang to me during my visits with you. I have been deeply touched by you and the message you carry. My life has unfolded and continues to transform in mysterious ways. On March 3, 1997 in the early dawn hours I was laying half awake and half asleep when I heard your voice. It was as if you were sitting next to me. You said, "You may not want to do it now, but when you want to do it, it will come." I know this message regards my place in the arena of work. Since returning from India I have not had the physical energy or mental energy to focus on where my place is in the work force. I am not sure what the "It" is, but I feel comfort in your words. Living with the unknown is a double edged sword of fears and wonderment, but I let them all go when they come my way.

Ramesh, I have been truly Blessed to have you in my life.

Your Beloved Disciple

Demetra

囟 囟 囟

21 February '97

Dearest Ramesh,
My Beloved Master,

This is the evening of my last but one day with you. Has anyone been visiting you for three and one-half months? I feel so lucky and graced by God, that He allowed me to stay here with you for such a long time.

What has happened during this period? It has become absolutely clear that I have come home, that I have found the Teaching which has made my life simple and transparent; that I have found the Teacher, my Guru, where spontaneous impersonal Love is happening. I was so happy that I could do a little "seva" for you.

It actually is not necessary to once again stay for so long. But if I can be of any help for you in some future time, I will be here again for long.

The search is over, and there is already a great amount of peace. It may take more time till "Wolfgang" is annihilated totally, but the understanding is there that it is God's Will whether "Wolfgang" will disappear at all or not.

May God play His Leela as He wants!

LOVE

Wolfgang

🔲 🔲 🔲

Bombay, 2.9.95

Dear Ramesh,

There is a deep gratefulness and thankfulness within me. Your gentle and patient hammering upon my "clay" shell is very much appreciated. You asked me the other day what my trip to you has brought me and then I couldn't really say.

It's difficult to put in words. It feels more like a process that is gently flowing on, rather than a big realization or sudden awareness. To me it seems as if my being was more receptive and open to the teaching and that the teaching has sunk deeper. I feel a deeper acceptance to what is in my role in life, thy will be done is sinking into the heart. I feel with this a peacefulness, like coming home . The concept of I am the doer has been very well hammered on and it seems to be full of cracks.

I appreciate also the opportunity I had to meet and learn from the lovely people around you. At the moment I can't say more. I feel as if I've been injected with a homeopathic medicine that will gradually show its effect.

Thank you for your hospitality, your gentleness, patience and directness and for giving many the opportunity to hear the truth.

In deep appreciation

Love Susanne

▣ ▣ ▣

July 97

Dear Ramesh,

Few days before I wrote you a letter. The question was "How to forget the teaching without losing it" and "flow to allow the teaching to go deeper." I didn't send it to you, because in some way I knew that "I" can't do anything and then the questions were with no sense. But something was asked without knowing "what."

An answer comes in the night, it was about the "me" and enlightenment. Even if I have listened to you "correctly," I saw that till yesterday, for me enlightenment was that "someone" lives in perfect love, eternity, understanding. Through the dream, instead, I saw that enlightenment was always there and that it is only the identification with the "me" that obstacles it to be seen and lived. This new understanding was in some way an experience that I put into words in the morning when I awoke.

I saw then that when you told it to me in India I had understood but not deeply and that now it was deeper: I really saw how a person disappears and how what remains is Consciousness, enlightenment. I think this is the answer to the question. Could it always be so easy!?

It was amazing for me to see that it was enough to ask you something and *not* send the letter and that the answer was coming anyway—"Consciousness talking."

Thanks for all, Ramesh.

I love you,

Claudia

व व व

Munich, March 17th 1997

Beloved Ramesh,

I hope you are doing very well. Since days I feel your presence so strongly and I have such a strong need to connect with You not really knowing what to say, feeling a little bit shy and also embarrassed because my English is not really good. Please forgive me my writing with the computer, but I always get feedback that my handwriting is hard to read.

I am now back from Bombay since more than two months. In the beginning I was just under shock, although I am an "old" seeker your teaching was very strong for me, though what you are saying is very familiar to me. To come in touch with my strong spiritual conditioning of how the Guru has to look, how he has to be, how I have to feel to be sure that I am on the right path, was very painful for me. Finally I realized that there is no way to know for me and that I just have to let it be like it is, that confusion is confusion and there is no need to make anything about. Slowly, slowly I have the feeling that things settle and go deeper and I enjoy so much to listen to the tapes, so much love and space I feel and I cannot understand anymore why it was so hard for me in Bombay.

My life really changed a lot, not so much the outer but the inner. There is a lot of acceptance and letting go happening, so that I sometimes have the feeling that everything is just sliding out of my hands, more and more nothingness is happening; importances, ambitions, desires just leave me and sometimes I must admit there is a feeling of panic to disappear without leaving any trace behind. My friends begin to find me strange because I am not so much interested in excitement and company, that does not mean that I live miserably, but I just do not need much to feel good and also I do not care so much to feel good or bad, there is a certain exhaustion to always run behind my feelings. For sure I do feel thankful when nice things happen but I do not feel in the position to create them.

For the first time in my adult life I spent a peaceful and good time with my mother. It just happened that I listened to your tape on my way to her and I understood very deeply that she is as she is meant to be and she does things exactly the way she has to do them and that she says the things she has to say. This was a big relief for me to realize that it is not in my hands and responsibility to change her life, even if most of the times things happen differently in my life. I had the picture that wanting to change people would be like to rush in a cinema and drag someone out of there to bring him to another cinema where another movie is shown.

It feels so good to share this with You. You are so precious to me and your presence gives me so much warmth. As this letting go of so many things is so new and fresh for me I am a little bit scared, actually to be honest I am scared to death. Would you please hold my hands and would you please tell me if something I have written feels strange. Thank you for Being.

Narayani

回 回 回

June 3, 1996

Dear Ramesh,

I feel moved to write to you, to make contact in some way. I would love to come to Bombay and see you in person, but circumstances are such at the moment that a trip like that seems unlikely.

I have been an ardent seeker for ten years, burning for truth, freedom, inner peace. I became involved with Buddhist-inspired meditation practices and thought, and spent considerable time immersed in the retreat setting. About five years ago I was drawn into Advaita through the teachings of Ramana Maharshi, Nisargadatta, Jean Klein, et al., and I traveled to Lucknow to visit Poonjaji.

I have investigated different forms of self-enquiry— whatever I have been guided towards. Living in the San Francisco Bay Area, there is no shortage of teachers, teachings, methods and practices! My thirst for inspiration was never far from being quenched.

For some time I deeply yearned for a guru, a teacher— someone who would know me and advise me along the way, someone with whom I could have a personal relationship. Although I longed for such a guide, the realization grew within me that my path seemed to be an eclectic one; that there would be different teachers at different times. I came to see that the outer teacher only points to what is already known deep within me. Each teacher, whatever the form, helped to light up the inner knowing and over time the desire for a personal teacher fell away.

A perceptible shift occurred within me as the understanding deepened. I started rereading *Consciousness Speaks*. (It was really like ingesting and digesting it!) It started to come alive in me, your words penetrating to the core, like a laser beam, perfectly aimed. For some time I have had a good cognitive and intuitive understanding of Advaita. Recently the understanding has been manifesting as direct experience—spontaneous occurrences that leave no doubt as to the nature of what I am.

A couple of weeks ago...I noticed a thought arise that had a very seductive quality to it. At that moment I saw that the experience of personal identification is like looking through a lens which has a very closed down aperture. As soon as I noticed that, the aperture flew open (no aperture, no lens) and there was just seeing but no one seeing. The knowing of no personal self seemed to be infused in awareness. It was so simple and NATURAL and there was the sense of seeing the big joke of it all. That everyone is trying to get to where they already are, and trying to become what they already are! I could see that whether the aperture appears closed or open makes no difference at all, because everything is simply as it is, whatever the view of the perceived person.

As the understanding deepens, I notice the mind reacting by playing old fear tapes, as if by creating a contracted experience in the body-mind, the ego can buy itself more time.

Last week as I was driving in my car, I was suddenly aware that another car was coming towards me, as we were simultaneously changing into the same lane. I automatically swerved the car away and saw that I honked the horn and gave the other driver an angry look. The next moment there was no trace of emotional residue and I immediately understood what you describe as vertical experience and horizontal involvement.

Your descriptions are like beacons, like flower buds embedded in the recesses of my awareness, ready to burst into bloom when mysterious forces beckon.

I write this letter to express my deepest gratitude. Though we may never meet (but I hope we do!) the light of your being shines within me.

In gratitude and appreciation,

Barbara

1.11.97

My Beloved Guru,

Coming with a lot and leaving with—nothing—or
coming with nothing and leaving with a lot doesn't
make any difference. The only thing to say is putting all
down to the feet of my Satguru and leaving with a heart
full of love for my Guru: to stay in deep connection or—
just be.

                    Love and gratefulness

                         Your Rosemarie

No word can ever describe—It.

                    ▣ ▣ ▣

30th May '96

Dear Ramesh,

        I feel so much gratitude that I am able to attend
the morning satsangs, that there is no resistance to the
teachings, and that I am in the presence of a living
example of Consciousness Speaking. Somehow your
presence and the interaction in the group does so much
to assist the understanding to go deeper. I never cease to
wonder at the *lila* unfolding, at the misconceptions
disappearing and at the fact that there are no questions
arising. During this visit, the only question I had was
about "'my' Enlightenment Experience," its validity, and
why the "me" hadn't been annihilated. Even this seems
to have been answered, or it no longer is important. I
had thought I needed to *do* something to drop the

Search, but I see that it will just continue until it isn't there any more. There is a gentle unfolding of the "I don't care if I'm Enlightened or not" attitude—not out of frustration as I'd imagined, but because the quality of daily life is such that there is really no need to be anywhere else but here. I wonder how I could house thoughts that enlightenment could give me any more than what is—what is has become O.K. Simple and effortless somehow—not that frustration and involvement don't sometimes happen, but that they are no longer seen as a problem. So I can't honestly say yet, that I don't care if I'm Enlightened in this life, or not, but if things continue like this—the need to be Enlightened may just disappear!

With much love and heartfelt thanks,

Pamela

回回回

Dearest Ramesh,

There is the deepest gratitude and love in my heart for you and the teaching. The Understanding deepens and I begin to disappear. There is only God, and Alexis is the Illusion. I have never had an original thought for all thoughts rise and fall in Consciousness. There is only God acting as Alexis, but It is the actor, the motivator and the doer. There is no me there has never been, only the illusion. It is the greatest joke and misperception to think that I can be separate from what only is. This I is a facade, a mask of who I was told I was and believed to be true, it is not. All there is is God, Consciousness, Totality, Love in all Its myriad of forms.

I love you with all my heart,

Alexis

June 6, 1997

Dear Ramesh—

You have been in my heart, in my consciousness, very much lately, and Sharda too. I am very sorry to hear the news that Sharda is so ill and in the hospital. I think of the few times I spent with her with great affection. Please give her my greetings if that is appropriate.

I am coming for Guru Purnima, if that is still possible for you and your household. But my heart is impatient to tell you certain things (which you probably already know) and that is the reason for this letter.

Recently I feel so much love for you. It seems to be on several levels. I want to thank you for being a good parent to me—though you may not know you have been— guiding me towards what was best by being clear and unwavering in what you know. Several times over the years you reached out and cupped my face with your hand. That tender gesture, pulled out of you by some need in me, reassured and soothed me. Some hurt place in me was healed by that.

The other level is the Guru, Sadguru role. I've never felt the urge to formally acknowledge that connection before, although I have always referred to you as my teacher. But those teacher/disciple roles have been tremendously important to me. I do not know if I have already told you this, so I may repeat myself here. I have written the dedication of the book to you. It will say:

> To Ramesh Balsekar—who untaught
> me all I needed not to know. In that
> emptied place peace and Presence grow.

The Presence grows. There is still a "me" who feels it almost constantly now, and need only think toward it for it to grow stronger—or rather, for my awareness of it to become more direct. And as it grows, my gratitude for you enlarges: that I met you, that I have the access to you that I have, and that consciousness created us meeting and me paying attention as I could (more focused each year) to what you are and what you say.

It has also been very important to me, Ramesh, that you have a Bhakti nature and that it expresses through you.

This all comes down to Thank You, I love You, and I am so grateful to have you for a teacher.

Love and Gratitude,

Mary

回 回 回

6-9-97

To Dear Ramesh,

> I was many miles away from you
>> When first I heard your voice.
> I fell in love then instantly
>> I really had no choice.
>
> For many years my heart had ached:
>> For what—I had not known.
> I ran. I searched. And all the time
>> The emptiness had grown.
>
> But now I come to you at last
>> And finally I find
> The peace the mind is searching for
>> Is freedom *from* the mind.

A paradox, yet simple.
      But this freedom still eludes.
I sit now with Ramesh to feel
      The peace which "he" exudes.

The wanting mind obstructs the peace
      Yet still the want is there.
At times it goes. At other times
      It feels too much to bear.

You say there's nothing "I" can do:
      Surrender is the key.
Surrender can't be brought about
      By effort from the "me."

So what to do but wait and see—
      This process can't be hastened.
The "me" must finally come to see
      It cannot be awakened.

"Do what you like!" Ramesh declares,
      "For what you like is God's will."
And though "you" cannot do it
      Be quiet, and just be still.

There is no individual.
      There is no me. No you.
But since hypnosis still remains
      May I call you my guru?

           With Much Love,

              Mandie

        ▣ ▣ ▣

Most Beloved Ramesh

I cannot say this is my last satsang with you because satsang is the very air I breathe, the very fragrance of this magnificent existence, the deliciousness of life itself.

I am going home to tend to my business and to tend to my garden. Every flower and vegetable and busy bee shall remind me of you.

From the depth of my heart I thank you for your patience (even tho you say you don't have much), your kindness, your gentleness, your compassion, your brilliance and your crystal clarity. And thank you for the final tap.

In gratitude, the I gave up.
Pranams.

Alu Seemanta

P.S.
The life of the potato follows.

The Final Tap: The Lucky Life of a Potato

This story appears as a result of another story told by a Great and Wise Sage of India. It is laid at his beautiful garden feet in gratitude to all the Saints and Sages, Gurus, Masters, Guides, Teachers, Shamans and Brother and Sister travelers encountered all along the way. They all pointed the way.

The original story was told thus: The Great and Wise Sage was visiting with a group of his devotees in California and they all went to a restaurant to take a meal. The Great and Wise Sage ordered a dish called "Clay Baked Potato" because he was curious what it would be. It was served looking like a large lump of clay accompanied with a hammer. The waiter, noting the Great Sage's confusion, gave the clay lump a thump and handed the hammer to the Sage. The Sage then proceeded to give the clay a few taps. Nothing happened. So he gave the clay a few harder taps, still nothing happened. Then he gave the clay a really good tap and the clay broke apart, revealing a fully baked and very delicious potato. The Great Sage then used the moment to point out to his devotees that this clay lump, just like the devotees, was pre-programmed to burst open with a certain amount or certain strength of taps with the hammer. And that is what he was doing; tapping on their hearts and minds so that they too could burst open and reveal the truth of their being.

So once upon a time, another potato came into being. It was planted during a very dark time in history when mad people believed that some people were inferior and therefore should not live. There was so much killing and torturing and suffering and the land was drenched with blood and pain and sadness. The father of this potato was a Nazi and the mother was a fundamentalist Christian and the potato was growing in great confusion as to what was good or bad, right or wrong. Her brother potato, growing right next to her, justified all this racism and hatred. But she had many doubts and questions and grew in an atmosphere of conflict and confusion. She didn't want to hate anybody because their skin was a different color, or they worshipped different Gods, or because they were growing in different gardens. After all, there seemed to be a very large variety of shapes and sizes and colors of potatoes and she wanted to be friends with all of them.

Her mother took her to a Sunday School where people sang songs about a Great and Wise Sage who was murdered and hung on a cross to bleed. The small potato was very afraid and she didn't want to go to Sunday School but she was forced to attend. So she joined in the singing and forgot about the words and what they meant and she lifted up her voice so that the dead man on the cross could hear her love for him.

Singing helped the little potato forget all her confusion and conflicts. One day the young potato was taken to the church to be confirmed as a Christian. She refused this act. She didn't know what it meant and she was sure she didn't belong to this group. She was criticized and ostracized and spoken badly of but she was sure she would find her way if only she could leave this family.

So she did. She spent many years looking for other potatoes with whom she could coexist. She had learned rebellion and sought other rebels. And there was much to rebel against. She joined many groups because so many were trying to change the world. The rebels were proliferating at a rate equal to the amount of things to rebel against. It was a time of more conflict.

And alas the times were changing and great healing began to take place in gardens everywhere. Potatoes were learning how to resolve conflict. A great Mahatma in India spread a message of non-violent resistance. And they were learning how to make love and not war. They were drinking magic dust and dancing to exotic rhythms and reading wonderful books about wisdom and philosophy and spirituality. It was a happy time in a happy garden and things were looking rosy.

Then one day the potato met a beautiful Yogi from a very faraway land called Sri Lanka. He was dressed in a long flowing orange robe and his hair and beard were as flowing as his robe. He invited her to come and listen to his talking and she gratefully accepted. She was opened to the teaching. She learned how to be a vegetarian, a very important lesson for a potato. She learned how to care for her body so she could grow strong and healthy. She learned how to sit still, be quiet and listen.

She learned and practised and read books and thirsted for knowledge. And she started longing for something she couldn't describe because she didn't know what it looked like, she wasn't sure what it was, she wasn't even sure it was an it. But she knew she had a yearning and a burning and no matter how much she learned and practised and read, this yearning wouldn't go away. It even seemed to increase.

Then one day the potato came to the great spiritual market place of India where people came to choose potatoes that would be taken to various ashrams, temples, monasteries and shrines and then cooked into different dishes. It was a great joy being brought to the bazaar in a bullock cart as the bullock faces were painted and they had bells on their horn tips and the driver was so kind and treated the animals with such care and gentleness. The potato was placed on display with such a wide variety of potatoes she wondered how, or even if, she would be selected.

The first shopper to come along was a great Jnani who was sitting across the way in a cigarette shop. He picked her up, gave her a little squeeze, and selected another kind of potato because he wanted to make a Masala Dosa. Then a very beautiful Saint with deer-like eyes and the smile of an angel gave her a look of pure love and bliss and walked away because she lived far away to the north on the banks of a great river and she didn't want to carry a potato on such a long journey. Then the potato heard of a Great Maharshi who had lived on a sacred mountain in the south and she started to see his picture in many places and many people told her about him and she was sure if she was patient and quiet and still he could come alive from his picture and bless her and whisper the truth in her ears.

But alas one day a very simple man in a white lungi looked at her and asked her if she would like to visit his ashram as he was brewing a stew. She didn't know what a stew was. She had heard of chips, dum alu, alu mata, alu gobi, alu chat, alu Baba and Mashed, but what was a stew? The simple man said he was painting all his potatoes red and putting malas on them that carried his picture and the stew would be a grand experiment in consciousness raising because he had created many techniques and methods to burn away the vasanas of all his vegetables. He said he would be known as the greatest chef the world would ever know.

Now our potato was very confused by all this but confusion was nothing new. Many potatoes and fruits and vegetables were going with this man so she felt she would be safe in numbers. And perhaps it was her destiny. So off she went on this grand experiment. Potatoes were arriving every day from gardens all around the world. The master chef took off his simple lungi and put on opulent robes and jewelled rings and watches. He wore a crown as if he were a king, and drove around his ashram every day in a very big car. Soon the ashram was too small to contain the enormous assortment of fruits and vegetables and cars of the master chef so they all flew off to America in a giant airplane. Our potato grew sullen and more confused. She was back where she started from and hadn't gone anywhere. The master chef assured her there was nowhere to go as there was no one going anywhere because nothing existed anyway. She was pretty sure this was right speaking but if this was true why did the master chef get in a different car every day and drive to the next village and drive back? Where was he going and what was he doing? And then one day he got in his airplane and flew away and never came back. A great city was built out of wood and stone and blood, sweat and tears. It was deep in a valley of a distant desert and now it was abandoned. The dam would break and wash away all the houses, offices, discos, boutiques, restaurants, pizzerias, go-downs, gardens and the beautiful meditation hall. The welcome center vanished. Ten years of dreaming was washed away in a minute or two. And then it evaporated as if it had never happened. Our potato felt older but not wiser. She washed off the red paint, put the man's picture away, and kept the mala. Perhaps the beads would remind her of meditation and prayer and gratitude. Perhaps they would remind her of better days in the past, or better days in the future. She had come so far to get nowhere and was more confused than ever before. But she needed a car and a place to live and new clothes and food to eat. So she concentrated on starting over. A new beginning was dawning. Out of ashes, stars are born. Out of mud, a lotus blooms. Out of chaos, an order can be created.

So she came back to the beautiful land of India. She looked for bells like the bullock wore on his horn tips and bought them. She bought small murtis of her Beloved Ganesh and Adored Hanuman. She bought an old man's begging bowl. She bought a beautiful dress from a village woman in the mountains. And she bought a blanket too. She brought them back to her native place and sold them and she came back to India to buy more. She did this manytimes and prospered and thrived. She was happy again and the old longing and yearning for something more than happiness stirred in her again. How is it a simple potato feels a desire for something unknown and indescribable? Why can't a simple potato be content being a simple potato? Perhaps she is longing to be a bigger potato, or a better potato, or a brighter potato. The yearning was such a mystery and she was searching desperately for a solution.

Then one night a very beautiful woman came to her village to speak. She was carrying a picture of the Great Maharshi and she also carried a picture of a disciple of this Great Maharshi. The woman spoke of freedom and liberation and consciousness. The words pointed to the termination of confusion and searching for the unknowable. Our potato wanted to end her desires and concepts and illusions and the nagging sense of separation. So once again she cast herself upon the river of words and poetry and came once more in search of a magician, a sage, a guru, a jnani. She was ready and willing to surrender if only someone could show her how to do it. She was full of hope and expectations and determination. She was earnest too. She could go the distance. She was reaching the end of her rope. It had to be now or never.

She came to the feet of Papaji. Please, please, Papaji, help me to freedom. Lift the veil. Give me light. Mash me, mash me, the potato begged. Finish me off, she implored. End my dreaming and yearning. Do it for me, do it for me. I am now helpless and hopeless. Papaji was kind and funny and spoke the truth. He loved singing and dancing and making jokes. She knew the potato who was able to laugh at herself would never cease to be amused. But she was still thirsty and she was exhausted. So much trying and efforting and yearning. So much searching and finding and losing again. Where will it all end? What will happen to me? Why can't I just rest?

She sat down by the river and cried. She wanted to drown and be carried to the sea. Her tears moistened the mud around her and the earth wrapped her in a blanket of clay. She felt warm and safe and secure. She fell asleep and dreamed she was on a train bound for Mumbai. It rocked her and lulled her and carried her to her date with destiny. When she awoke she was sitting in a room of immense peace and the air was fresh and cool. There was a picture of the Great Maharshi and the Great Maharaj who gave her a squeeze in the market place so long ago when she first came to her Beloved India home. There was a beautiful man sitting in a chair next to her and he was holding a hammer. She looked into his wondrous eyes and he tapped her gently with the hammer and her clay cover cracked apart. All the dreams she had ever known fell away. She heard the singing of God and it was her own voice singing the love song. She felt the joy of love surrounding and permeating the entire universe. She saw the beauty and perfection of the whole of creation.

A spontaneous bowing brought the potato to the feet

of her Beloved Master Ramesh and she hasn't been seen
again. She was absorbed back into the garden from
whence all comes, and into which all returns. God was
rooting for her all the time.

Om Shree Sat Guru Ki Jai Ho

She searched and looked everywhere
She grew tired and gave up
Then she was found.

🖾 🖾 🖾

When Seeking Ends

I can no longer read the Teachings
or visit those awakened on the path
who sit amidst flowers and incense
and eager seekers waiting for morsels
of Enlightenment food.

I can no longer sit on my black cushion
waiting for the moment to appear
when the big bang will occur
and blow this world of work and life
into the heavens of bliss.

I can no longer search for what is missing
nor can I say that I have found it.
I listen to the furnace blowing at dawn
and watch a feather dance before its music.

I work and eat and sleep and simply live my life.
I no longer wonder if I should dye my hair
or give up eating meat
or lose ten pounds before summer.
If I do, I do, and if I don't, I don't,
and who is there to care?

The sound of the garbage truck
chewing up the remains of my week
offers just as much stimulation to my soul
as a church bell or the song of a bird's melody
lilting from the distant hill.

My candles of devotion sit unlit
upon the altar to the gods,
the bell of mindfulness unrung
upon its cushion,
the incense resting in a drawer.

What has become of the one
who searched and chanted and read and prayed
and hoped for enlightenment?
She still laughs with her family,
Sips champagne with friends,
and sings in the shower.

What is life when the seeking ends?
Just what it is, nothing more or less—
an ordinary person doing ordinary things.
Not wishing to be more or less,
content to simply be herself.

Dorothy Hunt
San Francisco
10 May 1997

ADVAITA IN THE BHAGAVAD GITA

Chapter II/28

अव्यक्तादीनि भूतानि व्यक्तमध्यानि भारत ।
अव्यक्तनिधनान्येव तत्र का परिदेवना ॥

Beings are not manifest to human senses before birth. During the period between birth and death they are manifest. They again return to the unmanifest at death. In this natural process, what is there to grieve over?

囗

Chapter II/30

देही नित्यमवध्योऽयं देहे सर्वस्य भारत ।
तस्मात्सर्वाणि भूतानि न त्वं शोचितुमर्हसि ॥

The indwelling Consciousness within all living body-mind organisms is forever invulnerable, indestructible. Therefore there is really no need to mourn for anyone.

Chapter III/4

न कर्मणामनारम्भात् नैष्कर्म्यं पुरुषोऽश्नुते ।
न च संन्यसनादेव सिद्धिं समधिगच्छति ॥

Abstaining from action is not the way to gain freedom from activity, nor can one achieve perfection by merely ceasing to act.

॥

Chapter III/5

न हि कश्चित्क्षणमपि जातु तिष्ठत्यकर्मकृत् ।
कार्यते ह्यवश: कर्म सर्व: प्रकृतिजैर्गुणै: ॥

Actually, not even for a moment can one remain free of activity (including mental activity, both conscious and sub-conscious). The energy within the body-mind organism will automatically produce actions according to the natural characteristics of the organism.

॥

Chapter III/27, 28

प्रकृते: क्रियमाणानि गुणै: कर्माणि सर्वश: ।
अहङ्कारविमूढात्मा कर्ताहमिति मन्यते ॥
तत्त्ववित्तु महाबाहो गुणकर्मविभागयो: ।
गुणा गुणेषु वर्तन्त इति मत्वा न सज्जते ॥

It is the energy within the body-mind organism that produces actions according to the natural characteristics of the organism. Man, deluded by his egoism, thinks: "I am the doer."

But the one who has true insight into the working of the energy within the organism does not get involved in the actions which are the result of the senses attaching themselves to their respective objects.

◫

Chapter III/33, 34

सदृशं चेष्टते स्वस्या: प्रकृतेर्ज्ञानवानपि ।
प्रकृतिं यान्ति भूतानि निग्रह: किं करिष्यति ॥

इन्द्रियस्येन्द्रियस्यार्थे रागद्वेषौ व्यवस्थितौ ।
तयोर्न वशमागच्छेत् तौ ह्यस्य परिपन्थिनौ ॥

Even for a wise man, the energy within the body-mind organism produces actions according to his own natural characteristics. All living creatures follow their natural tendencies. What is the use of any external restraint?

The attraction and aversion of the senses for their respective objects are natural, but involvement with them should be avoided — that is the obstruction.

◫

Chapter V/15

नादत्ते कस्यचित्पापं न चैव सुकृतं विभु: ।
अज्ञानेनावृतं ज्ञानं तेन मुह्यन्ति जन्तव: ॥

The Omnipresent Lord does not take note of the merit or demerit of anyone. What Is is always perfect. The light of the *Atman* is covered by the darkness of delusion, and that is how the human beings are deluded.

Chapter VIII/20, 21

परस्तस्मात्तुभावोऽन्य: अव्यक्तोऽव्यक्तात्सनातन: ।
य: स सर्वेषु भूतेषु नश्यत्सु न विनश्यति ॥

अव्यक्तोऽक्षर इत्युक्त: तमाहु: परमां गतिम् ।
यं प्राप्य न निवर्तन्ते तद्धाम परमं मम ॥

Behind the manifest and the unmanifest (which concerns phenomenality) there is another Noumenal Awareness which is eternal and changeless — this is not dissolved in the general cosmic dissolution. This imperishable Unmanifest Awareness is said to be the highest state of Being. Those who reach It do not return.

Chapter X/20

अहमात्मा गुडाकेश सर्वभूताशयस्थित: ।
अहमादिश्च मध्यं च भूतानामन्त एव च ॥

I am the *Atman* that dwells in the heart of every mortal creature: I am the beginning, I am the lifespan, and I am the end of all beings.

Chapter XVIII/20

सर्वभूतेषु येनैकं भावमव्ययमीक्षते ।
अविभक्तं विभक्तेषु तज्ज्ञानं विद्धि सात्त्विकम् ॥

That knowledge is *sattvika* (pure) by which the one Imperishable Being, the deathless, is seen in all existences in the midst of all the diversity.

WHAT DID LORD KRISHNA TELL ARJUNA?

Chapter II/30

देही नित्यमवध्योऽयं देहे सर्वस्य भारत ।
तस्मात्सर्वाणि भूतानि न त्वं शोचितुमर्हसि ॥

The indwelling Consciousness within all living body-mind organisms is forever invulnerable, indestructible. Therefore there is really no need to mourn for anyone.

回

Chapter II/47

कर्मण्येवाधिकारस्ते मा फलेषु कदाचन ।
मा कर्मफलहेतुर्भूः मा ते सङ्गोऽस्त्वकर्मणि ॥

All you can do is to work for the sake of the work. You have no right to the fruits of the work (the consequences of your actions are not in your control). But do not let this fact make you lean towards inaction.

回

Chapter XI/32, 33

कालोऽस्मि लोकक्षयकृत्प्रवृद्धः
लोकान् समाहर्तुमिह प्रवृत्त: ।
ऋतेऽपि त्वां न भविष्यन्ति सर्वे
येऽवस्थिता: प्रत्यनीकेषु योधा: ॥

तस्मात्त्वमुत्तिष्ठ यशो लभस्व
जित्वा शत्रून् भुङ्क्ष्व राज्यं समृद्धम् ।
मयैवैते निहता: पूर्वमेव
निमित्तमात्रं भव सव्यसाचिन् ॥

I am come as Time, the ultimate eroder of the people, ready

for the hour that ripens to their end. The warriors, arrayed in hostile armies facing each other, shall not live, whether you strike or stay your hand.

Therefore, arise and fight. Win kingdom, wealth, and glory. Merely be the apparent instrument for their end — they have already been slain by Me, O ambidextrous bowman.

⌘

Chapter XVIII/11

न हि देहभृता शक्यं त्यक्तुं कर्माण्यशेषत: ।
यस्तु कर्मफलत्यागी स त्यागीत्यभिधीयते ॥

It is indeed impossible for an embodied being to renounce action entirely, but he who has renounced the fruits of action is said to be truly non-attached.

⌘

Chapter XVIII/17

यस्य नाहंकृतो भाव: बुद्धिर्यस्य न लिप्यते ।
हत्वाऽपि स इमाँल्लोकान् न हन्ति न निबध्यते ॥

No act will create any bondage for him whose mind is free of attachment and whose understanding is untainted by the ego. Although he slays these thousands, he does not kill, nor is he bound by the action.

⌘

Chapter XVIII/47

श्रेयान्स्वधर्मो विगुण: परधर्मात्स्वनुष्ठितात् ।
स्वभावनियतं कर्म कुर्वन्नाप्नोति किल्बिषम् ॥

Better is one's own *dharma* though imperfect, than the *dharma* of another better performed. He who does the duty ordained by his own nature incurs no sin.

◙

Chapter XVIII/59, 60, 61

यदहङ्कारमाश्रित्य न योत्स्य इति मन्यसे ।
मिथ्यैष व्यवसायस्ते प्रकृतिस्त्वां नियोक्ष्यति ॥

स्वभावजेन कौन्तेय निबद्धः स्वेन कर्मणा ।
कर्तुंनिच्छसि यन्मोहात् करिष्यस्यवशोऽपि तत् ॥

ईश्वरः सर्वभूतानां हृद्देशेऽर्जुन तिष्ठति ।
भ्रामयन्सर्वभूतानि यन्त्रारूढानि मायया ॥

If, in your vanity, you decide not to fight, your resolve would be in vain: your own nature will drive you to the act.

Bound by your own *karma* born of your nature, you will do that very thing which your ignorance seeks to avoid.

The Lord lives in the heart of every creature, and by His *maya* He causes all beings to wander through life as though mounted on a machine.

PROGRESS—WHO CARES?!

Every month the disciple faithfully sent his Master an account of his progress.

In the first month he wrote: "I feel an expansion of Consciousness and experience my oneness with the universe." The Master glanced at the note and threw it away.

The following month, this is what he had to say: "I have finally discovered that the Divine is present in all things." The Master seemed disappointed.

The third month the disciple's words enthusiastically exclaimed: "The mystery of the One and the many has been revealed to my wondering gaze." The Master shook his head and again threw the letter away.

The next letter said: "No one is born, no one lives, and no one dies, for the ego-self is not." The Master threw his hands up in utter despair.

After that a month passed by, then two, then five months— and finally a whole year without another letter. The Master thought it was time to remind his disciple of his duty to keep him informed of his spiritual progress.

Then the disciple wrote back: "Who cares?"

When the Master read those words a look of great satisfaction spread over his face.

GLOSSARY OF CONCEPTS

The created object *cannot*
possibly *know* the Creator Subjectivity

abhanga
> Spontaneous outpouring of a keen devotee revealing the very core of Advaita; for centuries *abhanga*s have served as succinct and direct pointers to Consciousness; often put to music and sung as a *bhajan*; *see Advaita, bhajan*

Adi Shankara
> *see* Shankara

Advaita
> Nonduality; all there is is Consciousness, and all phenomenal existence is illusion, *maya*; the most important branch of Vedanta philosophy; *see* Consciousness, *maya*, Vedanta

ahankara
> Ego, *see* ego

Ananda
> Peace; *see Sat-Chit-Ananda*

Aum

> The sound of these three letters, now generally considered a word, denotes Consciousness, Brahman; believed to be the most sacred mantra; the letter *A* stands for the world of the senses, the letter *U* stands for the subconscious mind, and *M* stands for *Prajna*, the state beyond mind; usually written as Om; *see* mantra

avatar

> Incarnation; descent of a deity (i.e., Vishnu descending as Rama and Krishna)

awakening

> The *spontaneous impersonal event* at the end of the process of seeking in which there is the total, apperceived, intuited understanding *in the heart* that there is no doer and never was a doer or seeker; the ego, the "me," completely disappears; *see* doer, ego, seeker, seeking

Bhagavad Gita

> Literally the song of God; part of the *Mahabharata* in which a dialogue takes place between Lord Krishna and the warrior Arjuna just prior to the decisive battle; *see* Appendix II

bhajan

> Devotional practice, prayer; generally used to mean devotional words set to music and sung as a form of worship

bhakta

> Devotee; often used to refer to a seeker following the path of *bhakti*, as distinguished from that of *jnana*; *see jnana*, seeker

bhakti
> Devotion; adoration as a path to awakening; *see* awakening, *bhakta*, seeking

bhoga, (bhogi)
> Experience(er) of sensual reactions

body-mind organism
> Mechanism through which life and living happen; part of the totality of manifestation of Consciousness in which the ego may ignorantly assume the role of apparent doership and hence separateness; the body-mind organism, *not* the ego, has a destiny; *see* destiny, ego, manifestation

Brahma
> One of the gods of the Hindu trinity, *see* trinity

brahmachari (m), *brahmacharini* (f)
> One who leads the life of *brahmacharya*

brahmacharya
> Living in Brahman, enquiry into Brahman, or Consciousness; traditionally, although mistakenly, it has come to mean celibacy

Brahman
> Consciousness, Source, Totality, the Absolute; the ultimate Reality in Hinduism; *see* Consciousness

brain
> In the body-mind organism the mechanism which spontaneously reacts according to its conditioning, without judgment of thoughts received and input of the senses (it is the ego, thinking mind, which becomes involved and judges the unpremeditated reactions of the

brain); *see* body-mind organism, conditioning, ego, thinking mind, thought

Chit

Consciousness; *see Sat-Chit-Ananda*

concept

Anything that can be agreed to or disagreed with; *any* thought, idea, experience, name, thing, entity, or no-thing

conditioning

All the experiences of a body-mind organism, over which it has no control, of its entire environment (parents, family, society, culture, geography, school, etc.) which form the patterns and responses of the brain; *see* body-mind organism, brain, ego, programming

Consciousness

All there is is Consciousness; the basic perennial principle behind all religions and spiritual paths before corruption by interpretations and formal rituals; It has no aspects or qualities; It *cannot* be conceptualized but is given a name so It can be indicated or pointed to; It is *referred* to by many names—God, I-I, Noumenon, Potential, *Prajna*, Reality, Self, Source, Subjectivity, Tao, That, Totality, Truth, Unicity, etc.; unmanifested It is referred to as being "at rest" or transcendent, manifested It is referred to as being "in action" or immanent; Consciousness not aware of Itself becomes aware of Itself as I Am; *see* concept, I Am

consciousness

Not capitalized it indicates the illusion of a

personal identity with a "consciousness" of doership that is separate and fragmented from Consciousness, but there is *no* "doer," *no* "me"—Consciousness is all there is; *see* Consciousness, ego, I Am

Consciousness-at-rest

Consciousness unmanifested, transcendent; Potential unpotentialized; *see* Consciousness

Consciousness-in-action

Consciousness manifest, immanent; Consciousness reflected within Itself as the totality of manifestation; *see* Consciousness

darshan

Seeing, meeting

death

Death is *only* of the body-mind organism and ego, the sense of a separate and personal identity; at death the energies of Consciousness-in-action which had assumed personal identity in life as a body-mind organism return to the pool of Consciousness; *see* ego, body-mind organism, pool of Consciousness

deep sleep

The state in which the I Am is present without any aspect of manifestation, which also means no personal or ego identity; temporary death; *see* ego, I Am

destiny

All there is is Consciousness; there is no doer and no free will—all is the impersonal functioning of Consciousness, or God's will; life is a movie which is produced, written, casted, directed, acted, and watched by Consciousness on the screen of Consciousness; the body-mind organism has a destiny, the ego—which does not exist—has no destiny; the key, which is not in the control of the *apparent* individual, is the complete acceptance of What Is; decisions have to be   made, so live life *as if* there is free will, making   decisions with your standards of ethics, morality, and responsibility, and whatever the decision is will be God's will; *see* Consciousness, What Is

dharma

The programming of the body-mind organism; inherent property; natural characteristic; in Hinduism the firm code of conduct and duty of the individual; *see* body-mind organism, programming

dhyana

Meditation; *see* meditation

Divine hypnosis

Mechanism through which Consciousness expresses a sense of personal doership in a body-mind organism; *see maya*

doer, doership

For the impersonal functioning of Consciousness, or God, through manifestation or life as we know it to happen, the basis of life is the sense of personal doership; Divine hypnosis creating the illusory ego's belief that it has free will; the sense of doership is unhappiness; spiritual seeking is the process of getting rid of personal doership; *see* ego, free will

dualism

> The ego involved in making an apparent choice between interconnected opposites; *see* ego, doer, duality, free will, involvement

duality

> Pairs of interconnected opposites, neither of which can exist without the other (i.e., beauty-ugliness, positive-negative, male-female, etc.); one of the mechanisms by which the totality of manifestation operates; when the ego becomes involved, duality becomes dualism; *see* ego, dualism

education

> Accumulation of concepts; learned ignorance; *see* concept

ego

> The sense of personal doership; Consciousness-in-action assuming identification as a "doer," thinking mind, with a separate name and form; the user of the word ego must know that the primary meaning is the mistaken belief of being a "doer" because a sage continues to have name and form, a body-mind organism, but *without* a sense of being a "doer"; *see* Consciousness-in-action, body-mind organism, Divine hypnosis, thinking mind

enlightenment

> *see* awakening

free will

> All there is is Consciousness, there is absolutely no free will; everything is God's will, the impersonal functioning of Consciousness,

manifesting as destiny, individual or otherwise; decisions have to be made, so one makes them *as if* there is free will—the result is God's will; *see* destiny

Gayatri

A verse from the Vedas used as a mantra

God

Consciousness, Source; *not* an entity; *not* personal; *see* Consciousness

grace

The totality of manifestation is grace; the prevalent misunderstanding is the ego's involvement in dualism and thus not accepting What Is as grace; the ego refers to what is difficult as God's will and what is special and beneficial as God's grace; *see* dualism, involvement, What Is

gunas

Attributes, qualities; the three primary attributes of the totality of manifestation are *sattva, rajas,* and *tamas*; *see* each attribute

Guru

Spiritual preceptor; the living expression of the Sadguru that has no sense of personal doership and through which a seeker may experience his True Nature; *see Sadguru*

Guru Purnima

The full moon (*purnima*) day in July-August on which the disciple renews his or her dedication to the Guru

heart

> The understanding becomes complete when it is
> spontaneously intuited in the heart; in the heart
> there is intuited understand *ing*, there is no "me"
> to understand anything; *see* intellect

horizontal

> The involvement of the thinking mind; *see*
> involvement, thinking mind

I Am

> The initial manifestation of impersonal
> Consciousness in the awareness I Am, other than
> which nothing exists; the *only* Truth since It
> cannot be disputed—thus It is not a concept
> unless conceived by subsequent thinking based
> on the feeling of a personal identity; the interval
> between two thoughts, between two
> expectations; *see* Consciousness, I-I

I-I

> Ramana Maharshi's reference to Consciousness,
> Source, Totality; I-I and I Am are not two, I-I
> becomes I Am in manifestation, I-I becomes
> aware of Itself as I Am

intellect

> The understanding usually begins in the thinking
> mind—for the understanding to be complete and
> final it must be intuited in the heart; a well
> developed and concentrated intellect is necessary
> for the process of seeking on the path of *jnana*
> and dealing competently with the material; *see*
> heart, thinking mind

involvement

> The nonacceptance of What Is; the cause of

suffering; the ego's mistaken belief that it has free
will and consequently is in a continuous state of
judging, deciding, and beingconcerned about
consequences; this concept correlates to the
concept of attachment in Buddhism; *see* ego, free
will, thinking mind, What Is

Ishwara

In Hinduism, Consciousness-in-action deified as
in charge of the Universe

Janaka

King Janaka is the "superbly ripe disciple" of his
Guru, Ashtavakra, in the *Ashtavakra Gita*
translated by Ramesh in his book *A Duet of One*

japa

Repetition of the name or names of God, literally
"muttering"; when *japa* becomes natural it is
realization; constant, it repels all other thoughts;
vocal, it becomes mental and is the same as
meditation

jiva

The individual, identified consciousness; *see* ego

jnana

Knowledge, especially higher knowledge;
knowledge as a path to awakening; *jnana* and
bhakti are not mutually exclusive, however,
bhakti becomes *jnana* prior to awakening; *see*
awakening, *bhakti*, *jnani*

Jnaneshwar

A great Indian sage who was fundamentally a
jnani, but from the *abhanga*s he wrote it can be
seen that he symbolizes within himself a unity

not only of *jnana* and *bhakti* but also yoga in its various aspects; the Jnaneshwar classic *Anubhavamrita*, or *Amritanubhava*, is translated by Ramesh in his book *Experience of Immortality*

jnani

One who knows; currently used to refer to a seeker following the path of *jnana* as distinguished from that of *bhakti*; *see bhakti*, *jnana*, seeker

karma

Consciousness manifesting as *action* which is the principle of cause and effect; one of the fundamental mechanisms of the totality of manifestation for life to happen as we know it; a cause, action, leads to an effect which in turn becomes a cause leading to another effect, and so on

kriya

Spontaneous movement(s) or reaction(s) of the body-mind organism caused by movement of the *kundalini* energy

kundalini

In Hinduism, an aspect of the feminine creative energy symbolized as a serpent lying dormant at the base of the spine until aroused; a potentially dangerous practice; the arising of the *kundalini* is *not* a prerequisite for enlightenment; *see* awakening

liberation

see awakening

lila

In Hinduism, the play or game of God; the

totality of manifestation looked upon as the
Divine play; *see* destiny, manifestation

maha

Great; usually a prefix to a noun making it great
or superior

Maheshwara

see Shiva

manifestation

Consciousness unmanifest *reflected* within Itself
as the totality of What Is; *see* Consciousness

mantra

Instrument of thought; hymn, incantation; ideal
or sacred sounds of certain syllables or words,
the repetition of which may lead to material or
spiritual benefits—if it is the destiny of the body-
mind organism repeating them

maya

Illusion; delusion; the veiling power which
conceals Consciousness unmanifest from
Consciousness *reflected* within Itself as the
totality of manifestation; the false identification
with the body-mind organism as a separate
individual and doership; *see* Consciousness

"me"

see ego

meditation

When meditation happens you know it because
there is a feeling of emptiness; some body-mind
organisms are not programmed to meditate so
there is no question of right or wrong about

meditating; not a must but if it happens it is good; involves a doer if there is effort in meditation; for the beginner, meditate on the fact that "you" have no free will; that meditation is true meditation in which there is no doer of the meditation; *see* doer, free will

mind

Consciousness-in-action as a *functioning* of thoughts received and subsequent thinking (the *physical mechanism* for receiving and spontaneously reacting to thought is the brain); the *processing* of thoughts received takes place in either of the two aspects of mind—working mind or thinking mind—in the latter the ego is involved; the destruction of the thinking mind, which can only be God's will, is the intuited understanding in the heart that there is no doer, no separation from Consciousness, which is the *essence* of mind; *see* brain, thinking mind, thought, working mind

moksha

Liberation; *see* awakening

nirguna

Without form or attributes

Nisargadatta Maharaj

Ramesh's final Guru; his teachings can be found in Ramesh's book *Pointers from Nisargadatta Maharaj*

Noumenon

Consciousness unmanifest; there is no plural for this word; *see* Consciousness

Now
> *see* What Is

OM
> *see* AUM

play
> *see lila*

pool of Consciousness
> A concept referring to energies which may or may not have been manifested as matter or non-matter in general or specifically as a body-mind organism; at the dissolution of matter or the death of a body-mind organism the energies return to the pool of Consciousness and may or may not again appear manifested; *see* rebirth

pradakshina
> Devotional circumambulation of a sacred object or holy place

Prajna
> Unselfconscious Knowledge; *see* Consciousness

predestination
> *see* destiny

Present Moment
> *see* What Is

programming
> Genes plus conditioning, over which the body mind organism has no control, determines the way the brain reacts to all input; the mechanism by which the destiny of a body-mind organism is carried out; *see* body-mind organism, brain,

conditioning, destiny, ego

puja
Ceremonial or ritual worship

rajas
Motivity, activity, energy; one of the three *gunas*; refers to the activating aspect of manifestation without which the other constituents could not manifest their inherent qualities; *see gunas*

Ramakrishna
The great Bengali *bhakta* sage who lived at Dakshineshwar in Calcutta in the nineteenth century

Ramana Maharshi
The great *jnani* sage of Arunachala who lived all of his adult life in Tiruvannamalai, Tamil Nadu; Ramesh said in *satsang*, "To me, in phenomenality, there is nothing higher than Ramana Maharshi."

realization
see awakening

rebirth
There is no individual so there can be no rebirth of that which does not exist; there are past births and from them, at the deaths of the body-mind organisms, the functioning energies return to the pool of Consciousness to perhaps again, in another combination, pass into a future body mind organism—thus there are apparent past-life memories of some body-mind organisms of prior births; eventually, energies of such refinement may come together in a body-mind

organism in which the process of seeking ends in awakening; *see* awakening, body-mind organism, ego, pool of Consciousness

rishi

Ancient sage

Sadguru

The Guru within you—-the Self, or Consciousness

sadhaka

A seeker who practices *sadhana*; *see sadhana*

sadhana

Spiritual practice or practices involving a doer (seeker) which *may* precede the goal of awakening; the goal may or may not happen depending upon the destiny of the seeker; if *sadhana* happens, let it happen; traditional *sadhana*s are meditation, yoga, and selfless service (*seva*); a body-mind organism may be programmed to do one type of *sadhana* and not another

sage

A body-mind organism in which awakening has happened; a sage may be regarded as saintly, but a saint is not necessarily a sage; *see* awakening

saguna

With form and attributes

saint

see sage

samadhi

A state of meditation beyond mind; absorption in the Self

Sat

Existence, Being; *see Sat-Chit-Ananda*

Sat-Chit-Ananda

Being-Consciousness-Peace; in Hinduism the three attributes of "attributeless" Brahman, or the Source; *see* Consciousness

satsang

Association with one who is always in the Beingness

sattva

Being, existence, reality; one of the three *gunas*; it stands for equilibrium and manifests itself as light; *see gunas*

seeker

The ego mistakenly believing it is a doer and separate and thus a seeker seeking something sought; *see* ego, seeking

seeking

One of the innumerable and *impersonal* processes of Consciousness manifest; "from the first moment a baby seeks its mother's breast intuitively, life is nothing but seeking," regardless of what it is for; that there is no doer and no thing done and thus no seeker and no thing sought is the final understanding prior to the end of the process of seeking; *see* awakening, ego

Self-realization

see awakening

seva

Selfless service, service without *any* expectations

417

shakti

Power, energy, capacity; in the totality of manifestation of Consciousness, or Shiva, within Itself, *shakti* is portrayed as the female energy of duality, Shiva-Shakti; she is deified, often with the name of Parvati, as the wife of Shiva; *see* Shiva

Shankara

Also called Adi Shankara and Shankaracharya; an eighth century philosopher and reformer of Hinduism who established the school of unqualified *Advaita Vedanta*

Shiva

Consciousness unmanifest; when manifest he is portrayed as the male energy of duality, Shiva-Shakti; he is deified as the husband of Shakti; one of the gods of the Hindu trinity; *see shakti*, trinity

siddha

Refers to a perfected sage (but with the understanding that *siddhi*s are not necessary or prerequisite to awakening); often used to refer to one who has psychic powers

siddhi

The final "accomplishment" or awakening; has come to mean psychic power (which is often an obstruction to awakening because the ego becomes involved)

silence

Noninvolvement or nonidentification with thought(s); a sage is always in silence; silence between the Guru and the disciple is heart-to-heart speech; *see* involvement, sage

Source

    see Consciousness

tamas

    Darkness, inertia, passivity, restraint; one of the three *gunas*; *see gunas*

Tao

    see Consciousness

thinking

    The functioning of thoughts received by the brain which can either be uninvolved as the working mind or involved as the thinking mind; *see* brain, thinking mind, thought, working mind

thinking mind

    The horizontal aspect of mind in which the ego is involved with thought and concerned with *future consequences* for itself—i.e. fear, hope, worry, or anxiety for whether an action will be beneficial or harmful, or for what others may think; not accepting What Is; *see* horizontal, thought, What Is, working mind

thought

    Thought does not originate in the body-mind organism, it comes from outside and a split-second later the brain spontaneously reacts according to its conditioning; a thought is an input which brings about an output which leads to causation; both thought and the reaction(s) of the brain are vertical, in the Present Moment—if the ego gets involved (the thinking mind) then there is horizontal involvement in time; *see* brain,

Present Moment, thinking mind, working mind

Tiruvannamalai
> The town in the state of Tamil Nadu in southeast India where Ramana Maharshi spent his entire adult life at the foot of the holy hill Arunachala

Totality
> *see* Consciousness

trinity
> The Hindu trinity is Brahma the creator, Vishnu the preserver, and Shiva—or Maheshwara—the destroyer

Tukaram
> One of India's greatest *bhakta* sages who, following awakening, wrote devotionally as a pure *jnani*; wrote *abhanga*s which have been set to music and are sung as *bhajans*

understanding, total
> The spontaneous, intuited understanding in the heart that there is no doer; *see* awakening, doer

Unicity
> *see* Consciousness

Upanishads
> Concerned with pure knowledge, these ancient philosophical texts are much later than the original Vedas; the texts from which all Vedanta philosophy originates; *see* Vedanta, Vedas

Vedanta
> Literally, the end of the Vedas, the culmination of knowledge; philosophy based upon the Upanishads; Advaita Vedanta is the most well-

known branch of Vedanta; *see* Advaita,
Upanishads

Vedas

The most ancient of the sacred literature of
Hinduism; they start out as mythical and ritual
texts and culminate in the pure philosophy of
Vedanta; *see* Vedanta

vertical

Being in the Present Moment, or What Is; cuts off
horizontal involvement; only the working mind
is functioning; *see* horizontal, What Is, working
mind

Vishnu

One of the gods of the Hindu trinity; *see* trinity

What Is

Outside of space-time It neither is nor is not—
past, present, and future and all of their
apparent contents are *spontaneously* happening
simultaneously; this state/non-state is also
referred to as Present Moment and Here and
Now; cannot be "experienced" by the ego

working mind

The vertical aspect of mind which is *only* in the
Present Moment—the ego is *not* involved with
concerns for the future; the working mind uses
judgment and consideration of consequence to
do the best it can with the knowledge it has
for a task, but the judging and consideration of
consequence are *in the Present Moment*, or What
Is, and there is *no* personal concern for *future*
consequences; while the working mind is
functioning there is little or no sense of time and
place unless such consideration is part of the task
at hand; in the sage there is *only* the working
mind, there is *no* thinking mind; *see* thinking
mind, vertical, What Is

INDEX

Also By Ramesh S. Balsekar

A Duet of One
Here Ramesh uses the *Ashtavakra Gita* as a vehicle for an illuminating look at the nature of duality and dualism
Softcover — 224 Pages $16.00

Experiencing The Teaching
In this book many facets of Advaita (non-duality) are examined and illuminated through a series of 24 dialogues. Ramesh's ability to cut through to the simple heart of complex ideas is a joy to experience.
Softcover — 142 Pages $11.95

The Final Truth
A comprehensive and powerful look at Advaita from the arising of I AM to the final dissolution into identification as Pure Consciousness.
Softcover — 240 Pages $16.00

Your Head In The Tiger's Mouth
A superb overview of the Teaching. Transcribed portions of talks Ramesh gave in his home in Bombay during 1996 and 1997.
Softcover — 472 Pages $24.00

A Net Of Jewels
A handsome gift volume of jewels of Advaita, selections from Ramesh's writings presented in the format of twice daily meditations.
Hardcover — 384 Pages $25.00

Consciousness Speaks
Ramesh's most accessible and easy to understand book. Recommended both for the newcomer to Advaita and the more knowledgeable student of the subject.
Softcover — 392 Pages $19.00

Ripples
A brief and concise introduction to Ramesh's Teaching. Perfect to give to friends.
Softcover — 44 Pages $6.00

If unavailable at your bookstore, these titles may be ordered directly from Advaita Press.

Send check or money order or Visa/Mastercard or American Express number (include expiration date and billing zip code) for the indicated amount plus shipping as noted below to:

Advaita Press
P.O. Box 3479 CS3
Redondo Beach, CA 90277
USA

Shipping & Handling:
In U.S. — — — *Surface mail*: First book $3.00. Add 50¢ for each additional book.
  Airmail: First book $5.50. Add 50¢ for each additional book.
Outside U.S. — *Airmail:* $10.00 per book. *Surface mail:* $3 per book Payment in U.S. dollars via check or money order payable on a U.S. bank. No Eurochecks please.

More Books About Advaita

NO WAY -
for the Spiritually Advanced
by Ram Tzu
Blending paradox, wit, satire and profound insight Ram Tzu creates a view of spirituality that is truly unique.
"Ram Tzu is accessible from several levels of misunderstanding." ~ *Ram Tzu*
Softcover — 112 Pages $13.00

Consciousness and the Absolute
edited by Jean Dunn
The final translated talks of Sri Nisargadatta Maharaj, recorded just before his death in 1981. Includes four b/w photos.
Softcover — 118 Pages $12.00

I Am That - Conversations with Sri Nisargadatta Maharaj
A compilation by Maurice Frydman of Maharaj's conversations with seekers who came to him from around the world. This is the latest high quality American edition.
Softcover — 576 Pages $24.95

Seeds of Consciousness
edited by Jean Dunn
More translations of conversations with Nisargadatta Maharaj. This is a NEW EDITION of a once out of print title.
Softcover " 216 Pages $14.00

Prior To Consciousness
edited by Jean Dunn
Further insights into the teachings of Sri Nisargadatta Maharaj via translated accounts of his talks. NEW EDITION includes 5 new photographs.
Softcover —159 Pages $14.00

If unavailable at your bookstore, these titles may be ordered directly from Advaita Press.
— See previous page for ordering information —

Audio and Video Tapes Are Also Available

— Write Us For a Free Catalogue—

Or visit us on the Internet at: www.advaita.org